New International Business English

Updated Edition

**Communication skills
in English for business purposes**

Teacher's Book

**Leo Jones
Richard Alexander**

CAMBRIDGE
UNIVERSITY PRESS

PUBLISHED BY THE PRESS SYNDICATE OF THE UNIVERSITY OF CAMBRIDGE
The Pitt Building, Trumpington Street, Cambridge, United Kingdom

CAMBRIDGE UNIVERSITY PRESS
The Edinburgh Building, Cambridge CB2 2RU, UK
40 West 20th Street, New York, NY 10011–4211, USA
477 Williamstown Road, Port Melbourne, VIC 3207, Australia
Ruiz de Alarcón 13, 28014 Madrid, Spain
Dock House, The Waterfront, Cape Town 8001, South Africa

http://www.cambridge.org

© Cambridge University Press 1989, 1996, 2000

First published 1989
New Edition 1996
Updated Edition 2000
Fifth Printing 2002

Some of the names of companies and individuals in this book are
fictitious. In these cases any resemblance to an actual company or
person is coincidental.

Printed in the United Kingdom at the University Press, Cambridge

Typeface Sabon 10.5/12pt. *System* QuarkXpress®

A catalogue record for this book is available from the British Library

ISBN 0 521 77471 3 Teacher's Book
ISBN 0 521 77472 1 Student's Book
ISBN 0 521 77469 1 Student's Book Cassette Set
ISBN 0 521 77468 3 Student's Book Audio CD Set
ISBN 0 521 77470 5 Workbook
ISBN 0 521 77466 7 Workbook Cassette Set
ISBN 0 521 77467 5 Workbook Audio CD Set
ISBN 0 521 77441 1 New Video Cassette (VHS PAL)
ISBN 0 521 77443 8 New Video Cassette (VHS NTSC)
ISBN 0 521 77442 X New Video Cassette (VHS SECAM)
ISBN 0 521 42735 5 Video Teacher's Guide
ISBN 0 521 42732 0 Video Cassette (VHS PAL)
ISBN 0 521 42734 7 Video Cassette (VHS NTSC)
ISBN 0 521 42733 9 Video Cassette (VHS SECAM)

Contents

Thanks

We'd like to say a big 'Thank You' to everyone who helped us, made comments and suggestions, and who encouraged us while we were working on this project:

Will Capel, our editor, started the ball rolling and kept the project moving along. His critical comments encouraged us to incorporate innumerable improvements.

Alison Silver guided the project smoothly, efficiently and cheerfully towards its publication. Her eye for detail, good humour, encouragement and thoroughness enhanced the book enormously. Working with her was, as always, a delight.

Amanda Ogden devoted great care and attention to researching the photographs and obtaining permission for us to use the copyright materials.

Ruth Carim for her eagle-eyed proof-reading.

Nick Newton and Randell Harris designed the book with good taste and flair.

Martin Williamson produced the recordings and the engineer was Jerry Peal at Studio AVP.

The actors who participated in the recording sessions.

All the teachers who gave us feedback on the First Edition – and contributed their own suggestions and ideas for improvements. In particular, thanks to:

Stephen Berg and Paulo Gilberto de Araujo Galarti in Brazil;
Alison Haill and Sue Pedley in England;
J. Dantreveaux, Patrick Foley, Robin Forrest, Susan Hendrie, Jeffrey Hill, Matt Norton, Carolyne Occhuzzo, David Podger, Jeanette Ramos, Anita Subtil, J. Vernon and M. Weber in France;
Irene Bruntsch, A. Dördelmann-Stappert, Christine Frank, Sarah Jones-Macziola, Eberhard Kelin, John Riach, Inge Spaughton and Douglas L. Sperry in Germany;
Aouda Au, Jonathan Hull, Regina Lo and Raymond Ng in Hong Kong;
Péter Koronváry and Monika Szabó in Hungary;
Anne Brindle and Christine Calvert in Italy;
Leonard Crawford and Tessa Pacey in Japan;
Peter Ellis, Nick Flynn, Joanne Foxford, Thérèse Kennedy, Richard Lane and Cees Sier in Spain;
Pam Scott in Thailand;
Colin Sowden in Wales.

Finally, thanks from Leo to Sue, Zoë and Thomas, and from Richard to Gerlinde, for their support behind the scenes.

The Updated Edition was designed by Barney Haward and Jo Barker.
Hilary Fletcher researched and commissioned the photos and cleared the permissions.
Jackie Pritchard did the proof-reading.

From the First Edition

In preparing this book we've had generous help and advice from a large number of teachers and business people: our thanks to all of them.

In particular, we'd like to thank the following for their assistance during the research for this book, for using and evaluating the pilot edition and for contributing detailed comments and suggestions:

Sue Gosling; Lesley Stéphan in Lyon; Sandra Bennett-Hartnagel at Hewlett Packard in Böblingen; Pauline Bramall-Stephany at Braun AG in Karlsruhe; the British School of Monza; Business English Programmes in San Sebastian; CAVILAM in Vichy, France; the staff of Calor S.A. in Lyon, France; the English School of Osaka; Christine Frank at Sennheiser in Hanover; Eileen Fryer; Stephen Hagen at Newcastle Polytechnic; International House Executive Courses in London; ITCS DELL'ACQUA in Legnano, Milan; ITCS PACLE G. MAGGIOLINI in Parabiago, Milan; Christine Johnson; Peter Kirchhoff; Des O'Sullivan; PERKS Enseñanza de Idiomas in Barcelona; Francis Pithon of SETARAM in Lyon; Nic Underhill; the VHS Language Centre in Nuremberg.

RA would also like to thank Gerlinde for her support and sustenance while the book was being written.

Last but not least, special thanks to Peter Donovan, Peter Taylor and Avril Price-Budgen for their patience, good humour and expertise whilst *International Business English* was being planned, written, recorded and edited – and to Derrick Jenkins who brought us together, and encouraged and helped us throughout the project.

Acknowledgements

The authors and publishers are grateful to the authors, publishers and others who have given permission for the use of copyright material identified in the text. In the cases where it has not been possible to identify the source of material used the publishers would welcome information from copyright owners.

p. 99 article adapted from the *Financial Times* (18.9.92); p. 99 (photo) Louis Vuitton Malletier; pp. 209–11 Telford Development Agency; pp. 212–14 Wigan Metropolitan Borough Council Economic Development Office – as this information is of a historical nature it should not be used outside this exercise.

Introduction

About the course

New International Business English is a course in communication skills in English for students who need, or will soon need, to use English in their work. There are 15 units, each centred around a different business situation, divided into sections, many of which involve students in a variety of task-oriented 'integrated activities'. The situations reflect the kind of standard business practice that most students of Business English are likely to encounter in their working environments.

We have called this course *New International Business English* because English is the major means of communication between business people in different countries. This may involve, for example, a Swede talking to a German or a Japanese talking to an Italian in English – and not just foreigners talking to native speakers of English. As there's no international standard form of English, we have incorporated both British and American usage into the book.

The recordings include a wide variety of different speakers, not all of whom are native speakers of English. The standard business situations covered in the course are ones that are common to all businesses. We have ensured that even in an activity that seems to focus on a special skill like, for example, taking an order over the phone, the kind of language practice that students are getting will also be relevant and useful to students who are themselves unlikely to need to use the phone in this particular way. Similarly, in role-plays that involve buying and selling (a central part of any business), even a student who is a professional salesperson will benefit from playing the role of buyer and seeing a familiar process from a different point of view.

Who the course is for

New International Business English is suitable for a wide variety of learners: ranging from young students or trainees with no work experience to senior business people with a lot of experience of dealing with foreign business partners – and ranging from intermediate to more advanced level classes, including mixed-ability classes.

This may seem an ambitious claim, but as so many of the activities are open-ended, students can perform them according to their own abilities, experience and knowledge. As we have discovered from teachers who have been using *International Business English* (the First Edition of this course) this material really does work in a surprisingly wide range of classes. Of course, the teacher may need to adapt material to suit particular students' needs – this may involve selecting particular activities and leaving out others, and it may sometimes involve supplementing this book with material from other sources. Sometimes this may involve using exercises from the Workbook with your students in class.

New International Business English is extremely flexible. It's designed to be used with all kinds of people who need to be able to use English effectively in their work.

New International Business English is suitable for students who:

- are still studying business and who have little practical experience of business practice
- are participating in a training course and have had no work experience

and for business people who:

- all work in the same field or in entirely different fields
- work within the same company or in different firms
- are managers – or people who hold more lowly jobs

and for students who intend to take an examination in Business English, such as:

- the International Certificate Conference (ICC) *English for Business Purposes* examination
- the University of Cambridge Local Examinations Syndicate (UCLES) *Certificate in English for International Business & Trade* (CEIBT) or *Business English Certificate* (BEC)
- one of the London Chamber of Commerce and Industry (LCCI) *English for Business* examinations
- or a local, national, college or university examination in Business English or Commercial English

and for people from different walks of life who:

- will appreciate a practical and purposeful approach that a 'general English' course may not offer, and who may need to use English in their work as well as in social situations

'Business English'

Business English isn't a special language with a special grammar – it's simply ENGLISH USED IN BUSINESS SITUATIONS.

The words professional people tend to use and understand when talking about their own or other people's working lives might justifiably be defined as 'Business English'. But such language is nowadays also widely used in contemporary industrial societies. Hence vocabulary like *marketing*, *fax*, *report*, *memo*, *order*, *correspondence*, *customer*, *product*, *profit*, *proceeds*, *paperwork*, *negotiate*, *expenditure* and so on are words that practically every adult English speaker uses or understands – they aren't specialized terms only used by business people. Presumably a ballet dancer or a forestry worker might not use the terms so frequently as an office worker, but he or she would certainly have them at his or her disposal.

Most of the vocabulary that's used in business situations is, by any definition, 'general' English vocabulary. Students must strive to widen all aspects of their vocabulary and grammar if they want to improve their communication skills beyond the survival level and be respected and appreciated for their contributions when talking with foreign people in English.

When commentators wish to point up the 'special' character of business language, they normally allude to the specialized, and even 'academic', terms used by people working in a particular profession. Every trade (including forestry and ballet) and every firm has its own jargon and its own ways of doing business – and every department within a company may use its own special terminology to describe what it does and its products.

This course doesn't cover this kind of technical, academic or specialist vocabulary, but it does cover the basic business or commercial terms that most business people use in the course of their work. Any specialist or technical vocabulary that your students require they may either know already or will have to research for themselves, perhaps by using a technical dictionary or by consulting colleagues at work. We assume that students already know (or can be relied upon to learn) all the English terminology they need to talk about their own firm's product or services. This terminology is best learned 'on the job' – which may have to wait until your students are employed if they're still training and have no experience of working yet.

Active focus on business

The emphasis of *New International Business English* is on performing tasks and carrying out activities, not just discussing what you WOULD do. Students should be encouraged to use their judgement, business or general knowledge and skills as they participate in the activities. In speaking and using English in business settings, students should try to be creative in both their actions and their thoughts. Students won't only be improving their English, adding to their vocabulary and language skills, but actually using their English throughout the course. The course thus aims to be both stimulating and motivating.

The course aims to help students to improve their English so that they'll be able to use English effectively and confidently in their work. Using English in business always involves drawing on both business skills and language skills – someone whose English is excellent, for example, may not be able to make a phone call complaining about poor service as effectively as someone who has the appropriate knowledge and experience. Using English in business involves both knowing how to use English and knowing how to do business.

While the course does not presuppose any previous business experience, students who do have work experience are encouraged to apply their business knowledge and experience as they work through the book. The course draws on the insights of management training techniques as well as the communicative approach in language learning. Students without work experience will benefit from the opportunity to practise and rehearse the kinds of business skills required in a wide range of professions and business organizations.

Many sections are devoted to language skills and revision of language points: punctuation, functions, etc. However, particularly in the integrated activities, students will have the opportunity to sharpen their business and management skills – we have incorporated this element into the course because we want students' work in class to be both challenging and interesting. We believe that students who are using their intelligence, imagination and knowledge, as well as their knowledge of English, are more likely to remain highly motivated throughout a long course. We have also included a lot of discussion in the course – we believe that one of the main benefits students get from working in a class is exchanging ideas with other students and learning from each other – not just sitting attentively, trying to absorb all their teacher's knowledge.

How the course is organized

The Student's Book contains 15 units. Units 1 to 4 introduce the basic business skills, and Units 5 to 14 are centred on integrated skills, each organized round a different business situation. Most of the units contain a functions section, reading and listening material, and ample discussion opportunities. The way that the different types of section work is explained below.

To complete the material in a typical unit will take about four 90-minute lessons (a total of roughly sixty 90-minute periods). The exact time required depends on the length of the unit and the level of your class. If your students have less time available, you'll need to select the units and activities that will be most useful for them. The material is designed to be used selectively in this way.

Units 1 to 4

These units introduce the 'basic Business English skills' that students are expected to have some experience in before they embark on the work in Unit 5 onwards: Talking to people face-to-face, Writing letters, memos and faxes, Using the telephone and Writing summaries, notes and reports. These are skills that are fundamental to all business contexts where English is used, and will be practised throughout the course.

Students who already actually *use* these skills in English in their work might not need to spend quite so long on these units as students with less experience of using English at work. We recommend, however, that *all* students should do most of the work in these units – it will help to refresh their minds about the skills they use and build up confidence for the more demanding activities they'll be doing in later units.

If your students are finding a particular section in the first four units very easy, or if you anticipate that they will, we recommend that they do the section quickly rather than leave it out altogether. If your students are having difficulty with a particular basic Business English skill in a later unit, you may decide to return to one of the first four units to do some remedial work.

Units 5 to 14

Each unit contains at least one integrated activity lasting 45 to 90 minutes. There is a progression towards more open-ended simulations from Unit 11 onwards. Students should be aware that it's not just that they learn more English as they progress, but they learn a different way of employing and dealing in and with English. 'Progress' implies not only learning more English words and developing fluency and accuracy but also pushing the use of one's English language resources to their limits and feeling more confident about using English in a wide variety of situations.

At the same time the extended role-plays, integrated activities and simulations are the means towards testing out the communication skills in Business English we have been dealing with.

In these units we have attempted to cover all the necessary basic skills (including vocabulary, standard business situations, reading, speaking, listening and writing skills) and these skills are practised in task-based activities and role-plays.

The extended role-plays, the integrated activities and the longish to full-scale simulations in later units reflect the reality that communication in business is multi-dimensional, many-sided, variable – and unpredictable. The purpose of a simulation is to provide opportunities for students to rehearse dealing with the unknown by employing the known means at their disposal.

In the same way as the first four units are the transition from the world of 'general' English for many of our students into the realm of Business English, the simulations in Units 11 to 14 provide a springboard from the classroom to the real business world of actually *doing it*!

Unit 15

Unit 15 is rather special: it takes the form of a full-scale simulation and revises the skills introduced and practised in the earlier units. The simulation can be spread over three 90-minute lessons. The procedure for the simulation is described in detail in the teaching notes for Unit 15.

No special equipment or facilities are required for this simulation, but some documents have to be photocopied from the Teacher's Book and given to selected participants. If you can manage to requisition an extra room for the simulation, the scenario may seem more realistic; if there's another class in your college or institute doing *New International Business English* you could arrange to combine the two classes at that stage and use both rooms.

Types of activities and exercises

In *New International Business English*, the various language skills are integrated into task-directed and communicative activities, wherever possible. In many of the speaking, writing, reading and listening activities students are expected to work together in pairs or groups. They are encouraged to play roles and to co-operate purposefully in solving a problem or performing a task.

Integrated activities

In these activities a variety of skills are used: for example, after reading a short text, students listen to a recorded phone message, discuss what they should do and then role-play a telephone call or draft a letter, e-mail or fax, and then receive further information which will lead to further discussion, role-playing or writing.

These activities contain tasks that are similar to the kind of tasks students will have to perform in business life, where they'll be using a wide range of skills (language skills as well as business skills and knowledge) to operate effectively in English.

Each SECTION is sub-divided into several STEPS (**A**, **B**, **C** and so on) and sometimes the steps are sub-divided into smaller steps (**1**, **2**, **3** and so on). A recommended **Procedure** for each activity is given in the Teacher's Book. If you decide to diverge from this procedure and leave out a step, for example, make sure everyone is fully aware of what they have to do and which step you're asking them to skip.

A real-life setting involves very detailed knowledge of the product, circumstances and personalities involved. The scenarios we have used are deliberately GENERAL and IDEALIZED – so that they can be swiftly understood and then discussed and dealt with. Any missing information that students request for the case or the activity may have to be sorted out by mutual agreement before work starts. We can't supply a full set of recent sales figures, complete customer files or personnel records! But in real life such information *would* be available – plus a whole range of other documents and data, colleagues with special knowledge to be consulted and background knowledge of company policy and practice. In real life, clearly, an enormous amount of information from all kinds of sources would be taken into account in reaching a decision.

So, find out if members of your class have specialist knowledge to contribute. If, for example, a knowledgeable member of the class says, *'I think we need to know whether the firm's cash flow is healthy before we can reach a decision'* or *'I need to know what the warehouse capacity is and whether the goods will deteriorate during storage'*, then be prepared to reach a consensus on this and perhaps make a ruling before resuming the activity. The alternative is for you to say, *'You can assume this aspect of the scenario works in the same way as it would in your own company'*.

Role-play

Many of the activities in *New International Business English* involve students taking on specified ROLES in pairs. These role-plays range from fairly simple activities, such as acting out face-to-face visits in **2 5B**, to more elaborate tasks, such as explaining how to do something in **12 2E**. The roles are explained in the main text of the Student's Book or explained in the **Files** (see below). Students are asked to play a role in order to simulate the kind of situations in which they may find themselves in business life.

Some of the role-plays involve TELEPHONE CONVERSATIONS. Students should sit back-to-back for telephone role-plays, to simulate the essential fact that we aren't able to *see* the person we're talking to on the phone, and have to communicate only with our voices, not gestures and eye contact.

During a role-play, you should go round the class monitoring, listening in to what is going on and offering individual advice and vocabulary suggestions. Make a note of the errors you overhear so that you can draw everyone's attention to them in the feedback/follow-up stage at the very end of the activity or section.

If you have a video camera and recorder available, many of these role-plays can be recorded for playback, analysis and discussion later. This will enable students to 'see themselves as others see them', which may be slightly traumatic at first, but very beneficial in the long run. If you are going to do this, keep a copy of one of the recordings you make at the beginning of the course – then you'll be able to play it again later in the course to show your students how much progress they have made. An audio cassette recorder (with a good directional microphone) can be used in the same way.

Files

Many of the role-play activities involve an 'information gap'. Here students are directed to separate sections at the back of the book, called 'FILES', where each person is given some information but they can't see the other's information. Their purpose is then to find out what their partner knows and to tell him or her what they know.

The Files are on pages 146 to 175 of the Student's Book. As you'll see, they are jumbled up in random order, so that it's not possible to find your way through them easily. This means that students will find it difficult to 'cheat' by looking at each other's information. However, many of the Files are 'colour-coded' to show that they go together. For example, Files **6**, **37** and **64** are all printed on a green background to show that they are part of the same activity, whilst Files **7**, **38** and **65** are printed on a yellow background.

In these information-gap activities two or three students are each given different information, such as two halves of a price list or different role descriptions, and then have to bridge the gap in a conversation or phone call: the Files work in the same sort of way as role cards. An example of this is **6 1C**, where one member of each pair looks at File **12** while the other looks at File **44**: by asking each other questions they build up a complete picture of the price list.

Some of the Files contain information that students don't need to see until they have completed a certain number of steps in an activity. An example of this is in section **8 2**, where students are only given the information required for step **B** (in File **75**) when they have completed step **A**.

Some of the Files provide model answers to written tasks, which students aren't supposed to look at until they have completed the task. An example of this is in **2 5A** where students see a model memo in File **63**, but not until they have attempted the task themselves. Model answers to some of the other tasks are given in the Teacher's Book and you may photocopy these if you think your students will find it helpful to see them.

The Teacher's Book contains a brief summary of each activity where the Files are involved and a description of what will happen.

Guide to the Files in the Student's Book

As the Files are deliberately 'jumbled up' in the Student's Book, here is an index to help you find your way through them, showing which sections have Files belonging to them.

Section number	File contents	File numbers		
1 1E	Information for A Team and B Team	A: **1**	B: **31**	
2 2B	Addresses	**57***		
2 2C	Names and addresses	A: **2**	B: **33**	
2 5A	Improved version of memo	**63***		
3 2C	Europrint & Utopia Products	A: **3**	B: **34**	
3 3D	Medusa S.A. and head office – first call	A: **4**	B: **35**	
	– second call	A: **5**	B: **36**	
3 4C	Tanaka, Suarez and 'Observer'	A: **6**	B: **37**	C: **64**
	Peterson, 'Observer' and LaRue	A: **7**	B: **38**	C: **65**
	'Observer', Steiner and Restaurant	A: **8**	B: **40**	C: **66**
	Robinson, Hotel and 'Observer'	A: **10**	B: **41**	C: **49**
4 2B	Model report on health and safety	**67***		
4 3E	MD's memo	**69**		
5 1D	Telephone role-play about Ms Trosborg's visit	A: **9**	B: **39**	
5 3C	PacifiChemCo charts	A: **11**	B: **43**	
5 4B	Hyundai advertisement	**70**		
6 1C	Price lists	A: **12**	B: **44**	
6 2D	Jim Dale's role	**13**		
6 3D	Agencia Léon and AntiSpy Products – first call	A: **14**	B: **42**	
	AntiSpy Products and Agencia Léon – second call	A: **15**	B: **45**	
6 4B	Order from Costa Rica	**16**		
6 4C	Faxes from anchor suppliers and freight forwarders	**46**		
6 4D	Reassuring fax from Costa Rica	**71**		
6 4E	Memo from Mr Richardson	**22**		
6 4G	Merry Christmas from Costa Rica!	**52**		
7 1D	Air waybills	A: **17**	B: **47**	
7 3B	Finntech and Julio Martinez roles	A: **18**	B: **48**	
7 3C	Letter from Julio Martinez	**85**		
7 3D	Fax from Julio Martinez	**72**		
7 4A	Letters of Credit: correct answers	**73**		
7 5C	Credit controller and Customer roles	A: **19**	B: **27**	
7 5D	Letter from Wilhelm Becker	**74**		
8 2B	Fax from Uniplex and computer records	**75**		
8 3E	Criticisms and apologies	A: **20**	B: **51**	
8 6A	Apologetic fax from Mr Reynard	**76**		
9 2B	Hotel reservation role-play	A: **21**	B: **50**	
10 5B	Questionnaires for Groups A, B and C	A: **23**	B: **53**	C: **77**
11 3C	Staff committee meeting	A: **24**	B: **54**	C: **78**
11 3 4	Tips for chairperson	**80**		
12 1D	Hard disk and fax machine	A: **26**	B: **56**	
12 2C	Diagrams to explain	A: **62**	B: **68**	
13 2B	Application letter	**81***		
13 4B	Guidance for interviewers	**82**		
14 3C	Telephone recorder & Customer role	A: **28**	B: **83**	
	Bulldog alarm & Customer role	A: **58**	B: **83**	
14 4B	Customer, Supplier and 'Observer' roles	A: **29**	B: **59**	C: **84**
14 5D	Buyers and Sellers roles	A: **30**	B: **60**	
	Seller, Buyer and (optional) 'Observer' roles	A: **32**	B: **61**	C: **84**

---

* This File contains a Model answer for students to refer to after they have completed a writing task.

Listening

Within the integrated activities, recorded information is given to provide input or stimulus for a discussion or role-play, shown by ▣◎. This may be a message recorded on an answerphone, or an overheard telephone call or a conversation. These aren't 'listening comprehension exercises' with questions to answer, but essential components of the activity. An example of this is the telephone message in **8 2B**, where further information is supplied for the next step in the activity.

You may well need to play a recording to the class two or three times, while they take notes and concentrate on understanding the information given in the recording. In most cases, they won't need to understand every word that is spoken. If students listen to the recordings in pairs, rather than as individuals, they can help each other to understand. You may decide to introduce a few helpful questions to guide your students towards recognizing the relevant information, and often they are expected to make notes on the main points that are made (as they might do in real-life situations).

In the recordings of *New International Business English* you'll hear a wide variety of speakers – both British and American accents are heard and some of the speakers are non-native speakers with foreign accents.

Most of the recordings are simulated authentic conversations or telephone messages. Some of these recordings were improvised, some are loosely scripted and others are more closely scripted – though all the features of real conversations, telephone calls or messages (hesitation, false starts, slightly unclear phraseology or pronunciation, etc.) have been retained and not 'edited out'.

There are also some self-contained listening comprehension exercises in the Student's Book, with accompanying tasks. There are two kinds of listening exercise:

- Some exercises consist of extracts from conversations with questions to direct students' attention to the relevant information – an example of this is **8 1B**, where students have to listen very carefully to pick up the information.
- Some listening exercises are complete conversations. The procedure for these listening exercises usually involves a pre-listening step to prepare students for the text and establish certain expectations about its content, followed by a main task, then followed by a post-listening step where students compare notes with a partner and then discuss the topic in a larger group.

In the Workbook and on the Workbook recordings, there are further listening tasks, some of which you may like to use in class. These introduce a different aspect of the theme of the unit and may be used as a lead-in for a discussion, for example.

Reading

Reading is integrated, like listening, into the units as an intrinsic part of the activities. For example, extracts from letters, faxes, e-mails, news articles or information on a database may provide the input for a speaking or writing activity. These aren't 'reading comprehension texts' with questions to answer but sources of information that will help students to cope with the task they are involved in. An example of this is the advertisement in **6 3A** which provides essential information for the steps that follow.

Clearly, in such activities, a skill like reading does not play an isolated role. Nor is this the case in most business situations: participants in a business situation switch from the spoken medium to the written medium and vice versa, frequently having to transfer information from one to the other, with little or no conscious focusing on the medium they are using. It is their COMMUNICATION PURPOSE that affects which skill is being used. So it is a tenet of this course that the practising of such skills needs to be as organic as the classroom situation allows.

At the same time, we have included some longer reading texts, involving aspects of the business world, which are of interest in themselves and relevant to the topics dealt with in the unit. Here different aspects of the reading skill are focused on: reading for gist, extracting specific information and reading to find particular details. Examples of this are in **13 1** and **13 2**.

These passages are accompanied by tasks, which are fully explained in the Teacher's Book. There are questions and tasks to help students to develop their reading skills. There are three basic types of tasks in these exercises:

- Reading for gist: to get the basic information from the text
- Scanning: looking through the text to find specific information as quickly as possible
- Reading for detail: understanding more detailed information in the text

And finally there's a discussion activity. The reading of the text – perhaps an advertisement or a longer passage – provides ideas and vocabulary input for a subsequent discussion.

Writing

The integrated activities contain all kinds of writing tasks, including making notes and drafting memos, letters, faxes, e-mails and short reports. Students are usually asked to 'DRAFT *a letter, e-mail or fax …*' rather than '*write*' one, since a first draft may be the most that students can realistically achieve in class. However, for homework, students can be asked to produce a revised final draft – perhaps word-processed or typed. The writing that they'll do within an activity is communicative and an integral part of the activity: what they have written is usually 'delivered' to another pair who have to reply or react to it.

Students are often expected to do their written drafts in pairs, so that they can help each other, and then the completed draft is shown to another pair for their comments. The purpose of this is to encourage co-operation within the class and to give students a chance to benefit from each other's ideas and experience. Usually such written drafts would then be collected and marked by you. Alternatively, students may be asked to prepare revised drafts for homework, and these are what you would collect and mark.

Students who are taking an examination may need to be encouraged to write letters during their course, rather than faxes or e-mails. This is because faxes and e-mails tend to be shorter, more informal and obey the conventions of style and layout less strictly. Moreover, with faxes or e-mails the reader's tolerance of errors is rather higher – business people are sometimes quite surprised if they get a fax or e-mail from another country with no mistakes in it!

Over the past 25 years or so, business letter writing in English has undergone something of a transformation: the traditional Dickensian style of business letters, using a multitude of formulae and clichés ('*We are in receipt of your esteemed favour of the 14th inst. …*'), has been replaced by a much more straightforward, informal style of writing.

Moreover, many firms have come to realize that even a fax or e-mail message is a personal as well as a corporate piece of communication: a brief personal greeting often helps to maintain a relationship between two people in different parts of the world – and the closer the relationship, the more likely it is that the customer will remain loyal or that the supplier will do his or her best to satisfy the customer.

In some activities, there's a letter, e-mail or fax to read or reply to, which itself in turn becomes the model for a letter, e-mail or fax that the students will have to write later in the same activity. An example of this is **8 4**, where the students read an apologetic letter from a supplier in step **A3** and later use it as a model for their own letter of apology to a customer in step **B3**.

Model versions of some of the writing tasks are given in the Teacher's Book. You may photocopy these to give your students further ideas. If there's an overhead projector in your classroom, you could photocopy these model versions onto OHP transparencies (most modern photocopiers can do this impressively well) and project them for the whole class to see.

In some cases, where it's essential for students to see a model version, this is hidden among the Files, so that students don't get to see the model until after they have completed the task.

Discussion and follow-up

At the end of every section, you should allow enough time to discuss with the class how they got on in the activities and give them time to raise any problems or queries they may have. This is a significant activity in its own right and can contribute much to the learning process. It may sometimes be better to skip the final step of an activity so as to allow time for this before the lesson ends.

Where an integrated activity raises any controversial issues, there are questions in the Student's Book for a follow-up discussion. At this stage you should also give feedback to the class on their performance in the activity and allow them to step outside their roles and consider the value of the tasks and how real-life business situations are different to (and usually more complex than) the simplified or idealized scenario they have enacted. A real-life setting involves very detailed knowledge of the product and situation you're in, whereas the scenarios we have used are more general, so that they are easier to understand and deal with. Like case studies in a training course, the issues that are raised must be localized to students' own circumstances.

Some discussions are provoked or led into by short recorded texts or interviews, shown by ◉◯, or by short reading passages. The discussions are designed to work best in small groups – though if your whole class is small, a whole-class discussion may be best. An example of this is **8 6C**, where the value of good customer relations is discussed.

Students should be encouraged to reflect on the issues and activities they have been dealing with. One reason why this is particularly important is that the language required in a discussion to express opinions, evaluate ideas, agree and disagree and so on is fundamental to much business interaction – as well as contributing to one's broader educational development. You'll find that discussion naturally arises after many of the activities throughout this course, such as reading a text, and particularly after students have taken part in an integrated activity.

Discussion about business topics is a regular feature of *New International Business English*. Participation in a language class gives everyone a valuable opportunity to exchange ideas with other people who may be in similar or in very different situations and this will perhaps encourage them to re-examine their own ideas and prejudices. Discussion, particularly in small groups, also gives everyone a chance to use and consolidate the vocabulary that they have encountered in the unit.

At the end of each section of *New International Business English* students should be given a chance to raise any queries or doubts they have. Sometimes it may be a good idea to ask them to explain how they benefited from doing a particular section. This may sound like asking for trouble, and in some classes you might really be opening a can of worms by asking this kind of question! But it's very reassuring for students to find out that the other members of the class have had similar difficulties and that others have found the activity useful.

You should also provide the students with feedback, pointing out errors you have noted down and congratulating them on the activities they have performed well.

In some sections we have suggested extra discussion ideas in the Teacher's Book, in the form of further questions you can present to the class.

Functions

Some units contain a complete section dealing with functions. The following groups of functions are covered:

Getting people to do things **3 2**
Exchanging information **6 1**
Complaining and apologizing **8 3**
Possibility, probability and certainty **10 4**
Explaining how to do something **12 2**

Others contain a function step within another section:

Agreeing and disagreeing **5 5C**
Telling stories **9 4B**
Taking part in meetings **11 1B** & **11 2A**

One major emphasis of these sections in *New International Business English* is to make students aware of the need to select appropriate exponents to suit different situations they may encounter. This may often entail choosing an appropriate exponent (and commensurate tone of voice) which matches up with the type of people you're dealing with – whether they are complete strangers, superiors, familiar colleagues, valued clients or acquaintances.

To a great extent, success in business depends on creating the right impression. Politeness and formality are often keys to achieving a desired communicative effect, whether you're apologizing for the late delivery of a product or attempting to sell something to a customer. The kind of language used also marks or characterizes the speaker as friendly or unfriendly, helpful or unhelpful. We are all aware of how such signals tend to aid (or hinder) the smooth running of everyday social interaction: in business situations this tendency may often be magnified. Unit 1 emphasizes various aspects of how to create the right impression.

These sections begin with a presentation step with recorded examples, shown by 🔘, in which the function and some typical exponents are introduced. Students are asked to look at the speech balloons and to listen to the recording. Here the recording can also be used for pronunciation practice, using a PLAY-PAUSE-REPEAT technique: students hear each exponent, the recording is paused and the class repeat it, trying to copy the intonation and tone of voice. This may sound slightly demeaning for more advanced students, but it's an extremely effective way of focusing attention on aspects of phonology that are difficult to define, such as 'sounding polite' or 'being deferential'.

This is followed by a series of activities in which students practise using the exponents in role-plays or a discussion. While they are doing these activities, you should go round the class listening in and discreetly offering advice, making notes on any points that should be made to the whole class afterwards.

In the Teacher's Book we also suggest an Extra activity to involve students in further communicative practice.

The Workbook contains follow-up exercises on all the functions covered in the Student's Book. If your class are having a lot of difficulty with a Functions section, you could supplement their work by using an exercise from the Workbook in class. Some of these Workbook exercises are recorded on the Workbook recordings.

Vocabulary

In the Teacher's Book you'll find a list of Vocabulary items for each section in the Student's Book: these are Business English terms and other English words and phrases which your students may be unfamiliar with. From these vocabulary items you should select the ones which your students need to remember: encourage them to highlight these items in their books. In some cases, if any of the words are likely to confuse or disconcert your students, you might decide to write up some of them on the board and discuss their meanings before everyone starts work on a particular section.

The reason why we have taken this approach is because *New International Business English* is used with so many different kinds of students with varying levels of English and varying levels of business experience. It's impossible for us to predict which vocabulary items are 'new words' for your students – you are the only person who can judge what vocabulary your students may need to learn. But the final choice about which 'new words' to highlight should be made by the students themselves, guided by you, their teacher.

Highlighting vocabulary in their Student's Book turns each person's book into an INSTANT REVISION AID. Every time they look back at sections they have already done, the vocabulary they want to remember 'jumps out from the page', reminding them of the vocabulary items and showing the words in context. Just leafing back through previous units in a free moment (on the train, tram or bus, for example) will help them to revise vocabulary really easily.

What students should NOT DO is highlight whole paragraphs of text (as if they were memorizing passages from a textbook for an exam). The selective approach of highlighting just a few chosen words on each page is much more effective.

Most of the recordings are designed to encourage students to listen for information and not try to spot unfamiliar vocabulary. Indeed, students should be discouraged from worrying about vocabulary when their main task is to understand the information that the speakers are communicating – which is what happens when we really listen to people in the flesh or on the phone. Nevertheless, the Vocabulary lists in the Teacher's Book include the 'new words' used in the recordings. You may find it helpful to go through the Transcript of the recording before the lesson, highlighting in your Teacher's Book any vocabulary which you think your students need to know before they hear the recording – these might be key words they don't know, or unfamiliar words that might distract them from concentrating on understanding the gist or from performing the task.

Vocabulary storage Apart from highlighting new words, students should be encouraged to store vocabulary in other ways: a loose-leaf personal organizer or Filofax is particularly useful for this. This is best done by topics, with each new topic starting on a new page. Fresh pages can be inserted whenever necessary and the pages and topics can be rearranged easily.

This example shows a suitable method of organizing a vocabulary notebook:

> Buying and Selling
>
> a supplier /səplaɪə/
> (to supply)
> – Acme Inc is our sole supplier
>   of those components
>
> a contract /kɒntrækt/
> – We signed the contract with
>   Acme Inc to supply…

Technical vocabulary or jargon that is special to a particular trade, industry or firm isn't covered in *New International Business English*. The texts, instructions, exercises and recordings contain much of the 'business' vocabulary that students will require, thus enhancing the active nature of the book. The majority of this vocabulary is assimilated as students carry out a task-related activity and should not be taught 'separately' out of context.

In addition, the Workbook contains exercises on the vocabulary related to the particular theme of the unit. These exercises are designed to introduce business-related vocabulary and terms which have not occurred elsewhere in exercises or texts. Given that some of these exercises are to a certain extent test-like, they'll appeal variously to different types of students. Students should do these exercises on their own, checking their answers in the Answer Key and raising any problems they have in class. You should always allow time in class for students' questions arising from the exercises they have done in the Workbook.

As we are dealing with English as an international language, we have tried to show no normative bias towards one specific national variety of English. Both British and American vocabulary items are used in the text, in the vocabulary exercises and on the recordings.

Students should be encouraged to buy a general dictionary such as one of the following:

Cambridge International Dictionary of English
Collins COBUILD Learner's Dictionary
Longman Dictionary of Contemporary English
Oxford Advanced Learner's Dictionary of
  Contemporary English

In class there are considerable advantages in having SEVERAL different dictionaries available, so that when students look up words a larger number of examples of the words used in different contexts can be seen.

In monolingual learners' dictionaries, it's the examples which are usually more enlightening than the definitions!

A pocket-size bilingual dictionary (English-German, English-French, etc.) is liable to be more annoying than helpful, except perhaps when away from your desk or travelling. Such dictionaries contain so few examples that it's impossible to discover from them how a new word is used in context. Preferable to these might be a pocket-size learner's dictionary, such as the *Oxford Learner's Pocket Dictionary*, though it is no substitute for one of the larger general dictionaries listed above.

We feel that, for students at this level, a special dictionary of Business English terms is NOT NECESSARY. This is because all the Business English vocabulary students are likely to need is covered in any of the general dictionaries listed above anyway – together with the vast amounts of non-business vocabulary they are likely to come across. Your students probably need to learn far more 'general' multi-purpose English vocabulary to become more effective speakers and writers of English than 'Business English' vocabulary, after all.

However, for your own purposes it may be helpful to have one of these specialized Business English Dictionaries to refer to:

A Dictionary of Management by Derek French and Heather Saward (Pan Books)
Oxford Dictionary of Business English for Learners of English
Longman Dictionary of Business English

Extra activities

The Teacher's Book contains a number of Extra activities which you can do with your students if time allows, and if they would benefit from or enjoy more work on a particular topic.

Some of the Extra activities can be presented directly to the students (for example, the activity at the end of **6 1** on page 87 in the Teacher's Book).

Others are designed to be photocopied from the Teacher's Book and handed out to the students. These photocopiable activities look like this in the Teacher's Book:

New International Business English   This document may be photocopied.

An example of such an activity is at the very end of **6 4** in the Teacher's Book, which is particularly suitable for students with work experience.

Another example is *Flying down to Rio* at the very end of Unit 9 in the Teacher's Book, which is an extra integrated activity.

© Cambridge University Press 2000

Mistakes and correction

Although accuracy is an important aspect of language learning and should never be ignored, it's far more important for learners to be able to communicate effectively. To speak English fluently it's important to develop confidence and this is impossible if you're afraid of making mistakes. Students shouldn't be corrected too often as this may have an inhibiting effect and make them 'mistake-conscious'. You can't learn a language without making mistakes, and mistakes are a useful indicator of what students still need to learn. In real life, after all, people have to communicate with each other IN SPITE OF the mistakes they may be making and the limited amount of English they know.

Students should certainly be corrected when they make serious errors, but it's usually best to point out any mistakes that were made AFTER the class have completed an activity, rather than interrupting DURING the activity. While students are working in pairs or groups, and you're going from group to group listening in, you MIGHT be able to make the occasional discreet correction without interrupting the flow of the conversation, but normally it's better to make a note of some of the errors you overhear and point them out later.

You may overhear your students making mistakes in pronunciation, intonation, grammar, vocabulary or style, but rather than mentioning every single mistake you've noticed, it's more helpful to be selective and to draw attention to certain points that you think your students can improve. It's less confusing to focus on just one type of error at a time by, for example, drawing attention to pronunciation errors after one activity and then to vocabulary errors after another and to grammar errors after another. Accuracy is something that takes a long time to develop and it can't be achieved overnight!

Written work

In writing, where errors are more noticeable, accuracy is much more important. When marking students' written work, you can't really overlook some of their mistakes as you might do if they were talking. However, it's helpful to show students which of their mistakes are more or less serious and to distinguish between different kinds of mistakes.

Give students a chance to correct their own mistakes by underlining the relevant parts or showing in the margin whether there's a mistake in grammar (**G**), word order (**WO**), vocabulary (**V**), punctuation (**P**), spelling (**Sp**) or style (**St**).

A tick (✔) is a nice way of showing that an idea has been well expressed.

Background information for the non-business person

Many of the units in *New International Business English* depend on a certain amount of knowledge about the business world or business practice. This is why we've included in the Workbook a section of Background information for students (and perhaps teachers) who aren't specialists or who lack work experience.

Don't worry about your own lack of business knowledge: you are the English language specialist and your students are the business specialists (or are studying business in the vocational parts of their course). Don't be tempted to bluff them into thinking you know more than you do – be frank about your lack of knowledge of business, and let the class explain to you how business works. Say things to them like:

'I've read that in business people often do so and so. Is that true in your experience?'
rather than:
'In business you should always do so and so.'
And looking at the Background information in the Workbook may also fill you in on some of the basic concepts.

The Teacher's Book gives you enough information to understand the content of all the activities and exercises that your students will be doing – but remember that they are bringing to the activities and the discussion experience and knowledge that you, as language teacher, may lack.

To keep in touch with developments in the business world, we recommend that you look regularly at either *The Financial Times*, *The Economist*, *Fortune* or *Business Week*. Alternatively, you should regularly inspect the business section of one of the 'quality' daily newspapers (in the UK: *The Guardian*, *The Times*, *The Independent* or *The Daily Telegraph*) or Sunday papers (in the UK: *The Observer*, *The Sunday Times*, *The Independent on Sunday* or *The Sunday Telegraph*). All of these publications have web sites.

Using *New International Business English*

Many of the activities in *New International Business English* are open-ended and hence unpredictable. A course full of predictable, controlled exercises would be much less exciting and challenging.

It's always difficult to predict how long any activity will last in a particular class. The level and enthusiasm of the class as well as the time you have available will control this. Nevertheless, in the Teacher's Book, we have given a rough indication of how long each section will take to do – each section takes either 45 or 90 minutes to complete, and the 45-minute sections are arranged in pairs so that you can do two of them in one 90-minute lesson.

You may well find that there's more material in the book than you can cover in the time you have available, in which case you'll need to SELECT the units and sections within a unit that will be of most benefit to your students. Indeed, we recommend that you do select among the activities, since not everything in the book is likely to be equally relevant to every group of students. Many of the sections are 'free-standing' and don't depend on having done the work in a previous section. You may decide to deal with units in a different sequence from the way they are presented in the Student's Book and this won't affect the way that the course works. However, the units do become progressively more difficult.

It's important to adjust the emphasis of the course to suit your students' level and their experience of the business world – as well as to suit their individual needs and interests. Using the Workbook will enable slower students to keep pace with their colleagues, and will provide extra practice in all the main language points dealt with in each unit. The Workbook is an integral part of the course, as explained below.

The teaching notes for Unit 1 in the Teacher's Book explain the rationale behind the different types of activities you'll be using and are rather more detailed than subsequent ones.

The Teacher's Book

Each unit in the Teacher's Book starts with an outline of the contents and aims of the unit. This is followed by detailed notes on each section, beginning with a list of the vocabulary that students may find difficult to understand in the section. There is a step-by-step procedure for the section, including correct or suggested answers and a transcript of the recorded material. Some sections also have an optional extra activity for the class to do.

We recommend that you always read the teaching notes for each section and prepare ahead what you'll be covering in class. This is particularly important in the role-plays and the integrated activities where you'll need to know who's doing what and when. You may also need to make photocopies in advance.

The Workbook

The Workbook and the Workbook recordings are an integral part of *New International Business English*, consolidating and extending the work that is done in class using the Student's Book.

We have designed the Workbook to be helpful, stimulating and sometimes challenging. The exercises are all 'self-correcting', with an Answer Key at the back. The material in the Workbook provides follow-up exercises and additional material to accompany each unit in the Student's Book for students to do as homework.

The units in the Workbook contain:

- Background information on the topic of the unit
- Vocabulary exercises and puzzles revising some of the essential business vocabulary connected with the topic of the unit
- Functions exercises, some of which are recorded speaking exercises
- Word-building exercises
- Listening comprehension tasks and note-taking exercises, based on the Workbook recordings. (Listening to an interview or noting down a telephone message is often best done alone, rather than in class. Working at their own pace, students can listen to the recording as many times as they wish and pause it frequently, without feeling embarrassed that they might be wasting their colleagues' time in class.)
- Reading comprehension tasks, based on articles and texts connected with the topic of the unit
- Exercises on prepositions and prepositional phrases
- Writing tasks, with model answers in the Answer Key at the back
- Grammar review and revision exercises

Many exercises in the Workbook can be used in class to supplement the work in the Student's Book. We have not suggested a procedure for using them in class, as the exercises are all self-explanatory. However, some exercises (such as the Speaking exercises) are less suitable for classroom use than others (such as the Reading exercises).

Students will find that it's useful and reassuring to SHARE their experiences of using the Workbook with their classmates, and we recommend that a little time be set aside on a regular basis for queries and discussion on what students have done in the Workbook.

The Workbook should be viewed as a means for sustaining interest and maintaining momentum in the learning process during the time in which the students aren't in class. This also serves the purpose of helping students to grasp the importance of attaining a degree of autonomy in their language learning and of creating a motivation to persist.

Home study

We believe that, however busy your students are, they must spend about as much time studying at home as they spend in class. This homework should consist of:

- Written work stemming from activities they have done in the Student's Book – this might include writing final drafts of letters, e-mails or faxes they've done first drafts of with a partner in class
- Follow-up work, revising material they've covered in class, particularly vocabulary and functional exponents
- Preparation for sections they're going to do in class next time, to save time in class – particularly reading texts and studying preparation steps in the Student's Book
- Workbook exercises – you may recommend particular exercises for everyone to do before the next lesson or leave it to your students to choose when to do these exercises
- Self-directed reading connected with the student's own trade or industry. Such material can be found in the trade press, on web sites or in more general business (and non-business) weeklies like *The Economist*, *International Business Week*, *Time* or *Newsweek*. The kind of books, web sites, newspapers or magazines you recommend will, of course, depend on a particular student's interests and line of business.

The *New International Business English Video*

There are 15 programmes on the *New International Business English Video,* each of which accompanies the equivalent unit in the *New International Business English* coursebook.

- Programmes 1, 2, 3, 4 and 9 are scenarios introduced by the Presenter. The Presenter raises questions for discussion. These programmes include interviews with business people talking about their experiences.
- Programmes 6, 8, 11, 13 and 14 are scenarios introduced by the Presenter, but without interviews.
- Programmes 5, 10 and 12 are documentaries, filmed at Swatch AG in Switzerland, where English is used as an international language.
- Programme 15 is a scenario focusing on *Giving presentations.* The Teacher's Guide provides pages of extra material for photocopying so that this skill can be covered in more depth. This programme includes interviews.

Each programme lasts between 2½ and 7½ minutes, and is designed to be viewed several times, with questions and tasks photocopied from the Teacher's Guide. The questions and tasks help students to understand the content of the programme, and provoke discussion or provide role-play activities. The Presenter introduces the main topics for discussion by asking viewers to reflect on what they have seen and to analyze the way the performers behaved.

The material can be used flexibly, according to the level and interests of each class and the time available. A classroom session on each video programme might typically take up to 45 minutes in the classroom.

The aims of the *New International Business English Video* are:

- to provide students with examples of English being used by business people in business situations
- to focus on examples of successful and unsuccessful communication
- to encourage students to discuss various aspects of business and work, comparing their experiences and sharing their opinions
- to enable students to appreciate the ways in which intonation, tone of voice, facial expressions, gestures and demeanour contribute to communication
- to encourage students to discuss cultural and cross-cultural issues
- to provide a 'window on the world', giving students an insight into other people's lives and ways of thinking, and opening up the classroom to other people's ideas and experiences
- to supplement the material in the equivalent units of the Student's Book, and to provide further variety in the classroom

The video may be shown at various stages in relation to the equivalent unit in the book.

- The video can be shown before you start the unit in the book, as an introduction to the theme of the unit. This is usually the best stage to show the video.
- If you prefer, the video could be shown about half-way through the unit, as a break from using the book.
- Alternatively, the video could be saved up until all or most of the unit has been done, perhaps as a follow-up to revise some of the work that has been done in the unit — or as a 'treat' to encourage less motivated students.

You may wish to show different programmes at different points, depending on the contents of each programme and the equivalent unit.

The Teacher's Guide (packaged with the *Video*) contains a general introduction, guidelines for use, short warm-up activities, transcripts of all the programmes, and tasks for photocopying for each programme (with answers).

The original *International Business English Video*

The original *International Business English Video* contains seven (longer) sequences. If you have the original video, you may still wish to use sequences from it.

Sequence 1 *Face to face* relates to Unit 1 in the Student's Book.
Sequence 2 *Communication* relates to Units 2 & 3 in the Student's Book.
Sequence 3 *A portrait of a company* relates to Unit 5 in the Student's Book.
Sequence 4 *An important order* relates to Units 6 & 8 in the Student's Book.
Sequence 5 *Travel and hospitality* relates to Unit 9 in the Student's Book.
Sequence 6 *A manufacturing process* relates to Unit 12 in the Student's Book.
Sequence 7 *Meetings* relates to Unit 11 in the Student's Book.

The tasks and questions for the original *International Business English Video* are in the original Teacher's Guide.

Face to face

To some extent, this unit can be considered as a 'comfortable introduction' to the rest of the course – it also introduces the types of exercises and activities that students will be doing during the course and shows the degree of student autonomy expected. But this is not just a 'getting to know your classmates' unit: the emphasis throughout is on encouraging students to consider and re-evaluate the social functions of English. In business, this is particularly important, as students may be dealing with all kinds of people in English: clients and colleagues, friends and strangers, superiors and subordinates – all of whom have to be talked to in different ways.

The whole of Unit 1 comprises material for about four 1½ hour lessons. We have given approximate timings for every section in the book, based on a 'standard' 90 minute 'double lesson'. If your timetable is divided into shorter lessons, it will take you two of these to cover the same ground – where to make the break between lessons is up to you in this case. Some sections take 'about 45 minutes'. These timings are approximate and, depending on the level of your students and what interests them, you should be prepared to take more time over some sections – and if necessary skip some steps altogether.

This and the other three introductory units are 'compulsory' for students without work experience. But work-experienced students should also go through them, perhaps more quickly, before they start Unit 5. This is because many of the language skills taken for granted in Unit 5 onwards are introduced and practised in Units 1 to 4.

➡ The teaching notes for this unit are much more detailed than subsequent units. This is because we're introducing some of the methods and ideas underlying the course. It's advisable to read the notes through before each lesson.

Background information

For students who have no first-hand experience of business the Workbook contains Background information on the topic of meeting people and developing relationships. Draw their attention to this section in their Workbooks.

Video

Programme 1 on the *New International Business English Video* introduces the theme of this unit.

1.1 First impressions ...

This section introduces the idea that, in business life, it's important not just to be efficient and do your job but also to look and sound friendly, confident, sincere and helpful ... and not unfriendly, insincere, shy or unhelpful! People in different countries have different ideas of what sounds friendly, polite or sincere. Further aspects of the way in which people behave differently in different cultures are developed in **1.2** and

1.4. In **1.1** we focus more on verbal behaviour and smiling; **1.4** focuses more on non-verbal behaviour: gestures, paralanguage and body language.

This section also covers first meetings, establishing contact with people and taking the first steps in developing a relationship, which is taken further in **1.5.**

By approaching the topic through students' everyday experiences the aim is to sensitize them to the need for friendliness, TACT and 'smoothness', which are needed in business dealings.

> ⚠ Some students need to be made aware of how their 'natural' way of talking might sound to a native speaker of English – some nationalities (e.g. some Cantonese speakers and some German speakers) may sound rather abrupt or rude to speakers of other languages. Some students may need to make a considerable effort to smile more than usual and be extra polite to compensate for the way their tone of voice sounds to a foreigner!

Vocabulary

In each section of the Teacher's Book you'll find a list of important **Vocabulary** items: these lexical items are business and non-business terms that are introduced in the section, some of which students may not have come across before.

Your students may be unfamiliar with the following words and expressions in this section. You may need to explain some of them – or you may prefer to ask the members of the class who *do* understand them to explain them to the others. Or you may prefer to wait until your students ask you to explain them.

Students should highlight the items they want to remember in their own books – this means vocabulary which is new to them as well as words and phrases they already understand but which they (or you) feel they should try to use more often in their own speech.

Among the items in the list will be some which are less relevant to your students, or which they don't really need to remember and use – as well as many that some or all of them already do know and use.

visitor	*sincere*	*Whereabouts ...?*
(un)welcoming	*aggressive*	*head of department*
appointment	*co-ordinator*	*small talk*
efficient	*sales office*	*superior*

And in the Files for step **E**:

1

surname	*personnel*
badge	*public relations*
vice-chairman	*colleague*

– But, if possible get your students to choose a job title they do understand, rather than one they don't!

31

Many of the place names (*Geneva*, *Milan*, etc.) will be different in English from your students' language.

First of all

If the members of the class are together for the first time, get everyone to introduce themselves by answering these questions:

> *What's your name?*
> *Where are you from?*
> *Where do you work?*
> *What do you do?*
> or *What are you studying?*
> *Why are you doing this course?*

> *My name's …*
> *I'm from …*
> *I work in …*
> *I'm a …*
> *I'm studying …*
> *Because …*

Remind everyone that we usually answer the question:
> *What do you do?*

by saying:
> *I'm a student.* or *I'm an export clerk.* or *I'm a secretary.*

Introduce yourself in the same way too.

Don't spend too long on this, as students will be talking in more detail about the kind of work they do in **1.3**. If everyone already knows everyone else, start straight in with the recording.

Procedure – *about 90 minutes*

A This is a warm-up activity. If your students already know each other, and you haven't done the 'First of all' activity above, this step might be a good whole-class activity.

At the end, try to reach a consensus as to which person looks the most welcoming and which the least.

B 🎧 Play the recording. Perhaps point out that the people greeting the visitors are not all receptionists, some are people who happen to be in the office when the visitor arrives – a situation all members of the class may find themselves in. We suggest that you play the recording through three times, though you may wish to pause between each brief interaction for your students to make comments and ask questions.

1 Play the recording all the way through so that students can imagine each of the situations, get used to the voices and get the gist of what is being said.
2 Play the recording again and this time ask everyone to decide on their answers to the questions in the Student's Book. Then get everyone to discuss their answers. Why did some speakers sound more friendly or efficient than others? Was it the language they used or their tone of voice or what? (The man in extract 5 and the woman in extract 9 are particularly impolite.)
3 Finally, play the recording for a third time and ask them just to sit back and listen. Maybe they could note down any questions they want to ask you at the end, or note down vocabulary or expressions that were used – or just relax and enjoy the conversations while soaking up ideas and vocabulary.

Transcript [2 minutes 40 seconds]

1 *Woman:* Good evening, Mr Green, how nice to see you again.
Man: Good evening, it's nice to be back. How are you?

2 *Man:* Good morning, madam, can I help you?
Woman: Yes, I've got an appointment with Mr Henry Robinson.

3 *Woman:* Good afternoon, sir.
Man: Good afternoon. I'd like to see Mr Ferguson, please.

4 *Man:* Hello, madam, can I help at all?
Woman: Yes, I'd like to know what time . . .

5 *1st man: (brusque)* Er...good morning, sir. Do you have an appointment?
2nd man: Yes, I've arranged to see Ms Shapiro. I think I may be a bit early . . .

6 *1st man:* Good morning, sir. Do you have an appointment?
2nd man: Yes, er...I've arranged to see Ms Shapiro. I think I may be a bit early . . .

7 *Woman:* Good morning, Mr Rossi. How are you today?
Man: Just fine, thanks. Is Mr Grady in yet?
Woman: I'll just find out for you . . .

8 *Man:* Er...hello, Miss Macdonald, I'm afraid...er...Mrs Sanderson isn't back from lunch yet.
Woman: Oh, that's OK, I'll sit and wait if that's all right.
Man: Oh, certainly, would you like some coffee?
Woman: Mm, that sounds a good idea, thanks.

9 *Woman: (off-hand)* Yes?
Man: Good morning, my name's Martin. I'm here to see Mr Suzuki.
Woman: Who?
Man: Mr Suzuki.
Woman: Oh, he's busy I think.
Man: Could you let him know I'm here, please?
Woman: OK.

10 *Woman:* Good morning, sir.
Man: Good morning, my name's Martin, I'm here to see Mr Suzuki.
Woman: If you'll just take a seat, Mr Martin, I'll let him know you're here.
Man: Fine, thanks.
Woman: Mr Suzuki, Mr Martin's in reception for you . . . He's on his way down.

C The conclusions the groups may come to are that giving a good impression reflects your company's image (no company wants its customers to think it's unpleasant!) and that if you start off a relationship in a friendly, pleasant way it's likely to go on in the same way, which will be to everyone's advantage.

Ask the groups to announce some of the adjectives they added to the lists. Be prepared to help with supplying unknown vocabulary here.
Some possible additions to the 'try to be' list are:

alert distinct friendly confident calm honest skilful intelligent nice helpful polite

And for the 'try not to be' list:

sleepy unclear lazy dishonest clumsy stupid prejudiced inefficient nasty unhelpful off-hand rude

Once you have decided as a class on the 'top five' or even 'top ten' adjectives, these can be written on the board in **LARGE LETTERS** and henceforth considered as 'Golden Rules' that can be referred back to later in the unit.

The answer to the last question will depend partly on the established practice in a firm: usually *'Good morning/afternoon, can I help you?'* or *'Good afternoon, Mr Brown ...'* are more common than *'Hello, can I help you?'* or *'Hi, Mr Brown ...'*. But the most important thing is a nice smile and friendly eye contact.
If necessary, draw students' attention to the point made above about smiling and being extra polite.

D This step introduces some expressions that are used when meeting someone for the first time, or meeting them again after an absence. The recording illustrates and presents various exponents of the functions of meeting and greeting, used in context.

1 Before you play the recording put the students in pairs and ask them to predict what the people might be saying, considering the situations described and illustrated.

2 Play the recording through once to give everyone a chance to get used to the voices and accents, and to get the gist of what's going on. After the first hearing of each conversation, ask the class to suggest who and where the speakers are.

3 Next, play the recording again, pausing it as necessary, while everyone notes down the missing phrases in the gaps. Allow time for everyone to compare what they've written and to ask any questions they would like to. Ask them to 'study' the expressions they have noted down, and the ones in the speech balloons, and highlight the ones they think will be most useful or the ones they feel most comfortable with. Remind them that the only way to remember new expressions is by using them in class and revising them at home.

4 Finally, play the recording again and encourage the pairs to speculate how each conversation might continue. We'll be returning to the topic of small talk in **1.5**.

Transcript [2 minutes 10 seconds]

1 *Alex White:* Oh, good afternoon.
Chris Grey: Good afternoon.
Alex White: Er…I'd just like to introduce myself. Er…the name's Alex White and I'm the new export sales co-ordinator.
Chris Grey: Oh, yes. I've heard of you. How do you do? I'm…er…Chris Grey. Pleased to meet you. Er…have you just arrived?
Alex White: Er…no, no, I got here…er…it was yesterday morning, but it,…it's the first time I've been up to this floor. So, Chris, what do you?
Chris Grey: Well, I'm not very important really. I'm…er…Jenny Santini's assistant. She's head of personnel – have you met her?
Alex White: Oh, yeah. I was introduced to her yesterday. Actually, I'm looking for Jim Price's office. Am I on the right floor for that?
Chris Grey: Er…well, no actually, Mr Price is on the fifth floor. Er…if you take the lift over in the corner you . . .

2 *Tony Harris:* Ms Smith…er…I'd like you to meet Mrs Jones. Mrs Jones is from our sales office in Toronto.
Liz Jones: Hi!
Claire Smith: How do you do, Mrs Jones? I've been looking forward to meeting you.
Liz Jones: Oh, please call me Liz.
Claire Smith: And I'm Claire.
Liz Jones: Hi.
Claire Smith: Well, Liz, did you have a good journey?

Liz Jones: Yeah, not too bad. God, there was all this fog at Heathrow, though.
Claire Smith: Oh no, what happened?
Liz Jones: Oh, it was…my flight was diverted to Bournemouth, ye…and then we had to go by bus from there to London. So…I didn't get to my hotel till lunchtime, it was crazy . . .

3 *Mrs Green:* Mr Evans, um…have you met Miss Lucas? She's from Argentina.
Mr Evans: Yes, I think we've met before. It's good to see you again!
Miss Lucas: That's right, hello again. How are you?
Mr Evans: Fine, thanks. Er…must be, what, a couple of years since we last met?
Miss Lucas: Oh, even longer – four years ago I think. In Miami, wasn't it?
Mr Evans: Yes! Yes, that was an interesting conference! Ha…W…would you both like some coffee?
Miss Lucas: Oh, yes, please. Black for me.
Mrs Green: Oh, thanks a lot, Mr Evans. Er…white with sugar for me.
Mr Evans: Right.
Mrs Green: Er…Miss Lucas, er…whereabouts do you come from in Argentina?
Miss Lucas: Er…well…mm…I live in Buenos Aires, but I was raised in Mendoza.
Mrs Green: Oh, was it…that's in the north . . .

E Now it's time for the role-play activity. As this is the first use of Files in the book, you may need to explain the 'information-gap' principle underlying this kind of exercise. The activity simulates what might happen when a visitor is passed from person to person within a company, being introduced to each other and taking part in a social conversation.

➡ Some sticky labels or pin-on badges are required for this activity. Small Post-it™ notes work well as temporary badges and are easy to remove later.

1 Divide the class into two teams. The A Team look at File **1** on page 146 in the Student's Book, where they discover that they are to play the role of COLLEAGUES working in the same firm, ACME Industries. The B Team look at File **31** on page 156 in the Student's Book, where they discover that they are to play the role of VISITORS to ACME Industries.

2 Make sure everyone understands more or less what they have to do, according to the instructions given in Files **1** and **31**. If necessary, go through the instructions with the class. It all looks complicated but once they've done steps **1** and **2**, step **2** keeps repeating itself.

3 To start off with, all the members of the A Team ('colleagues') should choose a name and job title and write their own first name and title with their chosen family name on a label or badge. Meanwhile, the members of the B Team ('visitors') will choose names and places of origin, but they don't need badges.

4 Start off the activity: the steps below are numbered in the same way as the steps in both Files in the Student's Book.

The steps in the Files in the Student's Book are as follows:

1 A 'visitor' finds a 'colleague' and introduces him or herself. They strike up a conversation until they receive a SIGNAL from you to stop and begin the next step. One way of doing this might be switching the classroom lights on and off or rapping sharply on the board, or even using a bell (a hotel reception bell is ideal and can be used regularly to interrupt pair and group work).

2 The 'colleague' then introduces his or her 'visitor' to another 'colleague'. They hand over their 'visitors' and the new pairs strike up a conversation until they receive a signal from you.

3 So it goes on with 'colleagues' handing over 'visitors' several times.

4 When everyone has met and talked to several other people, tell everyone to stop and go back to their seats.

5 Now, the roles are reversed and the 'colleagues' become 'visitors' and vice versa. First, they should choose names and the 'colleagues' should make badges. Then, exactly the same procedure is followed as above.

F Arrange the class into groups of three or four and get them to ask each other the questions in the Student's Book. This is a good opportunity for students to compare their experiences and get to know each other's attitudes and personalities.

At the end of the discussion (which could last between two and five minutes, depending on how much the groups have to say on the subject), ask each group to report its most interesting ideas to the rest of the class. There are, of course, no 'correct answers' to these questions – but your students may be interested to hear your own answers to some of the questions at the very end of the discussion.

Further discussion questions:

• What might happen if you don't introduce people to each other?
• What might happen if you don't mention their position in the company? Is it important that women are introduced with the same 'weight' or emphasis as men?

Finally, ask if anyone has any questions or comments on what they have done in this section.

Extra activity

If you have a smallish, fairly advanced class, you could ask everyone to record their own voices on a blank cassette. Working in groups, each student records a short monologue introducing themselves, as if talking to a small group of strangers: '*My name's ____ and I come from ...*'. Once they have done this they should pass the cassette to another group who will then comment on the impression they get. Students who are judged to sound abrupt or unfriendly should be recommended to smile more and be extra polite!

This activity may also be done by students working together in pairs as part of their homework, and would be suitable for a larger class in this case.

1.2 It's a small world ...

This section involves some essential vocabulary and a discussion based on a reading passage. Steps **A** and **B** could be prepared at home before the lesson – and if possible the article in **C** should be read through at home beforehand too.

➡ A large wall map of the world would be useful in this lesson.

Vocabulary – most of this is in the article in **C**

behaviour	demanding	chewing	disaster
manners	gymnastic	apparently	syllable
offence	demonstrations	counterparts	aperitif
increasingly	tricky	offensive	surname

Procedure – *about 90 minutes*

A This step introduces some of the principles involved in forming nationality words and introduces some of the one-off exceptions. It should be done in writing, as spelling is important here. Students could do this alone and then compare what they've written with a partner.

Answers

an Australian

a Brazilian

a Canadian

a Frenchman or Frenchwoman or French person

a Dutchman or Dutchwoman or Dutch person

a Hungarian

an Indian

a New Zealander

a Norwegian

a Saudi Arabian

a Swede

an American

Before going on to the next step, make sure students know the names of all the countries that surround their own country and can spell the name of each country – and also what they'd call a person from each country and the language(s) they speak there.

B Students should work in pairs. They may need to consult a map of the world to get ideas if their geography isn't very good!

Suggested, but not exhaustive, answers

AFRICA: Kenya   South Africa   Egypt   Tunisia   Algeria   Morocco   Ghana   Gabon   Senegal   . . .

ASIA: Japan   Korea   China   Indonesia   Malaysia   Thailand   India   Pakistan   . . .

MIDDLE EAST: Syria   Saudi Arabia   Kuwait   Lebanon   Egypt   Abu Dhabi   Iraq   . . .

LATIN AMERICA: Brazil   Argentina   Venezuela   Chile   Peru   Uruguay   Guyana   Colombia   . . .

EU countries: France   Italy   Luxembourg   the Netherlands (Holland)   Germany   Spain   Portugal   Belgium   Greece   Ireland   Denmark   United Kingdom (UK)

Non-EU countries (some of these may be EU countries by the time you read this!):   Poland   the Czech Republic   Slovenia   Bulgaria   Albania   Hungary   . . .

C It may be necessary to remind your students that they don't need to understand every single word of this (or any) passage to understand what it's about. The questions in **3** are intended to direct their attention to the main points in the article – if they can answer those, then they've understood the passage adequately.

If you do think they need help with vocabulary before reading the passage, spend a few minutes going over this before they read it – but if possible encourage them to read the article *before* the lesson, so as to save time in class for questions and discussion.

Don't worry if your students fail to appreciate the humorous tone of the magazine article – it's the information content that they should be concerned with in this case. The article raises serious issues in a light-hearted way.

1 Don't spend too long on this step – it's just a warm-up for the reading comprehension exercise and the longer discussion in **4**.

2 If possible, the article should be read through at home before the lesson. You may feel it's necessary to explain some of the vocabulary beforehand (see above).
   Discuss which of the headlines seem more suitable than others – the original article was titled *Good manners, good business*, but *When in Rome …* or *I didn't mean to be rude!* might be equally suitable and stylistically appropriate. *Problems that business people face* is too general, *Doing business in Europe* seems very dull and *Travelling abroad* isn't really a relevant headline.

3 Answers
True: 1   4   7   8
False: 2   3   5 (*never* is an exaggeration)   6   9

4 To help with this discussion, put a list of headings on the board as cues:
*greeting and saying goodbye   addressing people   clothes   table manners
visiting someone's home   giving gifts or flowers*

➡ The theme of non-verbal behaviour and body language is taken further in **1.4**.

Extra activity – *You may photocopy the activity in the box below.*

Part of the purpose of this activity is to explore national stereotypes and re-examine them. Hopefully, students will agree that it's *not* a good idea to presuppose that everyone from a country is going to behave in the same way – but let them decide this together.
   If, after some discussion, everyone still seems to think that there really is such a thing as a typical Italian, Swede or American, then ask them if they would like to be typecast as a 'typical' citizen of their own nation, or would prefer to be treated as an individual. National stereotypes are quite dangerous and can hamper developing a relationship with a foreign business partner.

New International Business English   This document may be photocopied.

Work in groups   Some people have stereotyped ideas about foreigners – and even about people from other parts of their own country …

Ask the other members of your group to describe 'a typical person' from:
the USA   Great Britain   the North of your country   the South of your country
the capital of your country   the second city of your country
– and other countries from the list you made in **1.2B** earlier.

➡ To what extent are such stereotypes useful? To what extent are they dangerous?

1.3 What do you enjoy about your work?

The speakers interviewed on the recording are speaking naturally and at their normal speed. Your students will probably need to hear the recording two or even three times. These are authentic interviews, and students shouldn't expect to be able to understand or even 'catch' every single word they hear. Perhaps reassure them on this score. The speakers all work for a software company, but there's no need to have any specialist knowledge of computers to understand the main points they each make.

Vocabulary – some of these are computer terms, which don't all need to be understood to do the task in **A2**

accountant	generate	solve problems	applications
day-to-day	(computer) systems	hectic	environment
tackle a job	trouble-shooting	be confronted with problems	ambitious
deadlines	back-up	encounter problems	prospects
finance	data	resolve problems	
business development	loose cable	hands-on	
responsibilities	challenge	programming	

Procedure – *about 45 minutes*

A

1   The purpose of the first listening is to let students get used to the voices and get just some of the basic information from the texts. It's a good idea to stop the recording after hearing each speaker.
  There may be a few tricky vocabulary items (see above) which, although not necessary for answering the questions and getting the gist of the passage, might just cause your students some trouble. Writing some of these up on the board and explaining some of them beforehand might help to speed up the listening process.

2   Play the interviews again, pausing between each one to give everyone time to note down their answers.

3   Depending on how difficult your students find the interviews, be prepared to play them through again so that they can fill in any remaining gaps.

Suggested answers

Ian McShane is an accountant

He is responsible for:
day-to-day accounting

He enjoys:
1 Different jobs
2 Deadlines
3 Dealing with finance

He doesn't enjoy:
Being difficult with people to get money out of them

Lesley Trigg is an administrator

Her responsibilities are:
1 Correspondence
2 Arranging meetings
3 Organizing travel

She enjoys:
The people she works with

She doesn't enjoy:
Not being busy (She has to wait for people to generate work)

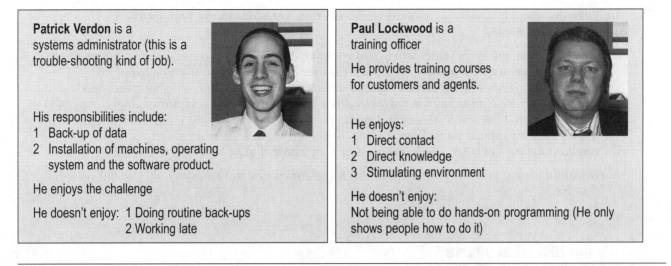

Patrick Verdon is a systems administrator (this is a trouble-shooting kind of job).

His responsibilities include:
1 Back-up of data
2 Installation of machines, operating system and the software product.

He enjoys the challenge

He doesn't enjoy: 1 Doing routine back-ups
2 Working late

Paul Lockwood is a training officer

He provides training courses for customers and agents.

He enjoys:
1 Direct contact
2 Direct knowledge
3 Stimulating environment

He doesn't enjoy:
Not being able to do hands-on programming (He only shows people how to do it)

Transcript [4 minutes 20 seconds]

Ian: My name's Ian McShane and I'm the group accountant for Small World-wide. I'm responsible for the day-to-day accounting for the group, covering financial management, management accounting, cash books, purchase ledger, sales ledger, credit control and so on.

Virtually every day you've got a different kind of…er…job to tackle, it's *always* without exception urgent. I'm always up against deadlines and therefore I'm never bored. I find the whole of finance fascinating anyway and the whole exercise is very, very interesting.

It's not very pleasant being difficult, or having to be difficult with people to get money out of them. I don't particularly like doing that.

Lesley: My name's Lesley Trigg. At Small World I work as an administrator for the international business development group. My responsibilities are responding to correspondence, making sure that meetings are scheduled for the right rooms at the right places. Um…also I deal with organizing people's travel in the company to various different countries throughout the world.

The most important thing that I enjoy is actually the people that are here in Small World. The people are very friendly and I enjoy the work.

I wish at times I was a little bit more busier. Um…I have to wait for people to generate work for me and, as working within the international business development group most of the people actually work in…within other countries, because they're going out into other countries to find partners that will assist Small World. And when they're out of the country they're not generating the work for me back in the office, they generate the work when they're back in the office for me to deal with.

Patrick: My name is Patrick Verdon. I deal with the systems administration for Small World. I think the best description of systems administration is that it's a trouble-shooting kind of job, there are all kinds of responsibilities, such as back-up of data, installation of new machines, installation of the

operating system and the installation of the product that…er…Small World actually produces. It's quite a challenge, because there's such a variety of problems: sometimes it'll be a loose cable on a…on a machine that's a problem, another time it'll take hours to solve.

I think the nice part of systems administration is the challenge. Um…sometimes it's very quiet, but on the other hand you can have a day when it's completely hectic and all kinds of different problems come up. So y…you're always being confronted with…with different problems, which is nice.

The things I don't enjoy are the routine back-ups of all the data, these take a bit of time. The other thing that I don't quite like is the…the out of hours concept of system…systems administration, because the best time to actually fix problems is when people aren't working, which means that ideally we should do that after six when everybody's gone home, so, yes, we can be here until the early hours of the morning at the extreme.

Paul: I'm Paul Lockwood, and I'm one of the training officers at Small World and my job is to…um…run and provide training courses for our customers and agents.

The thing I enjoy most about my work is…um…being able to have direct contact with customers and…er…direct knowledge of the sort of problems they encounter and how to resolve them.

The things I don't enjoy so much is that I feel that I…I…um…tend to be spending a lot of time either teaching or preparing training material, and I don't get enough chance to do hands-on programming that I would like to do. I do have to have the skills of programming but what I don't get the opportunity to do at the moment is to actually use them to develop real applications for customers, I'm just showing other people how to do it.

Generally speaking, I…I enjoy my job. I…I enjoy the company that I work for. Um…it's a very good environment, a very stimulating environment.

B 1 Everyone continues working in pairs to discuss their reactions to the four speakers they've just listened to.

2 Then students 'interview' each other. While they're doing this, go round offering advice and encouragement. Persuade students who are replying too laconically to expand on their answers. Encourage students without work experience to reminisce about vacation work they've done, or times they've 'helped out' in the family business, for example.

Rather than do this as a whole class, perhaps rearrange the class into groups of four (each pair with another pair). Each student should tell the new partners about his or her original partner – in other words, no one is talking about him or herself at this stage.

Before finishing, give everyone a chance to make comments and raise any queries they may have.

1.4 It's not just what you say ...

Following the issues raised in **1.1** about sounding and looking friendly and polite, here we focus on specific ways in which your non-verbal signals and body language may influence the way people see you. The reading passage in **1.2C** also leads in to this section.

Social behaviour is an important aspect of dealing with people face-to-face. There may be national standards of appropriate behaviour, but many of these are by no means universal (see question 7 in the quiz, for example).

Appropriate behaviour partly depends on the various signals you give, mostly unconsciously, to the people you meet:

- The style of language you use and the words you choose: it's important to make sure that other people feel comfortable talking to you and don't feel that you're competing with them.
- Your tone of voice ('*Why?*' or even '*Why is that?*' can sound like a challenge or disagreement if spoken sharply).
- Your expression: an unchanging silly smile looks insincere, but it's better than a frown (which looks like aggression even if to you it means puzzlement).
- The noises you make: sighing, clicking your pen, tapping your foot all mean something – often much more than the words that are spoken. Imagine being told by a salesperson: '*It's very good of you to see me . . .* yawn . . . sigh . . . *Now, if I could just take up five minutes of your time . . .*'!
- Your body language and the way you stand or sit: if you have your arms crossed you may look defensive, if you slump in the chair you may look sleepy, if you sit upright with your shoulders back you may look eager and alert (maybe too much). Overdoing any of these signals may seem like play-acting and make you look insincere.
- Your appearance: different business clothes are acceptable in different countries and in different companies. What impression does a man in your business give if he doesn't wear a tie? Or if he wears his hair very long?
- Even the way you smell! Millions of pounds are spent by men and women on perfume, after-shave and deodorants to combat body odour. Different cultures find different smells unpleasant.

Vocabulary

conference	*concentrating*	*yawning*	*co-workers*
delegates	*sigh*	*clicking*	
quiz	*indigestion*	*sniffing*	
conversationalist	*reliable*	*tapping your fingers*	
blinking	*business card*	*body language*	

Procedure – *about 45 minutes*

A **1** This short exercise makes students aware that first names and surnames are used differently in different countries. Begin by pointing out that both Howard and Thomas could be a surname or a first name. One shouldn't assume that everyone uses the same conventions. If you aren't sure which name is a surname and which is a first name, you may need to find out – and this may be a particular problem with people from overseas with names which are strange to your ears.

In this case, the other delegates would probably be addressed as Mr Lo, Ms* Burgos, Ms* Kryskiewicz and Mr Ivany.

(On an envelope the last two would be Ms* Grazyna Kryskiewicz and Mr László Ivany.)

* Or *Mrs* or *Miss*, depending on the title she prefers. People tend to play safe, if they don't know, by using *Ms*.

2 To forestall any vocabulary problems when doing the quiz, demonstrate the expressions and noises by:

blinking   sighing
and miming *indigestion* by holding your chest and showing pain

There are no 'correct' answers to questions 1 to 6, but suggested answers to the last two questions are: 7c and 8c.

While the discussions are going on, go round the class listening in and making notes on any language points you think students need to be made aware of. At the end of the discussion, mention these points to the whole class.

B The pairs could combine into groups of four. You may need to help students with vocabulary for describing the pictures. Demonstrate the expressions and noises by:

yawning   clicking your pen   tapping your fingers   sniffing   and so on

Some of the pictures are deliberately rather ambiguous, so encourage everyone to use their imaginations when interpreting them and deciding how the people look and the impressions they're giving. Point out that if you can't think of the terms *with his tie at half-mast* or *well-groomed hands*, for example, it's easy enough to say *with your tie like that* or *with fingers like those*.

C Perhaps change the members of each group round, to give more points of view.

Further discussion questions:
- Think of someone you know who is a bad speaker or conversationalist: what qualities make that person dull?
- Think of someone you know who is a good speaker or conversationalist: what qualities make that person effective?

1.5 Developing relationships

Following the issues that were raised in **1.1** about starting off on the right foot when meeting people for the first time, the three steps in this section concern the way a relationship changes, generally becoming more intimate and friendly, as time goes on. We also consider the different ways of talking to different kinds of people, depending on your relationship.

Particularly important in this section is 'small talk': talking about things that are not connected with business.

Vocabulary

flu	*sketch*	*junior*
figures	*border*	*business associates*
on-going	*common interests*	
terminal	*senior*	

Procedure – *about 90 minutes*

A 🔊 Play the recording. Students will hear five extracts from some typical interactions that might be overheard in an international company.

Students should note down their answers to the questions in their notebooks, rather than rely on their memories. Point out that they will have to guess some of the answers, basing their guesses on their own interpretation of the situations. For example, no one in the first extract actually says 'I am a sales rep' – you have to work this out from what they say. There are no definitive right answers to this exercise: describing relationships can only be done in an impressionistic way – so students are asked here to form impressions as they make notes.

Pause the recording after each extract, so that students can compare their notes with a partner. At the end, replay the whole recording so that everyone can see who was right. If you think your students will find this difficult, pause after each extract and ask everyone in the class to contribute their theories. Then replay the extract and decide whose theory was right.

Suggested answers

1 Tony and Bob have a cordial, informal relationship. Tony is an overseas sales rep and Bob is the Export Sales Manager. They're talking about problems Tony encountered on a visit to a client in Copenhagen.
2 Mr Allen is very friendly and informal but is superior to Barry and Susanna, who are new to the company. Mr Allen is probably office manager and the other two are clerical staff. Mr Allen is explaining who is who in the office.
3 Mr Green behaves very much as Martin's boss (he is quite authoritarian). Mr Green is probably the transport manager and Martin is a driver. They are talking about Martin collecting someone at the airport.
4 Geoff is more experienced and probably senior to Mandy. They have an informal relationship. They are probably commercial artists or designers. She's asking him to evaluate some work she has done.
5 Tony is junior to Mrs Lang, she is his boss and they have a fairly formal relationship. We can't tell what their jobs are. They are talking about Tony having time off on Friday.

Transcript [3 minutes 10 seconds]

1 *Bob:* Er...Tony?
Tony: Mmm.
Bob: Er...I'd like to see you for a minute, would you come into the office?
Tony: Oh, yeah, right.
Bob: Good. Now, how did you get on in Copenhagen?
Tony: Ah, yeah...er...well, Carlsson had the flu, so I couldn't see him.
Bob: Couldn't see him?
Tony: No, so I had to see his assistant. And, you know, we...er...we got along quite well, but...um...th...er... there are problems w...er...Crystals got in before us.
Bob: Oh Lord!

Tony: Yeah, they were in last week. So...er...they...you know, they...they spent days there and...er...it was all wrapped up really by the time I got there.
Bob: Is it...is it a question of...of...of supply? Are we... are we not producing enough for them?
Tony: Well, no, they didn't really look at the figures, quite frankly, and I showed them the figures and they...they weren't interested.
Bob: Yeah, well you see the trouble is that we've got a...we've got an on-going problem . . .

2 *Mr Allen:* Now, Barry...er...and Susanna, have you got your worksheet in front of you – fact sheet here?
Barry & Susanna: Yes.

Mr Allen: Now you can see here that Miss Henry is James Ferguson's personal assistant. That's pretty important to know. Ted Douglas is the chief export clerk.

Susanna: Ah, right.

Mr Allen: Er...Barry, you're going to be working with Susanna very closely here . . .

Barry: Good.

Mr Allen: And...er...I think it's very important, Barry, that you...er...get together with Susanna over there and try to work out the...the letter filing system here.

Barry: Uhuh.

Susanna: Mmm.

Mr Allen: Now, as you can see, we've...er...as you can see on your fact sheet here we've got it marked Urgent and Non-urgent.

Barry: Yeah.

Mr Allen: Er...anything essential I'll take care of, OK? Haha.

Barry & Susanna: Haha.

3 *Mr Green:* OK, Martin, er...let's go through it again. You go to the airport.

Martin: Right.

Mr Green: OK. Terminal 2.

Martin: Terminal 2.

Mr Green: Pick up Glenn Donaldson.

Martin: Glenn Donaldson.

Mr Green: Now I want you to write this down.

Martin: Yeah, I've got it down.

Mr Green: OK, he's arriving from Miami on the flight number LX432.

Martin: LX432.

Mr Green: Have you got that?

Martin: Yeah, I've got it.

Mr Green: Right, off you go. Get back here as soon as you can.

Martin: Yes, sir, Mr Green.

Mr Green: Thank you.

4 *Mandy:* Geoff, um...could you just come over here a minute and have a look at this sketch?

Geoff: Yes, sure.

Mandy: What do you think?

Geoff: Aha, yes, well you've put a lot of work into it, that's...that's very good. I'm not too happy about this border round here...um...

Mandy: No?

Geoff: Maybe you could try another go at that.

Mandy: I will, I'll try again. OK.

5 *Tony:* Mrs Lang, could I have a word, please?

Mrs Lang: Oh, yes, Tony, of course.

Tony: I wondered if I might have next Friday off. My sister's arriving from Switzerland...er...I'd like to meet her at the airport.

Mrs Lang: Oh, Friday's rather difficult. What time does she arrive?

Tony: Well, the plane gets in at four pm.

Mrs Lang: Oh, I know, Tony! Why don't you go off just after lunch, then you'll manage to get to the airport on time to meet her at four.

Tony: Oh, thank you very much, Mrs Lang.

B The issue of what topics are suitable when talking to strangers (particularly if they are foreign clients whom you must impress, rather than embarrass) is quite complex, and rather personal. Clearly there are no hard-and-fast rules about this, but probably politics and religion are no-go areas, and your own family might be too personal a topic to talk about at the start of the meeting.

If your students ask you for advice on this, tell them which of the topics *you* would feel comfortable talking about. Among the other topics might be: holidays, travel, traffic, public transport, and any other interests you and the other person have in common. Indeed the purpose of a social conversation with a new person is to discover what you do have in common, so that you can then exchange experiences.

If the other person is, for example, older and senior to you, you might be more deferential and ask her or him exploratory questions to try and discover what you have in common, or at best what you both feel comfortable talking about together.

C This role-play activity explores the theme of changing relationships and using small talk. Perhaps point out that there are no easy formulae for small talk. You have to use your own ideas. But as you get to know someone better, you learn what subjects are suitable for small talk with that person.

If you have a video camera available, all or part of the activity can be recorded on video for playback and analysis later. An audio recorder (with a good microphone) can be used in the same way.

Before they begin the role-play, students should work in pairs and note down some suitable subjects that they like to talk about with people they don't know terribly well.

◉ Ask everyone to look at the expressions in the speech balloons, and play the recording, which demonstrates how the role-play might go.

Transcript [1 minute]

Host: Mary, hello again. Do come in and sit down! How are you getting on?

Visitor: Hello. I'm fine, thanks. How are you?

Host: Oh, very well thanks. Did you...er...did you have a good journey? . . .

(more small talk)

Visitor: . . . Well, I know I'm lucky to be here this soon.

Host: Yes, haha. Right, let's get down to business, shall we?

Visitor: Yes, all right.

Host: OK, first of all if we could just look at erm . . .

(main business phase of the meeting)

Visitor: . . . Yes, right. Well, I think that's agreed then.

Host: Yeah. Yep, sure.

Visitor: Oh, and now I really must be going, I've...er . . .

Host: Sure you won't have...er...some coffee or something before you go?

Visitor: Oh, no, no, thanks. I haven't really got time. Sorry.

Host: OK, well, see you again soon, I hope !

Visitor: Yes, yes, I...I'm glad we were able to meet.

Host: Oh, so am I. Um...I'll come downstairs with you . . .

If necessary, demonstrate the whole conversation again with one of your more confident students while the others watch and listen. Show how the main business phase of the meeting (between steps **3** and **4**) should be skipped.

As the 'Visitor' is arriving at the 'Host's office', he or she should stand up and walk into the office and be offered a seat.

➡ Before they role-play a meeting six months later, discuss what's happened so far:

• What particular difficulties and awkwardness did they encounter?
• How could these problems be averted next time?

Give students who have experience of talking to clients or salespeople a chance to give the rest of the class the benefit of their experience.

Follow-up discussion

At the end, ask the class what conclusions they have drawn from this activity:

• What aspects of small talk do they find difficult? What aspects do they find relatively easy?
• Does anyone in the class have any useful 'tricks' that they use when meeting someone for the first time, to break the ice and establish a friendly relationship?

And to round off the whole unit:

• What would you (realistically) like to be able to do in English by the end of this course?
• What aspects of your English do you think you need to improve most of all?
• What have you learnt from this unit that you will be able to apply in future units and in your daily work?

Workbook contents for this unit

1.1 Dealing with people   *Background information*

1.2 Around the world   *Vocabulary*

1.3 Go along and get along   *Reading*

1.4 Have you met ...?   *Functions & speaking*

1.5 Asking questions   *Grammar review*

1.6 Do it my way   *Reading*

Letters, faxes and memos

This unit introduces and practises the skills required to deal with the writing tasks in Units 5 to 15. It covers:

- How to lay out a business letter or memo
- Some 'golden rules' for writing letters, faxes and memos
- Practice in writing routine letters, e-mails, faxes and memos

Written business communication may take the form of letters, internal memos, faxes and e-mail (electronic mail) – students need to be confident in using all these forms.

The various styles of writing that are used in formal business letters, memos, e-mails and faxes are covered. However, students who will have to write a lot of long, formal letters in their work will probably need to do further work on this.

We have taken account of the changes that have taken place in recent years in the style of business letters in English – your students may need to be made aware that the style that is now current is much less formal than the style used in some other languages.

Background information

Before starting on this unit, draw your students' attention to the Background information in the Workbook. This shows some of the basic rules of writing business letters, and of writing memos, e-mails and faxes.

Video

Programme 2 on the *New International Business English Video* introduces the theme of this unit.

2.1 Communicating in writing

By contrasting the recorded conversation and the written memo in **B**, we see how the different modes of communication are used and some of the limitations of both.

Vocabulary

correspondence	*memo*	*internally*
attend to	*e-mail*	*externally*
proportions	*relative merits*	

Procedure – *about 45 minutes*

A The different forms of correspondence shown are:

fax   airmail   first class post   handwritten letter   typed letter   internal memo
postcard   e-mail (on the computer screen)   Post-It™ note   magazine

There is no 'correct order' for dealing with the correspondence, though one might open the airmail letter first and deal with the internal memo last of all!

To answer the last question, students who aren't working should estimate what they think are realistic proportions or remember their work experience.

B **1** Begin by getting everyone to read the memo. Get them to explain roughly what it's about. 'HGW' seems to be in charge of staff training.

2 🎙️ Play the recording twice. Ask the class to spot what information was missing in each and which seemed the more efficient way of conveying the information.

(In the memo a lot more information is given and it's easier to follow – and you have a permanent record. In the conversation there is an opportunity for discussion and for questions to be answered – but the details would only be given if they were demanded.)

Transcript [1 minute 20 seconds]

Mr W: Ah, Maria, I wanted to see you, um...did I tell you that we're starting up the English classes again?

Maria: Oh, are you? Great, good. Where?

Mr W: Er...in the training centre, hopefully. We're getting Mr Roberts in again from ELS. So could you tell your people and let me have a list of names by...um...let's say Wednesday?

Maria: Yes, yes...um...Last time there was a bit of misunderstanding about the books they needed...um...who was going to pay for them.

Mr W: Oh, really? Well, no problem this time, we'll provide the books. But they will have to do some homework outside work, make sure they realize that. Um...or else there'll probably be some problems. Er...there'll be two classes, by the way: an intermediate class and an advanced one. But there will be a limit in each of the classes of...probably about twelve.

Maria: Oh, really, a limit of twelve? Ah, well, what if there are more people wanting to come? I mean, I can think of at least eight just in my department alone. Um...how will you decide who can attend?

Mr W: Er...mm, good point. Er...I think we'll have to play that one by ear really.

Maria: OK, well how about running another class . . .

C **1** The discussion may bring up some of the following points:

FACE-TO-FACE communication – Advantages & pleasures:
   more personal   more interaction and feedback possible
   can make more impact   cheaper if no travel involved   you can smile . . .

   Disadvantages & difficulties:
   once you've said something it can't be unsaid
   saying something once may not sink in or be remembered . . .

WRITING – Advantages & pleasures:
   a record can be kept for the files   errors can be changed
   you can write or read when you're in the right mood
   you can take your time over planning and how you'll express complicated or delicate details . . .

   Disadvantages & difficulties:
   writing takes longer   there is no feedback or the feedback is delayed
   no 'personal touch'   no smiles   no handshakes . . .

2 The discussion continues in groups of four or five. Some of these points may come up:

MEMOS are on paper: you have a permanent record which can be referred to when away from your computer; they may be a waste of resources, they have to be delivered . . .

E-MAIL is quick and easy: people are more tolerant of spelling (and even grammatical) mistakes; a hard copy can be printed out if necessary; e-mail can go to another branch in another country almost instantly . . .

LETTERS have to conform to accepted style: they take time to write; they take time to arrive; they seem less 'important' or urgent than faxes or e-mails . . .

FAXES are very quick; they can go astray; they can be sent to the wrong number; you have no record of receipt except 'TX DONE' or 'STATUS CORRECT' which don't tell you if it's been received intact by the right person; they get distorted or have lines missing – especially over long distances . . .

Try to avoid making didactic statements yourself – business people have their own ideas and experience, and customs differ from country to country. You are probably less of an expert than many of your students, so let them give everyone the benefit of their experience.

2.2 Names and addresses

In this section we look at the way addresses are laid out in the UK and the USA, but the main emphasis is on S-P-E-L-L-I-N-G A-L-O-U-D. If you're working in business you need to be able to use the alphabet fluently and understand other people when they spell words or names out loud to you.

If necessary, run through the alphabet with the class, reminding them of the tricky letters (A and R, G and J, E and I, etc.).

Vocabulary

envelope	*addressee*
spelt (US spelled)	*job title*

Procedure – *about 90 minutes*

➡ If your students have little experience of how addresses are laid out, even in their own country, take along to class a few envelopes addressed to yourself. Draw their atttention to, among other things, the use of titles, punctuation, commas, indentation, post codes or zip codes, and any striking national differences.

A Ask everyone to study the address labels in the Student's Book and detect the differences between the layout of addresses in other countries (including the use of post codes or zip codes and street numbers).

Note that nowadays commas are not commonly used at the end of each line, and it's now considered quite old-fashioned to write, for example:

```
Cyril Old, Esq.,
34, Traditional Way,
Old Felixstowe,
Suffolk,
IP86 OAP
```

(Esq. is short for Esquire and used only to address male addressees in Britain.)

B [recording icon] Play the recording (probably twice), pausing as necessary for students to take the dictation down. All of these addresses are read aloud, which may provoke further discussion and questions. The complete recording lasts three minutes and the correct versions of the addresses are in File **57** in the Student's Book.

Get everyone to check their work in File **57**. Did they make many mistakes writing down the addresses in this exercise? If so, tell them that the next section needs extra special attention!

C For this information-gap activity, ask everyone to imagine that they are reading a list of addresses over the phone (maybe prospective customers that a salesperson has to visit). There are three difficult addresses with hard-to-spell names, which they must dictate to their partner. One student looks at File **2**, the other at **33**. You may have to point out that these names and addresses are all genuine and typical of the kind that they might encounter in their work.

If you think this will be too difficult for your students, they could hear the recording first (to give them confidence) and then have a go themselves in pairs, before hearing the recording again at the end.

[recording icon] When they have finished, or had enough, play the model reading on the recording. You'll need to pause it frequently.

See Files **2** and **33** in the Student's Book for the text of this recording, which lasts 5 minutes 20 seconds.

Three extra activities

⚠ Incorrect spelling in a business letter gives a bad impression and can be confusing. (Even if you only dictate letters, you'll need to check them before you sign them.)

1 Spelling aloud

To give further, probably easier, practice in spelling aloud, ask the class to imagine they are filling in a form. Give them these instructions:

1 Write down on a slip of paper:
   your own *full* name (with title: Mr, Dr, Miss, etc.)
   your home address and telephone number
   the name and address of the place where you work or study
   your date and place of birth

2 Pass the slip to another student, who will dictate your personal details to the rest of the class.

3 Write down the information the other students dictate to you. When it's your turn, read aloud what's on your sheet. Spell out any long or difficult names.

4 Check that your own personal details have been taken down completely accurately.

2 British and American spelling

Here are some words in their British English spellings. Write them on the board and get the class to spell them out loud in their American English versions (here given in brackets):

centre (*center*)   *labour* (*labor*)   *licence* (*license*)   *catalogue* (*catalog*)
traveller's cheque (*traveler's check*)   *instalment* (*installment*)   *programme* (*program*)

Note that some alternative spellings, such as:

    inquire/enquire   dispatch/despatch   realise/realize   utilise/utilize etc.

are often a question of a company's 'house style', and there are no fixed rules. This book uses a variety of these in the letters and other texts but adheres to a house style in the rubrics and explanations.

3 Abbreviations

1 Write some (but not all) of these English abbreviations on the board and check if members of the class can explain them:

PS	postscript
p.p.	per pro (on behalf of)
c.c. or cc	carbon copy to (often now a photocopy) – or cubic centimetres
ref.	reference (number)
Rd	Road
St	Street or Saint
Sq.	Square
No. (US #)	number
c/o	care of
attn	for the attention of
POB	Post Office Box
eg or e.g.	for example
ie or i.e.	that is / in other words
etc.	et cetera / and so on
& Co.	and Company
plc or p.l.c.	Public Limited Company
Ltd	Limited
Corp.	Corporation
Inc.	Incorporated

> ⚠ The role of full stops (periods) in abbreviations is constantly changing. Many established abbreviations (eg, ie, Ltd, PLC, plc, etc) can be printed with or without periods these days. Less frequently used ones, especially ones that are just short forms of longer words (Dept., encl., misc., and so on) tend to have full stops. Reassure your class on this score, as it's a thing some students do tend to get out of proportion. Your own preferences (or the firm's house style) should be made clear to the class. Point out that it hardly takes any longer to type, say, 'Department' than it does to type 'Dept' or 'Dpt', and to write 'paid' rather than abbreviate it to 'pd'.

2 Get everyone to jot down some common abbreviations that are used in their language (S.A., GmbH, etc.). Then ask them to explain what each one stands for – as if telling an English-speaking colleague.

On the next page there are some of the most common abbreviations that your students may need to know. You may photocopy this list. Included among them are the ones you may have written on the board in step **1** of this activity.

Common abbreviations used in business

& Co.	and Company	lb or lbs	pounds (weight)
@	at (a price of) ...	Ltd	Limited
a/c	account	m.	meters (US) / metres (GB)
admin.	administration		or miles
approx.	approximately	MD	managing director
ASAP or asap	as soon as possible	misc.	miscellaneous
attn	for the attention of	N/A	not applicable
b/f	brought forward	No. (US #)	number
c.c.	cubic centimetres	oz.	ounces
c.c. or cc	carbon copy (usually now a photocopy) – or cubic centimetres	p.a.	per annum (per year)
		p.p.	per pro (on behalf of)
c/f	carried forward	PA	personal assistant
c/o	care of	par. or ¶ or §	paragraph
CEO	chief executive officer	PC	personal computer
Corp.	Corporation	PDQ	pretty damn quick(ly)
cu.	cubic	plc or p.l.c.	Public Limited Company
dept	department	POB	Post Office Box
do	ditto	PS or P.S.	postscript
doz. or dz.	dozen	Rd	Road
ea.	each	recd	received
eg or e.g.	for example	ref.	reference (number)
enc. or encl.	enclosures	Sq.	Square
etc.	et cetera / and so on	sq.	square (metres, feet, etc.)
ft	foot/feet	St	Street or Saint
ie or i.e.	that is / in other words	yd or yds	yards
in. or ins.	inches	®	registered trademark
Inc.	Incorporated	©	copyright
incl.	including/inclusive	TM	trademark

2.3 Layout and style

Even business people who don't actually have to type or word-process letters themselves still usually need to check them through before signing them – and as layout is something that can create a good (or bad) impression, they should be aware of the conventions used in British and American correspondence.

Vocabulary

ref. (reference number)
layout
house style
abbreviations
p.p. (per pro = on behalf of)
enc. (enclosure)
catalog (GB catalogue)
c.c. (carbon copy – more likely to be a photocopy these days)

training manual
heading
paragraph
concise
courteous
dot matrix
recycled
letterhead
logo

Procedure – *about 90 minutes*

A Encourage questions about the layout and stylistic conventions illustrated. Allow time for discussion of the conventions that apply in your students' country.

B Continue in the same way, encouraging questions from the class and comparisons with the conventions used in your students' country or countries. In this case, the typical American forms are:

`Sincerely` and `Best regards`

whilst these are more typically British:

`Yours sincerely`, `Best wishes`, `Kind regards` and `Yours faithfully`

C If possible, get everyone to treat these 'Golden Rules' with a certain amount of scepticism – some of the points are 'obvious' or common sense really. But highlighting encourages each student to pick out the advice they feel is most important for *them*.
   Find out what further rules they would suggest to a novice letter writer.

All of the tips apply to faxes and memos – particularly if you're taking the trouble to type or print them out nicely. But short note-style faxes, e-mails or memos can be dashed off more quickly, provided that you have established a suitably close working relationship with your addressee.

The discussion about styles of letters is to do with personal feelings, rather than any established 'rules'. Some of these points will probably be raised:

• The need for a certain amount of white space on a page (thus avoiding the so-called Zzzzzzz effect of long unbroken text)
• The way a document is divided up
• The use of headings and numbers
• The form and size of fonts (typefaces) used
• It's better if letters are 'attractive and clear', and not dull or confusing!

Extra activities

1 Ask the class to draft a letter to one of the people on the envelopes in **2.2**, requesting their latest catalogue.

2 This activity is probably more suitable for upper-intermediate and more advanced students. If you anticipate that your students will get quite involved in the activity and enjoy it, make sure you have enough time for them to do it adequately.

Work in pairs Imagine that you're setting up your own business. Design your own letterhead and logo.

2.4 Thinking about your reader

⚠ A long, impersonal letter may make you and your firm seem old-fashioned. Long sentences are difficult to read – and difficult to write.

This section looks at two aspects of letter writing: considering your reader at all times and adapting your style to suit the reader. The ideas apply to memos, short reports, e-mails and faxes too.

Vocabulary

wavy line	*additives*	*order form*	*relevant*	*extract*
utilize	*samples*	*prospective customer*	*irrelevant*	
artificial	*aromas*	*assemble*	*revisions*	

Procedure – *about 90 minutes*

A 1 Students should work in pairs for this discussion. They will probably consider the first letter to be rather old-fashioned, fuddy-duddy and dull.

2 Make sure they have time to find the actual turns of phrase that give the first letter its old-fashioned flavour and the second its more modern flavour. Many students may prefer something halfway between the two styles, particularly if they think the second one is too 'pushy' – but remember that it's a sales letter, designed to whet the reader's appetite!

Some rather dull or old-fashioned phrases in the first letter are:

'We enclose for your attention …'
'Should you require further information …'
'… your esteemed order …'

Some rather effective phrases in the second letter are:

'I am sure you will find plenty to interest you …'
'This year, for the very first time, …'

B Students should work in groups of three or four. First of all play the recording all the way through. Then play it again, pausing between each opinion while the groups discuss what they've just heard. Alternatively, pause between pairs of opinions – then the students may be less inclined to just say *That's a good idea* after each one.

Transcript [1 minute]

'Well, I use the back of an envelope or a beer mat.'
'Um…well, I usually sit back for a few moments and…um… think about what I'm going to do. And…well, then I just start writing.'
'I write on a word processor and I don't make notes before starting.'
'I write an outline of the letter and then do a final draft.'
'Er…I make notes on a large sheet of scrap paper.'

'Well, I just dictate it to my secretary and, well, let her sort out the details.'
'I do it all on my computer. Er…it's easy, I start by putting down the main headings, and then, well, start writing. I edit the document as I go along.'
'I sit for a few moments and then think about the person I'm writing to. Then I make notes before I actually start writing.'

C The '7 Steps' are from another piece of training material. Encourage students to give their views and to disagree with some of the points if they wish. If, however, they agree that planning is of great importance, this text can be referred back to again and again when letter-writing tasks are done in later units.

Highlighting the text will help to make the advice more memorable.

D The exercise is done in two phases: **1** finding the mistakes, and **2** rewriting the extracts (which could be done as homework).

Answers

There are 13 spelling and punctuation mistakes in the first extract:

> I noticed your advertisment in the Daily Planet amd I would be gratefull if you could sned me further infomration about your products My company is considering subcontracting some of its office services and I beleive that you may be able ot supply us with a sutiable service, Looking forware to hearing form you. Yours faithfully.

And with mistakes corrected:

```
I noticed your advertisement in the Daily Planet and I would be
grateful if you could send me further information about your
products.
    My company is considering subcontracting some of its office
services and I believe that you may be able to supply us with a
suitable service.
    Looking forward to hearing from you.
    Yours faithfully,
```

Here is the second extract with improved layout:

```
Thank you very much for your letter of 15 January, which we received
today.

In answer to your enquiry we have pleasure in enclosing an
information pack, giving full details of our services.

If you would like any further information, do please contact me by
phone or in writing and I will be pleased to help.

I hope that our services will be of interest to you and I look
forward to hearing from you.

Yours sincerely,
```

And here is the last one with shorter, clearer sentences:

```
There are a number of queries that I would like to raise about
your products. I would be grateful if you could ask a
representative to get in touch with me so that I can discuss these
queries.
    Hopefully, I will be able to place an order if the queries are
satisfactorily answered.
```

2.5 Sending messages

The style of memos can vary from scruffy handwritten notes to well-typed formal letters. Begin by finding out what kind of internal memos your students write and receive in their own work, if they are in employment.

Vocabulary

laptops	compile	agents	long-standing
feedback	come up to expectations	engineers	jeopardized
submit	benefit	puzzled	negotiating
informally	redraft	contract	

Procedure – *about 90 minutes*

A 1 If you anticipate difficulties with this task, begin by asking everyone what the purpose of KLJ's memo is: what action are you supposed to take after reading it? What information is not given?

(The main trouble with it is that it's imprecise and consequently liable to be misunderstood or, perhaps, disregarded.)

2 The redrafting should be a joint effort, with both partners contributing ideas. Perhaps point out that it should be made clear in the memo exactly what information KLJ wants from the staff and the deadline for its submission. Numbered paragraphs and headings may help.

While they're doing this, go round the class offering advice and checking spelling, punctuation and so on.

3 Before everyone looks at File **63** to see the model version of KLJ's memo, get each pair to show another pair their work and ask for comments.

(The model memo is better because it's more detailed, clear and precise. It's now absolutely clear what the reader is supposed to do as a result of reading it.) However, there may be some improvements or changes that can be made to this model!

B Allow plenty of time for this activity, but if time is short, it's better to skip one or two of the messages, rather than have no time to do steps **3** and **4**.

Divide the class into an EVEN number of pairs so that each pair will be able to communicate with another one in step **4**: this may entail having some groups of three.

Make sure each pair knows who their counterparts are. As the messages become progressively more complicated, students will build up confidence through experience.

You will need to announce a deadline for the transitions between each of the steps, so that all four steps plus the follow-up discussion can be done in the time you have available.

1 Everyone discusses how to transmit the messages. Go round from pair to pair asking for their reasons – as if you are genuinely interested, not as a challenge.

Students with more work experience should give advice to their less experienced classmates at this stage, perhaps in a brief whole-class discussion.

2 While students are planning and drafting their letters or faxes, go round offering advice and checking spelling and vocabulary.

3 The pairs read their counterparts' draft letters and faxes. They should apply the criteria given in the 'Golden Rules' in **2.3C** as they evaluate each other's work.

Then the pairs should join up with their counterparts and discuss each other's drafts.

If the drafts need to be rewritten, students should do this as homework. If they are satisfied with their drafts, collect up all the written work and mark it. There are no model answers here for this task.

➡ This might be a good source of material for you to photocopy and keep as a record of the standard of your students' written work at the beginning of the course. This can be compared with their (much improved) written work later in the course.

4 Rearrange the class into groups of four (each pair with another pair). The students who have phone calls or visits planned should role-play them, with one of each pair listening in and making notes, so that there can be feedback on the 'performance' afterwards. The partners should take it in turns here, and not let one do all the talking. (This activity could be recorded on video or cassette, and perhaps kept as a record of your students' spoken English at the beginning of the course.)

Workbook contents for this unit

 **On the phone**

This unit deals with basic telephoning skills and also receiving and noting down messages. These skills will be practised further in telephone role-plays throughout the book. Students are given a chance to discuss and develop their telephone techniques and practise making different kinds of business calls.

The functions of requesting, offering help and asking permission are also introduced and practised in this unit.

Background information

Draw everyone's attention to the Background information on telephoning in the Workbook. This is particularly important for students who have no experience of business calls – though we assume everyone is a user of the phone for social purposes!

Video

Programme 3 on the *New International Business English Video* introduces the theme of this unit.

3.1 I'd like to speak to …

This section introduces the topic of telephoning – and some of the difficulties that people encounter when trying to get in touch with someone on the phone. It focuses attention on the need for a good 'telephone style' and elicits some 'golden rules' for using the phone in English.

Vocabulary

mobile phone	*extension*	*applications*	*confirm*
phone booth	*connect*	*equipment*	*arrangements*
telephonist	*switchboard*	*literature*	
put you through	*laboratory/lab*	*agent*	

Procedure – *about 90 minutes*

A This warm-up discussion helps students to realize that they are already experienced telephone users. Some useful vocabulary is illustrated in the photos.

Further discussion questions:
- What are / would be the advantages and disadvantages of video phones in business?
- What about mobile phones: do you use one or know someone who does? What are the advantages and disadvantages of mobile phones?

B 1 ▢ The recording shows two attempts: an abortive phone call and then a rather unsuccessful call. Play both attempts through first so that students can get the general idea, then play it again pausing every so often for students to compare their notes.

Some of the places where problems and misunderstandings occurred are <u>underlined</u> in the Transcript. Some of the problems in the second attempt were partly the caller's own fault. (For example, she failed to double-check times and dates and she spoke too fast – she's the salesperson, so any misunderstandings are going to reflect badly on her firm.)

Your students with experience of making business phone calls will probably be keen to suggest many other ways in which the calls could be improved.

2 Most of the problems are due to people talking too quickly, not listening to each other and not checking back that they have understood or been understood correctly.

3 Combine the pairs into groups of four for this. Maybe ask the groups to come up with some 'golden rules' for making telephone calls – and at the end perhaps list these on the board. These might include:

- Plan your call by making notes beforehand.
- Talk slowly and clearly.
- Listen carefully to what the other person says.
- Note down important details (numbers, spellings, dates and times, etc.).
- Check back that you have understood important details correctly.
- Follow up the call with a fax, e-mail or letter, confirming the details.

➡ We return to the notion of 'golden rules' in **3.4A**, so don't spend too long on this.

Transcript   [3 minutes 30 seconds]

First attempt

Telephonist: <u>*(unintelligible)* and Company</u>. Can I help you?
Caller: Er...can I speak to Dr Henderson, please?
Telephonist: <u>Mr Anderson</u>. Just one moment, I'll put you through.
Anderson: Yes, Anderson, accounts.
Caller: Oh, er...hello, ...is that Dr Bill Henderson?
Anderson: What? No...no, this is Peter Anderson. You've got the wrong extension. You probably want Dr Henderson in R & D, that's...um...er...657. All right, 657.
Caller: Oh, um...well, c...can you connect me back through the switchboard, please?
Anderson: <u>Huh! Well, I'll try</u> . . .
(the line goes dead)
Caller: Hello?

Second attempt

Telephonist: *(unintelligible)* and Company. Can I help you?
Caller: Yes, I'd like to speak to <u>Dr Bill Henderson</u>, please.
Telephonist: Dr Henderson, putting you through.
Voice: 657.
Caller: Hello.
Voice: <u>Oh, hello</u>.
Caller: Um...is...is...is that Dr Henderson?
Voice: Er...no.
Caller: Oh, er...I'm trying to get hold of Dr Bill Henderson.
Voice: Oh, you want Bill. I'll just see if I can find him. Um...ju...just a moment.
Caller: Thank you.
. . .
Henderson: Henderson.

Caller: Oh, good. Um...good afternoon. This is Sylvia Perez. Er...I'm calling you from France.
Henderson: Sylvia who?
Caller: <u>Perez: P-E-R-E-Z</u>. Um...we met last month in...in Berlin at the trade fair. You expressed an interest in our <u>laboratory measuring equipment</u>.
Henderson: Oh, yes?
Caller: Well, the thing is I'm...I'm going to be in your area next month and I thought I might like to...um...call in and see you. I'd like to discuss the applications you might have for our equipment.
Henderson: Ah, I see. What's this about again?
Caller: Your enquiry about our laboratory measuring equipment. Didn't you get the literature that I sent you?
Henderson: Yes, yes. Um...that was very interesting. Um . . .
Caller: Well, the thing is: is it OK if I come and see you during my visit next month?
Henderson: I see. Yeah, all right.
Caller: Now what about the morning of Tuesday 10th April, is that OK? Say at about...er...11?
Henderson: I'll just see if I can find my diary . . . Umm, yes, here we are. Er...<u>April 11th at 10 o'clock</u> you said.
Caller: <u>That's right</u>. Now, um...is that OK? Is that convenient for you?
Henderson: The next day might be better. Just after lunch for preference.
Caller: Right, so that's...er...the Wednesday. In fact, that'll suit me fine, that's great. Now, shall we say...um...2.15?
Henderson: Er...certainly, yes, <u>2.50</u>, that's...that's fine.
Caller: Oh, and by the way, I'll be bringing our agent Don Reece with me i...if that's OK with you.

Henderson: Oh, certainly. Er...what was your name again?
Caller: Sylvia Perez: P-E-R-E-Z.
Henderson: Fine. I'll see you in April then. You know how to get to our lab, don't you? Goodbye then Miss <u>Perex</u>.

Caller: Goodbye Dr Henderson – and...er...actually it's *Mrs.* Oh, and I'll um...I'll write to confirm the arrangements just to make quite sure we've got everything . . . absolutely right.

C 🔊 In this step, students suggest how they might REPLY to the voices on the recording. Pause it after each bit, so that members of the class can make suggestions. This activity is best done by the whole class, so that all the suggestions can be discussed and evaluated.

Transcript [2 minutes 20 seconds]

1 *ring ring* 32543.
2 *ring ring* *(unintelligible)* and Co. Good morning.
3 *ring ring* . . . *(silence)*
4 *ring ring* Hello.
5 *ring ring* 33543.
6 *ring ring* Sales department.
7 *ring ring* Lines from Birmingham are engaged, please try later.
8 *ring ring* Richmond & Company, good afternoon.
9 *ring ring* Dr Henderson's office.
10 *OUR phone rings* Hello, this is Bill Henderson. You wanted me to get in touch . . .

Suggested responses – many variations possible

1 Is that Richmond & Co.? No? I'm sorry, I think I must have got the wrong number.
2 Hello, is that Richmond & Co.?
3 Hello? Hello?
4 Hello, is that 234 32453?
5 Oh, I'm sorry, I must have dialled the wrong number.
6 Oh, I wanted Dr Bill Henderson, can you put me through to him, please?
7 Oh, what a nuisance! How long should I wait?
8 Good afternoon, can I speak to Dr Bill Henderson, please?
9 Hello, this is … (*my name*) … Is Dr Henderson there, please? No? Could you ask him to call me, please?
10 Ah, Dr Henderson, thanks ever so much for calling back. I wanted to ask you …

D In **B** and **C** we asked the students to consciously recognize some of the 'problems' of making calls. Here in **D** we introduce some useful exponents, some of which have only been heard so far. Step **E** will be practice in the form of a role-play.

🔊 The recording illustrates most of the exponents given, but not in the same sequence as in the Student's Book. Play the recording through while everyone highlights the expressions they think will be most useful. Pause as necessary for any discussion of meanings and use. Unless time is very short, play the recording again before going on to the next step.

Transcript [1 minute 40 seconds]

First man: Hello, I'd like to speak to Mr Watson.
Woman: Oh, I'm afraid he's still at lunch. Is there anything I can do for you?
First man: No, no, it's all right, I'll call again later today. Thanks very much for your help.

Ms Johnson: Oh, hello, this is Alison Johnson. I'm calling from Cardiff.
Second man: Hello, Miss Johnson.
Ms Johnson: Is Mr Watson available, please?
Second man: Hold on a moment, please. I'll just find out if he's available . . . Hello. I'm afraid he's in a meeting. Is there anything I can do for you?
Ms Johnson: Er, no. Could you ask him to call me back, please? My number is . . .

Second woman: Hello, I'd like to speak to Mr Watson.
Third man: I'm afraid he's not available just now. Is there anything I can do for you?
Second woman: Could you give him a message, please?
Third man: Yes, certainly . . .

Ms Richardson: Hello, I'd like to speak to Mr Watson.
Telephonist: Er...I'll put you through to Mr Thompson, his assistant.
Ms Richardson: Thanks.

Mr Thompson: Hello, Mr Watson's office. James Thompson speaking.

Ms Richardson: Is Mr Watson available, please? My name's Anne Richardson.

Mr Thompson: I'm afraid he's not in the office at the moment.

Ms Richardson: Oh, what time do you expect him back?

Mr Thompson: Not until after lunch.

Ms Richardson: Oh dear, I need to speak to him rather urgently.

Mr Thompson: Right, I'll ask him to call you back as soon as he's free, Ms Richardson . . .

First man again: Hello, I'd like to speak to Mr Watson.

Mr Watson: Speaking.

First man: Oh, hello, Mr Watson. This is Anthony Buck from . . .

➡ If there is time, and if you deem it necessary, spend some time doing repetition practice of the exponents in the speech balloons.

E If you're running out of time perhaps postpone this role-play so that you can do justice to it in the next lesson.

If necessary, explain why it's important to sit back-to-back for this (and subsequent) telephone role-plays:

> In a real-life phone call you have to depend on your voice, not gestures and eye contact. You can't see the other person's reactions and the other person can't see how friendly you are – you have to show everything in your voice.

F For this discussion students should work in groups of three or four. If possible, make sure each group has someone with business experience in it.

Don't spend too long on this discussion – we'll be returning to this theme in the final section of this unit with 'Twelve telephone tips'.

Among the points that might be made are:

- A first-time call to a stranger often involves mutual suspicion and uncertainty.
- Maybe fax or e-mail ahead to say when you're going to call and what you're going to talk about – then both of you can be prepared and less time will be wasted.
- You can make everything easier if you speak clearly, slowly and carefully.
- The way that you speak (your tone of voice) has an enormous effect on the way your listener perceives you. Just saying 'Hello' abruptly when you answer the phone may sound unfriendly, brusque or impatient.
- The caller must try to establish links, such as mutual concerns or acquaintances and state his or her business clearly. Identify yourself or your department, so that the other person knows exactly who they're dealing with.
- It makes a big difference if the person you're talking to on the phone knows you – even if you've only corresponded.
- Always check back any important information you've noted down. Send a follow-up fax, e-mail or letter if necessary.

At the end, get each group to report to the class on the points that were made.

> ⚠ Both British and American people talk about *calling someone*, but *giving someone a ring* tends to be used only in the UK. If an American telephonist asks you *Are you through?* she means *Have you finished your call?* but a British telephonist means *Have you been connected?*

An American might answer *This is he* or *This is she* instead of saying *Speaking*, but this may sound abrupt or pompous unless spoken in exactly the right tone of voice.

The way you sound and the importance of a friendly, approachable tone of voice on the phone cannot be over-emphasized.

3.2 Getting people to do things   *Functions*

This section covers the functions of:

Requesting, and Agreeing to or Refusing requests;
Offering, and Accepting or Rejecting offers;
Asking permission, and Giving or Refusing permission.

Of course, these functions are not confined to telephoning, but are used in face-to-face situations and in writing too. This is why some of the steps in this section move away from telephone situations and focus more on face-to-face interactions.

Vocabulary

get in touch with	*non-smoking zone*	*package designers*	*courier*	*stick-on labels*
translate	*proposals*	*consumer goods*	*prototype*	*batches*
stuffy	*broken down*	*confirmation*	*quote*	
		receipt	*sub-contract*	

Procedure – *about 90 minutes*

A This is a warm-up discussion. The people in the pictures might be saying:

'May I use your car?'
'Could you photocopy these for me?'
'Would you like me to help you?'

Ask for suggestions for some other ways of saying the same things. This section is intended to encourage students to widen their repertoire of exponents to express these functions, rather than just stick with the simplest, most familiar exponents.

B The three recorded conversations illustrate how the exponents are used – these are underlined in the transcript below.

In each case, the recording should be played twice so that students can focus on the separate tasks. Pause between the conversations for students to ask questions about the exponents that were used.

Perhaps draw attention to the distinctions between formal/informal situations and direct/indirect ways of talking to people. Point out that it helps to be polite and friendly when dealing with people, even if you don't really get on with them.

> ⚠ Remind students that being over-polite can be interpreted as insincerity or sarcasm.

1 Terry only agrees to do the first two things.

2 The exponents that are used are <u>underlined</u> in the transcript – these don't match the phrases in the Student's Book *exactly*.

Transcript   [1 minute 20 seconds]

Requesting

Terry: Hello.
Jane: Hello, Terry. Are you very busy just now?
Terry: Not really, no.
Jane: <u>Do you think you could</u> help me with a couple of things?
Terry: Oh, <u>sure</u>.
Jane: Well, first of all: you know the German report?
Terry: Yes.
Jane: Well, <u>could you</u> send a copy of it off to Frankfurt for me?
Terry: OK, do you want me to fax it, or send it by mail?
Jane: Oh, fax, I think. Now, let's see, oh then <u>would you mind</u> arranging accommodation for Mr Berglund, he needs it for Friday night.

Terry: Friday night, <u>sure</u>. Er...Hotel Continental, as usual?
Jane: Mm, that's right. Oh, then <u>could you</u> get in touch with Sandy in New York after lunch and ask her to call me tomorrow?
Terry: Ah...I'll be over at the factory this afternoon, er...<u>I won't be able to</u> do that.
Jane: Oh, well, never mind. Another thing <u>I'd like you to do</u> is translate the technical documents into English.
Terry: Er...Jane, <u>I'm sorry but I can't</u>. I've got this report to finish by 11 o'clock and it's just not possible . . .
Jane: Oh, well, look, at least <u>could you just</u> check my spelling and punctuation in the sales literature if I bring it over to you?
Terry: But my spelling is terrible. I'll ask Annette to do it.
Jane: All right . . .

3 Sally accepts all the offers of help except the last two.

4 The exponents that are used are <u>underlined</u> in the transcript – these don't match the phrases in the Student's Book *exactly*.

Transcript [1 minute 20 seconds]

Offering to help

Bill: Morning, Sally, will you be in this afternoon?

Sally: Oh, hello, Bill. No, I've got to catch the three o'clock plane instead of the evening one.

Bill: Oh, goodness. Um…well, <u>would you like a hand with</u> some things you've got to do?

Sally: Oh, that would be great, <u>if you're sure it's no trouble.</u>

Bill: No, no trouble at all. Um…<u>would you like me to</u> check today's correspondence?

Sally: Oh, yes. Yes, <u>that's very kind of you.</u> Look if you do that, can you sign the letters for me as well, please?

Bill: Yeah, <u>of course,</u> no problem. And then shall I call you a taxi to the airport?

Sally: Yes. <u>Yes, please.</u> Now, let me think, I'll need to leave straight after lunch so…um…oh well, no, better make it 1.30, that'd be safe.

Bill: OK, 1.30. And…um…<u>would you like me to</u> do anything about your hotel booking?

Sally: Oh, heavens, yes, I'm glad you reminded me. I'm sure it's all right but would you mind phoning them just to confirm the booking?

Bill: Of course, of course, no problem. Um…and <u>shall I</u> deal with the weekly report?

Sally: <u>No, thanks. I think I can manage to</u> finish that now. It's nearly ready.

Bill: Sure?

Sally: Mm.

Bill: Um . . . Oh, I know, <u>would you like me to</u> call Amsterdam for you?

Sally: Oh, oh, <u>that's very kind of you.</u> Er…no. Let me think, n…<u>no, I think I'd prefer to do that myself because</u> there are some people I've really got to talk to.

Bill: Oh, OK, I understand. Well, um…<u>if you need any…any more help, just let me know,</u> OK?

Sally: Oh, terrific. Thanks, I will . . .

---

5 The host gives his permission for everything except opening the window, smoking and sending a fax (because the machine is out of order).

6 The exponents that are used are <u>underlined</u> in the transcript – again these don't match the phrases in the Student's Book *exactly*.

Transcript [1 minute 20 seconds]

Asking permission

Visitor: Um…<u>do you mind if I</u> open the window? It's kind of stuffy in here.

Host: Well, er…<u>I'm afraid we can't</u> open the window, because if we do open the window the air conditioning doesn't work!

Visitor: Oh, that's right, no, it's always that way. Er…<u>is it OK if I</u> take off my jacket then?

Host: Oh, <u>sure,</u> yeah. Make yourself at home.

Visitor: Oh, right. That's better. Oh, um…<u>do you mind if I</u> smoke? I notice nobody's smoking around here.

Host: Well, <u>I'm sorry, but</u> this is a non-smoking zone. We took a vote and then we came…

Visitor: Oh, I know. I've…that's OK. I'm trying to quit anyway, I figured it was something like that. Right, OK. Um…oh, by the way, <u>may I</u> use your phone to book a table…er…for lunch?

Host: Yeah, <u>sure.</u> Do you know somewhere good?

Visitor: Oh, oh yeah, absolutely.

Host: Great. Thanks.

Visitor: No, I'll do that as soon as we've finished this. Um…and…er…also…er…before we go, <u>is it all right if I</u> call my office, to see if there are any messages for me?

Host: <u>Sure. Go ahead.</u>

Visitor: OK, good, I'll do that as soon as…just a few more lines here. Um…OK, <u>do you think I could</u> get a photocopy of this leaflet done?

Host: Er…oh, <u>of course, yes.</u> Well, I'll get Tim to do it for you. Tim!

Visitor: Great. And also <u>can I</u> send a fax of these proposals to our branch in Canada?

Host: Er…<u>I'm sorry, but</u> the fax machine is broken down. We're waiting for somebody to fix it.

Visitor: Oh, that's OK. There's…there's one next door, isn't there?

Host: Ah…I don't know. I think so.

Visitor: Yeah, I saw one.

Host: OK.

Visitor: OK, fine.

Host: Right.

C In this role-play, students will make four separate phone calls. One student represents Utopia Products, a firm marketing consumer goods (File **3**), the other represents Europrint, a firm of package designers and printers (File **34**). The exchange of messages concerns packaging and printing for the first firm's products. There is a story line: each call leads on to another and Europrint gets closer to delivering the finished products to Utopia Products.

[icon] Before they embark on the telephone role-play, play the recording which sets the scene and demonstrates how the following phone calls will go – and how the information in the Files 'works'.

Transcript [50 seconds]

Woman: Hello, Utopia Products. Jenny Butler speaking. How can I help you?

Man: Good morning. Er…this is Tony Green of Europrint speaking. Could you confirm that you've received our samples?

Woman: Ah yes, the samples. No, I'm afraid they haven't arrived yet.

Man: Well, er…we sent them to you by airmail on February 6th.

Woman: Well, we haven't received them so maybe they've got lost in the post. Would you mind sending us a second set by courier? You see, we do need them rather urgently…

Man: Yes, all right, I'll see to it right away . . .

While they're making the calls, encourage students to experiment with the exponents in the speech balloons as they talk to their 'colleague', and discourage them from using the simplest forms, like *May I . . .* and *No problem . . .*!

D   Set the scene so that the conversation involves requesting:

Would you mind telling me . . .?
Could you tell me . . .?

as well as exchanging information.

To start everyone off, explain how you would use a public phone in an English-speaking country you know (UK, USA, Australia, etc.).

Then, if you know about the phone system in your students' country, write up on the board some numbers which are equivalent to the UK numbers in the list below.

Some facilities and services available in the UK are:

- 0891, 0839 and 0881 numbers are special information services charged at premium rates, such as weather or travel information.
- 0898 numbers, also charged at premium rates, may contain 'adult material'!
- 0860, 0850, 0836, 0831 and 0385 numbers are all mobile phones which are charged at high rates, even for local calls.
- Freefone numbers, 0800 (*O-eight-hundred*) and 0500 (*O-five-hundred*) numbers are toll-free (i.e. they cost nothing if you call them).
- 0345 and 0645 numbers are long-distance calls charged at local rates.
- Phonecards are obtainable from newsagents and many other shops.
- ADC calls: 'advise duration and charge' – the operator calls you back to tell you how much your call cost, which is useful if you're calling from someone else's house.
- Some useful numbers:
    local operator 100
    speaking clock 8081
    international operator for most countries 155
    international directory enquiries 153
    directory enquiries 192
    fax directory enquiries 153
    emergency 999!

Two extra activities

1 Ask everyone in the class to jot down some things they would like you or another member of the class to do, or which they would like permission to do. If appropriate, you can play the role of 'boss' while other members of the class are 'colleagues'. Then go round the class, asking each person to make his or her request or ask permission, by saying, 'Yes, Makoto?' or 'Maria, you wanted to see me?'

2 If you don't object to spending more time away from the telephone, this role-play, with separate role information, may be photocopied for students working in pairs.

New International Business English This document may be photocopied.

3.2 Getting people to do things

A Imagine that you're temporarily sharing an office with your partner while your own separate offices are being redecorated. You don't know each other very well so you should speak politely to one another.

Here are some of the problems you have. See if your partner can help, and offer to help your partner with his or her problems.

> 1 You think the office is overheated.
> 2 You are going to get some coffee from the machine.
> 3 You want to call home.
> 4 You want to have lunch in the canteen.
> 5 You can't understand these technical terms.
> 6 You want to leave early but you're expecting a call from Paris.
> 7 You can't find the file for the Hong Kong clients.
> 8 You have lost your diary.

© Cambridge University Press 2000

New International Business English This document may be photocopied.

3.2 Getting people to do things

B Imagine that you're temporarily sharing an office with your partner while your own separate offices are being redecorated. You don't know each other very well so you should speak politely to one another.

Here are some of the problems you have. See if your partner can help, and offer to help your partner with his or her problems.

> 1 You think the office is very hot and stuffy.
> 2 You are thirsty.
> 3 You want to call home.
> 4 You want to know the times of trains to the main station.
> 5 You have a headache.
> 6 You don't want to talk shop over lunch.
> 7 You won't have time to phone Toronto before lunch.
> 8 You need some photocopies made.

© Cambridge University Press 2000

3.3 Can I take a message?

This section covers the skills of taking notes and leaving messages (which may involve rewriting the notes).

Step **A** introduces the topic of taking messages. Step **B** practises actually taking messages, based on three messages recorded on an answering machine. Step **C** is a listening exercise involving listening carefully for important details, and step **D** rounds things off with a telephone role-play, in which students have to make notes (but they don't have to pass on any messages).

Vocabulary

answering machine	subsidiary
	head office
congress	contact
labelling	transaction
striped pyjamas	

Procedure – *about 90 minutes*

A We begin with a discussion on taking messages, based on an answerphone message and the note in the Student's Book, which lacks all the important details, though presumably Mrs Robinson would assume it was for her if the Post-it note was put on her desk or stuck on her computer screen.

Transcript   [50 seconds]

Herr Braun: Hello, this is Hans Braun – that's B-R-A-U-N. I'm supposed to be meeting Mrs Robinson on Tuesday afternoon at 4 pm. The problem is that I won't be able to make it. But I can meet her on Wednesday at 9.30, if that's all right. Could you call me back to confirm if this is all right, please? My number is 651 31473. Thanks, bye.

Before moving on to **B**, ask any students with practical business experience to say what kind of information they always note down and why. Confronted with an answering machine, when you expected a real person, it might be safer to ring back later when you've had time to think, and maybe even write out the message that you're going to dictate to the machine.

B **1** There are three phone calls to listen to, and each one will probably have to be heard at least twice.

In the transcripts of the calls, the important points that should be noted down have been underlined.

2 Allow time for everyone to compare notes – in particular whether they have done this concisely and clearly enough for another person to read and understand.

Extra activity – *for advanced students*

Play the calls again and ask everyone to make notes on the ways that the phone is used 'well' (effectively) and on the ways the phone is used 'badly' in each call.
Then join a partner and compare your notes.

Transcript [4 minutes]

1 *Telephonist:* REMACO, bonjour.
Mr Schulz: Hello, er...it's Peter Schulz here. Um...could I speak to Monsieur Février, please?
Telephonist: Oh, just a moment, I'll see if he's in. I'll put you through.
Secretary: Hello, Monsieur Février's office.
Mr Schulz: Could I speak to Monsieur Février, please?
Secretary: Oh, I'm very sorry, he's...er...out at lunch. Can I help you at all?
Mr Schulz: Ah. Um...could you ask him to call me today, please? Er...preferably before 4 pm...or...um...any time tomorrow. Er...it's to do with the arrangements for the July...f...for the congress in July.
Secretary: Yes, who's calling, please?
Mr Schulz: This is Mr Schulz – Peter Schulz.
Secretary: Peter Schulz. And can I take your number, please?
Mr Schulz: Yes, er...it's 01 456 9924.
Secretary: So that's 01 456 9924.
Mr Schulz: Yes.
Secretary: Peter Schulz. OK, Mr Schulz, I'll get Monsieur Février to call you as soon as he comes back to the office.
Mr Schulz: Thank you very much. Goodbye.
Secretary: Goodbye.

2 *Telephonist:* Green and Harding, good morning.
Paola: Oh, good morning. This is Paola Andreotti calling from Rome. I'd like to speak to Mr Guy Dobson, please.
Telephonist: Oh, certainly, ma'am, I'll connect you immediately.
Bob: Hello.
Paola: Oh, is that Guy Dobson?
Bob: Er...no, it...is that Paola?
Paola: Yes.
Bob: Oh, hi! This is Bob Swenson.
Paola: Oh, hi. Um...is Guy around?
Bob: Er...just a minute, I'll check . . . Um...no, he doesn't seem to be. He should be back...er...any minute. Er...can I help you?
Paola: Um...yeah. Look, can I leave a message with you?
Bob: Yes, sure.
Paola: It's urgent. There's been a mix-up about the labelling of product number 15437 B – that's the one for the Italian market.

Bob: Uhuh, I've got that.
Paola: And I'd like him to get in touch so that it can be cleared up.
Bob: OK.
Paola: Um...he can reach me at this number till tomorrow evening, OK?
Bob: Mmm.
Paola: It's 002 558 9847.
Bob: OK. He can reach you at this number till tomorrow evening: 002 558 9847.
Paola: That's right, great. Thanks Bob.
Bob: OK, bye-bye.

3 *Telephonist:* Hello, Santos Trading.
Mr Wong: Oh, hello, this is Mr Wong here, calling from Singapore.
Telephonist: Yes, Mr Wong, who do you want to speak to?
Mr Wong: Um...I'd like to speak to Mrs Cox, please.
Telephonist: Fine, putting you through.
Woman: Hello, can I help you?
Mr Wong: Oh, hello. This is Mr Wong calling from Singapore. Er...may I speak to Mrs Cox, please?
Woman: Oh, I'm afraid Mrs Cox is away. She has the flu and she may not be back in the office till Monday. I expect her assistant, Mr Box, can help. I'll just see if he's in his office. Hold on a moment, please . . . Hello, Mr Wong?
Mr Wong: Yes.
Woman: I'm very sorry, he's out just now, can I take a message for him?
Mr Wong: Oh, yes, please. Will you tell him I won't be arriving in Melbourne until quite late this Saturday, at 1 am local time. And will Mrs Cox still be able to meet me?
Woman: Right.
Mr Wong: And also inform the Royal Hotel that I'll be arriving very very late.
Woman: Sure.
Mr Wong: Oh, wonderful, thanks. Could you please...er...telex or phone me to confirm that this is possible?
Woman: Right, I...I'll take the message, I'll give it to Mr Box and I'm sure he'll be in touch with you. Thank you very much, Mr Wong.
Mr Wong: Thank you.

C 🔲🔍 This listening exercise will probably need to be played at least twice, but it isn't very long. Between the playings, students should compare notes with a partner, note any discrepancies and missing information and then listen again to have another go at the questions they didn't get right the first time. (See Transcript for the correct answers.)

Transcript [1 minute 40 seconds]

1 Could you please send us 300 kilos of white rice?
2 It's very good value at the moment: the price is only 18 cents per kilo.
3 We require two boxes of ripe bananas, please.
4 Er...the price per box is £115. Is that OK?
5 So the total price is going to be 4,295 francs, all right?

6 Our phone number is 456984 if you need to contact us.
7 So I'd like to order 40 kilos at £14 per kilo.
8 Our order number is JG 404.
9 Have you got that? 500 items are going to cost $900.
10 And...er...here's the item code: it's RAE 77 – got that? RAE 77.

D This role-play consists of two phone calls. Students will be working in pairs and should sit back-to-back for the calls:

Student A starts at File **4** and goes on to **5**.
Student B starts at File **35** and goes on to **36**.

The first call is between someone who works for a subsidiary of Medusa S.A. and someone at head office. They don't know each other. The caller requires information which the other person may be able to provide. Directions are given within each student's File on which File to look at next.

The second call is between the same people who have already spoken on the phone. The caller requires more information.

1 Allow time for everyone to prepare for the first call.

2 Allow enough time for each pair to have a reasonable conversation each time and to sort out all the sources of confusion in the information they are discussing (there are several potential problems built in to the role information).

3 Form groups of four (pairs of pairs) for the follow-up discussion.

Three extra activities

1 *Work in small groups* Think of some recent telephone calls (in English or in your own language) you have made or overheard. Describe them to your partners. Point out the things that sounded *strange* or *annoying* about the other person's use of the phone.

2 *Work in small groups* Imagine that you work for an international firm and that you need to appoint a new telephonist/receptionist as your present one is leaving soon.

• What qualities are you looking for in such a person?
• Are the required qualities of a telephonist and a receptionist different, and if so, should two different people fill such positions?
• What kind of training does such a person require?

Design a short advertisement for the position.

3 *Work in pairs* Design a form that will encourage your staff to take down all the necessary details when receiving messages on someone else's behalf.

3.4 Planning and making calls

This section starts by encouraging students to discuss and compare experiences on telephone manners and the need to plan phone calls. Even students with no business background will have personal experiences to contribute.

The main part of the section (step **C**) consists of four quite elaborate telephone role-plays, which are done with an 'Observer' eavesdropping and later giving feedback. Allow plenty of time for this.

Vocabulary

dial	*trade fair*	*staff sickness*
image	*dispatched*	*air freight*
	quality control	*at no extra charge*
	revised shipment date	*vegetarian*

Procedure – *about 90 minutes*

A 1   [recording icon] Form pairs or groups of three and play the recording. Pause between each pair of comments and ask the pairs to discuss their reactions to them before playing the next two comments.

Hopefully, students will agree that it *is* essential to plan phone calls they have to make in English, though they may not agree on the best method.

In later units in the course, make sure that students have time to plan their calls before they do any of the telephone role-plays.

Transcript   [1 minute]

'Well, um…a couple of lines on the back of an envelope are enough.'

'No, if I make notes before a call, I can't adapt to the other person's reactions.'

'Well, I get someone else to phone for me if I have to speak in a foreign language.'

'If I don't make notes beforehand, I'll forget what I need to say.'

'I try to "rehearse" an important call in my head before I make it.'

'I make much more careful notes before a phone call than I do before writing a letter.'

'I find a minute or two spent making notes before the call is better really than wasting time during it trying to think what to say.'

'I find it's a good idea to write down some of the phrases I want to use.'

---

2   Form groups of four (pairs of pairs). For this part of the discussion, students should refer back to **2.4C**, where the '7 Steps' for planning a business letter were discussed. Also, if they did come up with some 'golden rules' for telephone calls when they did **3.1** earlier, they should refer back to their notes on that section. The discussion continues in step **B**.

B   This group discussion continues the discussion that was started in step **A**.

C   This role-play works like a chain, with one part leading on to the next. It consists of FOUR separate phone calls. While two of the group are talking, the other(s) act as 'observers' and listen and take notes, so that they can make comments afterwards.

Allow plenty of time for this, so that everyone gets a turn at being caller, person at the other end of the line, and 'observer'.

The 1st call is between Mr/Ms Tanaka, a supplier (**6**), and Mr/Ms Suarez, a customer (**37**), concerning a lunch date. (Both coloured GREEN in the Files.)

The 2nd call is between Mr/Ms LaRue, a customer (**65**), and Mr/Ms Peterson, in charge of shipping orders (**7**), concerning some delayed shipments. (Both YELLOW in the Files.)

The 3rd call is between Mr/Ms Steiner (**40**) and the Provence Restaurant (**66**), concerning the reservation of a private room and special menu. (BLUE in the Files.)

The 4th call is between Mr/Ms Robinson (**10**) and the Hotel Cambridge (**41**), concerning the reservation of rooms and some special requirements. (ORANGE in the Files.)

If you think this sounds complicated, have a look at the flowchart opposite. Students have their own directions at the end of each File, which send them to their next File. Once they have started the activity, their own instructions will keep them going in the right direction.

The ideal group size is THREE, so have as many groups of three as possible. The 'chain' works equally well with groups of FOUR but make sure the students know which of them is Student A, which is B, which is C and which is D, so that they follow the right directions within the Files.

If students are working in groups of THREE:

1st call	A: **6** (Tanaka)	B: **37** (Suarez)	C: **64** (Observer)
	↓	↓	↓
2nd call	A: **7** (Peterson)	B: **38** (Observer)	C: **65** (LaRue)
	↓	↓	↓
3rd call	A: **8** (Observer)	B: **40** (Steiner)	C: **66** (Restaurant)
	↓	↓	↓
4th call	A: **10** (Robinson)	B: **41** (Hotel)	C: **49** (Observer)

If they're working in groups of FOUR:

1st call	A: **6** (Tanaka)	B: **37** (Suarez)	C: **64** (Observer)	D: **64** (Observer)
	↓	↓	↓	↓
2nd call	A: **38** (Observer)	B: **38** (Observer)	C: **65** (LaRue)	D: **7** (Peterson)
	↓	↓	↓	↓
3rd call	A: **8** (Observer)	B: **40** (Steiner)	C: **66** (Restaurant)	D: **8** (Observer)
	↓	↓	↓	↓
4th call	A: **41** (Hotel)	B: **49** (Observer)	C: **49** (Observer)	D: **10** (Robinson)

Make sure that the speakers are sitting BACK-TO-BACK – and perhaps the 'observers' could also have their backs to the speakers while they're listening in: some people don't like being watched while they're on the phone!

After each call, before the next call begins, make sure that the 'observers' give the speakers feedback on how they got on and advice on how they might improve their telephone technique.

Authors' comment:
Don't worry! This isn't actually as complicated as it looks – it will work! But it does need enough time.

D At the very end, besides the follow-up discussion, allow time for students to ask you questions and give them feedback yourself on their performances.

Workbook contents for this unit

4 Summaries, notes, reports

This unit deals with how to take notes in business contexts, how to summarize conversations and how to plan and write reports. It's a unit which can be used either as an introduction for students with little experience in report- and summary-writing or else as revision for students who are familiar with note-taking and report-writing already but need a swift review of the skills.

The emphasis throughout is on sharpening and practising note-, summary- and report-writing and on demonstrating that they can be viewed in a combined and integrated fashion. In particular the unit gives practice in the preparatory and planning stages of all serious and professional writing activities. The emphasis is on encouraging organizational and management skills, as in Units 1 to 3.

The unit gives some advice on making notes in different ways and also provides practice in punctuation.

> ⚠ **PLEASE NOTE** We haven't distinguished between NOTE-TAKING (taking notes *after* or *during* a conversation or meeting) and MAKING NOTES (noting down ideas *before* writing a report or letter or *before* a phone call or meeting). The processes aren't the same, but the techniques and styles we suggest are similar.
>
> LEAVING A NOTE or MESSAGE is different again, because such notes need to be understood by other people.
>
> Some ambiguity and even confusion is unavoidable, unfortunately!

Remind the students that in business we only write reports when we are asked to, normally by our boss or superior. Many people are afraid of writing reports. In this unit we want to show how note-taking and report-writing can be made easier. The unit takes up some of the elements of Unit 2 on letters, e-mails, faxes and memos, but it concentrates on the more specialized skill of writing reports and making summaries of conversations.

Background information

Draw everyone's attention to the Background information on report-writing in the Workbook. This is particularly important for students who have little or no experience of business report writing.

Video

Programme 4 on the *New International Business English Video* introduces the theme of this unit.

4.1 Summarizing a conversation

This section introduces the topic of using English for different purposes in business. Taking notes on information you hear and summarizing the main points of a conversation are very important communication skills when using English in business.

We begin by taking up what is in effect a transfer skill, proceeding from the spoken to the written medium. This section ties in with and recapitulates in part the skill developed in Unit 3, where taking a message was first practised in connection with telephone messages. This provides a transition to the rest of this unit.

Vocabulary

rely on	*trade exhibition*	*enquiry*	*consultation*	*card*
record	*summary*	*sales manager*	*procurement*	
record for the files	*company stand*	*sales representative*	*discount*	

Procedure – *about 45 minutes*

A This warm-up discussion aims to get students to realize that Business English is used in various ways. It reviews the distinction already made in **2.1** between communicating in speech and in the written medium. The division of labour between the different modes of communication and the crossover or the transfer from one to another is brought out.

Further discussion questions:

- Which of the methods are you familiar with?
- How often do you use the methods illustrated in your own work? How effective do you find them? How easy or difficult are they for you to do in English?

Extra activity

This provides further material for comparing writing and speaking. Give students a copy of these notes, which summarize some of the differences between writing and speaking. Ask them to read them through and then to do the tasks indicated below.

New International Business English   This document may be photocopied.

4.1 Summarizing a conversation

Communication in Business

☐ Keeping written records is helpful for future reference.
☐ If you make a mistake when you are writing you can correct it before sending the letter, e-mail or fax.
☐ It's a good idea to send a fax or e-mail with a summary of the points agreed in a telephone call.
☐ Once you've said something, you can't take it back.
☐ If the material is complicated it's sometimes easier to put it in writing than to say it.
☐ If you speak to someone face-to-face, it's much easier to be honest.
☐ Making a phone call is an easy way to solve a problem if you have no time to write a letter.
☐ If you're placing an order, you should do it in writing.
☐ If information is written down, you have more time to take it in and understand it.
☐ If someone owes you money, there's no point in phoning them.
☐ ....
☐ ....
☐ ....

1   *Work in pairs* Decide which points are most relevant to writing business letters, reports, messages, memos, etc. Number them in order of importance.

2   *Join another pair* Compare your results. Make a list of some of the DISADVANTAGES of communicating in writing, rather than in speech.

© Cambridge University Press 2000

B 🔊 Students work in pairs. Before they hear the conversation, students should look at the extracts from the three summaries of a conversation. Explain to the students that different styles of notes may be suited to different circumstances. Numbered notes may well be useful for 'easy reference'. More discursive notes may be appropriate as 'a record for the files'. Play the recording. It will be necessary to play the conversation a second time.

Transcript   [2 minutes 10 seconds]

Norman: How do you do, my name is Bob Norman. I'm with Rotaflex. Can I help you in any way?

Brown: Oh, hi. My name's Tim Brown. How're you doing? Pleased to meet you.

Norman: I'm fine...fine thanks and how about yourself?

Brown: Fine, thanks. I wanted to ask you about your rotary printer you have here.

Norman: Ah, yes, now you mean our R75.

Brown: Yes, that's right the R75. Now, what I'd like to know is can it deal with high quality embossed greeting cards? That's the sort of thing we're involved with.

Norman: Certainly. That's no problem at all.

Brown: Fine. Now...you see we're looking for replacements for our twenty-year-old machines.

Norman: Mmhmm.

Brown: So we need the latest technology. Now, if we were interested in making a firm order, how quickly could you deliver the machines?

Norman: Well, I can't give you a firm delivery date myself at this moment. But we can deliver pretty quickly.

Brown: My firm would be interested in ten machines.

Norman: Yes. Oh, that's very good.

Brown: So I was wondering, could we get a 15% discount on an order that size?

Norman: Well...er...as you can see from our catalogue here, we normally offer 12% on orders of that kind.

Brown: Yeah, yeah, I read that. But your neighbours down the hall there, they're willing to give me 15%.

Norman: Well, of course, we'd er...be delighted to do business with you, Mr Brown. And so, I'd like to draw your attention to the latest laser-driven technology which the R75 contains.

Brown: Yes, very interesting, but the discount is important.

Norman: Look, if you'd like to wait just for a few minutes er...I can get through to my head office and I'll enquire about any special arrangements which we might be able to make for you.

Brown: No, no, please don't bother about that just now. There's not that much of a hurry. I still have to report back to my board.

Norman: Oh, yes, I understand that.

Brown: Look here's my card. It'll be quite enough if you just drop me a line about things like the discount in the course of the next two weeks.

Norman: Yes, of course, yes er...very well, Mr Brown. I'd be only too pleased to do all that for you. It's been very pleasant talking to you.

Brown: Mmm.

Norman: Oh, and here's my card as well.

C **1** 🔊 Play the recording again. Students should draft their summary in the way which they find the most appropriate. The style they choose is immaterial. Particular offices may well have their own house styles. This is also a point which might be brought into the final discussion.

2 Reassemble the students in groups of four (each pair with another pair) to compare their summary and to discuss the reasons why they prefer one style to another. Allow time for feedback and queries.

➡ Further discussion question:
  • Discuss the reasons why you prefer one to the other.

4.2 Using notes to write a report

This activity gives practice in transforming notes into a connected text. At this stage the emphasis is on linking up ideas and adding missing elements, such as verbs and conjunctions.

   The approach adopted here is deliberately inductive rather than deductive. It's important to encourage students to use and summon up their already existent resources. To develop autonomy, learners need the opportunity to try things out. Most learners can already employ the basics of report-writing. By encouraging them to work in pairs and pairs of pairs they get the opportunity to learn co-operatively from each other.

Students should be encouraged to proceed by expanding the notes into paragraphs, as the instructions say. For students at this level the lesson to be drawn is that report-writing is not a mysterious activity but simply a case of writing a connected text. Learning how to write reports can thus proceed organically. In **4.3** the steps and formal elements are introduced explicitly and can then be discussed more meaningfully on the basis of having already attempted a similar task. Too often writing skills are presented as being 'formula-based', when in fact what learners require is the opportunity to engage in flexible trial-and-error activities.

Vocabulary

managing director (MD)	*physiotherapist*	*equipment*	*old-fashioned*
investigate	*union reps*	*procedures*	*eyesight*
health and safety provisions	*proposals*	*handling*	*lighting*
recommendations	*display*	*secure*	*complaints*
improvement	*regulations*	*ventilation*	*request*
paragraphs	*canteen*	*air-filtering*	*raised*
office bugs	*frequent*	*regular*	*concerning*
symptoms	*breaks*	*maintenance*	*appointed*
Repetitive Strain Injury (RSI)	*screen*	*replacement*	

Procedure – *about 45 minutes*

A Draw the students' attention to any difficult vocabulary they'll encounter in the notes.

Working in pairs, students expand the notes into paragraphs and connected text. Suggest that they add pronouns, e.g. *I* or *we*, and conjunctions, e.g. *first, then*, etc.

If you feel your students might benefit from it, you can give them a rough outline to follow on the OHP: (1) a general introduction: office health and safety provisions, (2) proposals numbered 1, 2, 3, etc.

The report-writing can be done as homework if convenient.

B Students work in pairs of pairs and compare each other's drafts. When they have done this they consult the draft report in File **67**. Draw the students' attention to the formal aspects of the model, in which the numbered notes are the basis for separate points, and the language is in full and connected sentences. You might wish to emphasize the neutral use of 'proposals' versus 'recommendations'. Clearly the relationship between the report-writer and the Managing Director will affect the language used in the task. Stress to the students that the model is only one possible version, and other variations would be equally good.

4.3 Planning and editing a report

With the experience now of having done **4.2**, the idea behind this activity is for the students to work through and 'think through' the preparation for report writing themselves in more explicit and conscious terms.

Vocabulary

edit	*separate*	*introduction*	*aim*	*conclusion*
items	*sheet*	*state*	*relevant*	*examine*
purpose	*body of the report*	*findings*	*rough*	*as a result of*

divisional personnel manager	*time-keeping*	*honesty*	*terminals*
clocking-in machines	*employees*	*salaried*	*overtime*
wasted	*workforce*	*grave*	*requests*
consultants	*clarified*	*undertake*	*efficient*
motivated	*extended breaks*	*review*	*intentions*
staff	*cover*	*selected*	
clerical grades	*department*	*switch on*	

Procedure – *about 90 minutes*

A Students work in pairs and follow the instructions in the Student's Book. In a business context there are many things you should do before you even think about 'writing' or drafting a report. You should first prepare or assemble your material and then plan how you are going to write the report.

The preparation and writing of a report falls into four stages, and some of the individual tasks involved are listed in this step.

B Reassemble the students in groups of four (each pair with another pair). Let the groups discuss what order they have arrived at, the reasons why and what they agree and disagree about.

After this you may find it helpful to get students to consult the document below for the recommended order and to let them respond to it. Remind them of the four broad stages of the process first and how each individual step fits in.

Perhaps to 'speed up the discussion' you could first draw the students' attention to the fact that of the 16 separately distinguished steps only four relate to the actual writing of the report! You can perhaps help to channel the discussion by giving them these four headings prior to the discussion (though not the answers!). Alternatively, you could do this *after* the group discussion.

1 Assemble the material (item 1 below)
2 Plan the report (items 2 to 7 below)
3 Draft the report (items 8 to 11 below)
4 Edit the report (items 12 to 16 below)

➡ Before moving on to the next step draw the students' attention to the four 'Golden Rules':

Be Accurate, Brief, Clear and Decisive.

C The purpose of this activity is to show that a clear statement of the aims of a business report is very important if anything sensible or useful is to be produced. Students work in pairs. They read the memo and imagine that it's addressed to them.

Suggested answers

• The MD is expressing dissatisfaction with time-keeping – in an indirect way.
• Perhaps the MD requires a report which will enable him or her to justify introducing clocking-in machines.

Draw attention to the fact that the intentions behind the Managing Director's memo are not explicit. They will probably have found that it's difficult to decide what the Managing Director really wants to be done.

D These are some of the possible points which might be raised:

• The MD's memo was fairly general in its aim. The report is correspondingly vague in parts. For example: there have been a number of problems connected with the motivation ....
• In parts the report is informative. But occasional long sentences make it difficult to

follow in places, e.g. the third sentence in the first paragraph: `We have also known for ...` , and the sentence in the second paragraph beginning: `The staff think that ...` .

A good feature is the high information content. For instance, the mention of the sister company's experience. A bad feature is arguably the closely typed text (cf. the Zzzzz effect). Numbered paragraphs could have improved this.

E Students work in pairs and draft an improved report together, basing this on the specification in File **69**, where the MD's wishes are somewhat clearer.

After this they compare their report with another group's report. Reading examples of 'bad' writing, such as the MD's memo, should act as a stimulus to be clear, explicit, and to follow the 'Golden Rules'.

After students have compared their reports you can show them the Model report on the next page and let them briefly discuss some of the things they find good about it.

Some of the reasons why the Model report is 'better' are:
1 Numbering sections helps
2 There is a clear introduction
3 There is a conclusion
4 In between there is the main body of the report

➡ Allow time for queries and problems to be raised.

New International Business English   This document may be photocopied.

Model answer

4.3 Planning and editing a report

This is the recommended order in which the planning and writing process can be best arranged:

Assemble the material
   1 Collect all relevant material – notes, documents, etc.

Plan the report
   2 Consider the purpose of your report: who is it for, why does he/she want it, how will he/she use it?
   3 State the aim and emphasis of the report briefly.
   4 Decide what information is important and what is irrelevant.
   5 Arrange the points of information in a logical sequence and in order of importance. Make rough notes.
   6 Draft a working plan on a separate sheet of paper.
   7 Decide where you might need illustrations or diagrams.

Draft the report
   8 Write the introduction: state the subject, state the purpose, summarize your findings.
   9 Write the body of the report.
   10 Write the conclusion (and recommendations).
   11 Summarize the report in a sentence.

Edit the report
   12 Examine the draft. Does it do what the report is expected to do?
   13 Check your grammar, spelling, punctuation and style.
   14 Read the text aloud to yourself, or, better, to someone else.
   15 Check your illustrations.
   16 Finally, if possible, let someone qualified to give constructive criticism look at your draft.

Model report
4.3 Planning and editing a report

```
FROM: Personnel Manager Division A
TO: Managing Director

DATE: 16 May 20__
SUBJECT: Proposed installation of clocking-in machines

1 Following your memorandum of 27 April we carried out a small
  study of staff views in three selected departments to see how
  the arrangements of breaks had been working. I here summarize
  the results:
  a) 65% office workers found the present break arrangements
     satisfactory;
  b) 25% would be in favour of a shorter lunch break and
     finishing earlier.
2 It is too early to say definitely how many machines would be
  needed. But at least one for every divisional office seems a
  reasonable estimate.
3 I also asked my personnel officers about the saving of time.
  They think that an improvement in time-keeping could be made.
4 The staff's reaction to the idea was not very encouraging. In
  the survey we carried out only 15% said they would be in favour
  of using clocking-in machines. If they had the choice they
  would prefer not to use them.
5 You also asked for my views on how to deal with the union. I
  had a meeting with the chief union representative. I mentioned
  that in some departments the lunch break was lasting a lot
  longer than is actually allowed. The representative's answer
  was not very helpful. She said the union would always insist on
  the lunch break being left as it is. There is a point beyond
  which no negotiation would be possible without asking all the
  union members in the company their opinion.

  In conclusion, it seems important to draw the Board's attention
  to possible difficulties which the rapid installation of
  clocking-in machines could bring. We need to discuss the
  problem a little longer and with more people before taking any
  action, it would seem.
```

4.4 Making notes

This section deals with making notes in general, taking notes on conversations using different styles of notes and finally with making notes as a way of planning and preparing.

> ⚠ We haven't made any distinction here between NOTE-TAKING (taking notes *after* or *during* a conversation or meeting) and MAKING NOTES (noting down ideas *before* writing a report or letter or *before* a phone call or meeting). The processes are not the same – but the techniques and styles we suggest *are* much the same. Making a distinction would be more likely to confuse students than help them, we feel.
>
> And LEAVING A NOTE or MESSAGE is different again, because such notes have to be written so that they can be understood by other people.

Vocabulary

abbreviations	*postpone*	*instead of*	*pattern*	*spot*
dash	*processing system*	*order*	*brainstorming session*	*arrows*
punctuation mark	*invoice*	*buyer*	*connect up*	*sequence*
layout	*bill*	*sets*	*branches*	*underestimate*
headings	*payment*	*production time*	*emerge*	*slow down*
increased bonus	*faulty*	*payment*	*conventional*	*rely on*
reduced	*deduct*	*batch*	*focus*	
flight	*lots*	*amount*	*note down*	

Procedure – *about 45 minutes*

A Students work in pairs and first look at the advice. Get them to compare their opinions with another pair. There are no correct answers.

B Encourage the students to read through the notes and raise questions concerning vocabulary *before* you first play the recording.

🔊 Play the recording twice, pausing after each extract to allow everyone time to decide which of the notes goes with which conversation.

Students put the notes in the order they think the best. The correct orders of the notes are overleaf. As you can see, the middle one in the Student's Book doesn't have a 'correct' order.

It can be helpful to use such methods as pattern notes, flowcharts and numbered sections when making notes for letters and reports. They represent some of the different ways of helping to prepare and plan what you wish to write.

Suggested answers

This is the correct order:

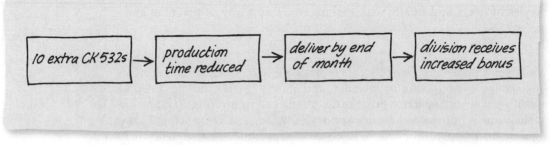

There is no 'correct order' for the middle one.

This is the correct order:

1 CK's last payment faulty
2 ...wrongly billed...
3 for two lots of T140s instead of one

4 reason for 532 figure
5 suggest sending new invoice...
6 deduct extra from total

Transcript [2 minutes 10 seconds]

1 It's about that order for Billingham's, John . . . Yeah. Er...their buyer rang to say they were willing to take ten more sets of the 532, because well it's really been so effective in their new processing system . . . Mm, yes, that's right . . . Yes, they've been able to cut their production time by nearly a third . . . Haha. Yes, it's good news, isn't it? Well, if you can get the stuff out and delivered by the end of the month, it could well mean that the div...the division will get an increase in the monthly bonus . . . Yeah, well I'm sure they'll all be glad to hear that!

2 Hello there, this is Bob Billingham speaking . . . Ha, yeah, yeah, I'm...er I'm just calling to let you know about my time of arrival. Er...let's see, I'm coming in on flight CK532 next Thursday . . . Yeah, yeah it gets in at...er...17.10 . . . Oh, yeah, yeah, yeah, that's good news, isn't it? . . . Yeah, I was hoping to come on the third of the month but...er...I had to postpone my trip for nearly a month. We've had so many problems with that new processing system. You know what I mean . . . Mm...yeah anyway, er...anyway...I...I can tell you all about that next week, OK . . . Mm . . . No, your division is going to have to help us out there . . . Ha, yeah, yeah, I'm afraid that's...that's the case. Right so...er...if you can be thinking about that . . .

3 Mm, but what we've got to do is find out what went wrong with the last payment. Er...now...er...I've been looking at the file for CKs and it seems as though we were billing them for two batches of T140s last month instead of one. Well, this may be how the misunderstanding arose...Well, yes, exactly. That could be how the...er...the 532 figure came up. Now look, what I suggest is that we send them a new invoice with the batch next month and simply deduct the extra amount from the total . . .

C Students work in pairs and follow the instructions in the Student's Book.

D [recording icon] Play the recording, in which a lecturer describes a method of making notes. After listening to the recording students work in pairs and draft a summary of the talk using one of the methods for writing personal notes they have encountered in this section. Then they show their notes to another pair and look at the other pair's notes.

Transcript   [3 minutes 30 seconds]

Speaker: . . . Now, then, I'd like to move on from *taking* notes (of what happened in a meeting or at a lecture) and to *making* notes using the technique of 'pattern notes'.

In the first place we usually make notes to prepare or plan some kind of writing, don't we? One of the ways one can do this is using what we call 'pattern notes'. It's a kind of individual brainstorming session, where you try to note down ideas as they occur to you and you show the way that they connect up. So one of the things you could probably do is to take a clean piece of paper and start with a topic you want to talk about written large in the middle. Mm...right in the middle of the sheet of paper. You can put a circle round this item, if you'd like to. And then the different aspects of the topic will form your first set of branches. So when you've got your first set of branches the ideas begin to emerge, to develop some of these further.

And, where you've got no ideas at all, there's a clear sign that certain aspects of the topic are either irrelevant or need to be thought about a little more. I suppose pattern notes are particularly useful because they're much quicker to produce than the conventional variety and they allow your mind to focus on the ideas without worrying about the correctness of the language you use. So you can note down ideas about different aspects of the topic as they occur to you and you can spot connections and contradictions since everything is laid out on the one page. You can, of course, mark these with arrows and question marks and there's no need to get into any complex arguments. Oh, and perhaps...perhaps I ought to add that psychologists also believe that they reflect the way we think more closely than the kinds of organized notes that run neatly down the page from the top to the bottom or...or from the left to the right.

You don't normally think about single ideas in sequence, rather you deal in whole groups and clusters of ideas – all at the same time. Some of this is done consciously and some of this is done unconsciously. And once you feel comfortable about doing these pattern notes – oh, and some people do feel very uneasy about dealing with what they first feel is...is an unstructured approach – and...and I don't want to underestimate this aspect – pattern notes shouldn't slow down your thinking as much as conventional note-making.

I believe that such notes can also be very useful for recording a fast moving discussion as the basis for minutes or a report to be written afterwards. So they also do have their use as a note-taking technique. So, as discussion jumps from topic to topic you don't have to keep, well, shuffling your notes from page to page to write extra points in.

4.5 Punctuation

This section provides practice in punctuation, which even some advanced students find tricky in English.

Vocabulary

apostrophe	*semi-colon*	*word-joining*
brackets	*single quotes*	*afterthought*
parentheses	*stroke*	*primary*
colon	*oblique*	*productivity survey*
comma	*slash*	*carry out*
dash	*double quotes*	*factory*
exclamation mark	*quotation marks*	*costs*
full stop	*inverted commas*	*competitive*
period	*doubt*	*avoid*
hyphen	*word-division*	*salary*
question mark		

Procedure – *about 45 minutes*

The four steps are straightforward. Any of these could be done as homework – but doing them in pairs gives students a chance to discuss the rules and exchange ideas.

A Answers

apostrophe ’   *brackets / parentheses* (...)   *colon* :   *comma* ,   *dash* –
exclamation mark !   *full stop / period* .   *hyphen* -   *question mark* ?
semi-colon ;   *single quotes* ‘...’   *stroke / oblique / slash* /
double quotes / quotation marks / inverted commas “...”

The punctuation mark within the brackets and quotes is an *ellipsis* . . . This isn't used in business correspondence, but can be seen in advertisements, notes, stories . . .

B Suggested answers

1 single quotes/single quotation marks/single inverted commas
2 full stop (British English)/period (American English)
3 question mark
4 hyphen
5 dash
6 exclamation mark
7 double quotes/double quotation marks/double inverted commas
8 semi-colon
9 colon
10 stroke/oblique/slash
11 brackets (parentheses)
12 apostrophe

C

Students work in pairs and decide which punctuation marks or Capital Letters are incorrectly used. Some of the punctuation is surplus to requirements and must be deleted!

Suggested answers – some variations are possible

1 It's important that your punctuation is correct because incorrect punctuation and capital letters used wrongly may confuse your readers.

2 Just like incorrect spelling, incorrect punctuation can be very annoying for your reader, who may pay more attention to the mistakes than to the content of your report or letter.

3 You probably know that exclamation marks are not used much in business letters. But they are used in advertisements, as well as in notes.

4 Contracted forms like *I've* and *we've* are a feature of informal writing. They are not found in most reports or business letters, which tend to be fairly formal. If in doubt use the full forms: *I have*, *we have*, etc.

5 It's usually easier for a reader to understand short, simple sentences rather than long, complicated ones.

D

Students work in pairs and decide where to add punctuation. Remind them that they will also need to add some Capital Letters.

In the Model answer opposite, notice that in a couple of places a semi-colon might have been used instead of a full stop.

Model answer

4.5 Punctuation

MEMO

From: The Managing Director
To: All Office Staff
Date: 25th November 20__

As a result of the productivity survey carried out in the factory, more rapid and efficient ways of operating are now being applied. In the factory, productivity has been increased by over 50 per cent. The management intends to apply these same methods to office staff in order to reduce costs. Our company must adapt in a competitive world. We aim to find ways of avoiding unnecessary actions by all staff. We therefore propose to pay a month's extra salary to any person who, in the management's opinion, has put forward the most practical suggestion to improve a particular office routine. All suggestions should be sent to the MD's office before the end of next month.

Workbook contents for this unit

4.1 **Writing reports**   *Background information*

4.2 **Punctuation**

4.3 **Summarizing**   *Listening & speaking*

4.4 **Getting it down on paper**   *Vocabulary*

4.5 **Dealing with a report**   *Reading*

4.6 **Rule Number One: Clear that desk**   *Reading*

4.7 **The passive**   *Grammar review*

5 Working together

This unit looks at various aspects of working in business and occasions when people may be expected to talk about their workplace. Firstly, one may have to show someone physically around the office or premises. Then, more generally, one may be asked to describe how the business is organized or structured. Furthermore, people in business may often be called upon to describe to outsiders or friends what their company actually does. The unit also looks at companies' backgrounds, and similarly, contemporary changes in company organization practices and manager-employee relationships are considered. The important issue of the role and status of women in working life rounds off this unit.

Background information

Draw everyone's attention to the Background information in the Workbook on different kinds of companies. This is important for students who have had little work experience.

Video

Programme 5 on the *New International Business English Video* introduces the theme of this unit. It deals with Swatch AG in Switzerland.

5.1 Getting to know the workplace ...

This section covers the important question of finding one's way about a company's premises either as someone who is new to the company or as a visitor. It concentrates on office life and how offices are laid out.

Vocabulary

employee	*trade union representative*
join	*union recognition*
installed	*recreational and sports facilities*
accounts	*child-care facilities*
pension scheme	*equipment*

Procedure – *about 90 minutes*

A 　Before you play the recording, students should work in pairs and study the floor plan and also the items in the box. Any vocabulary items should be dealt with. Get the students to say where they think particular rooms are likely to be.

This is the completed plan of the offices.

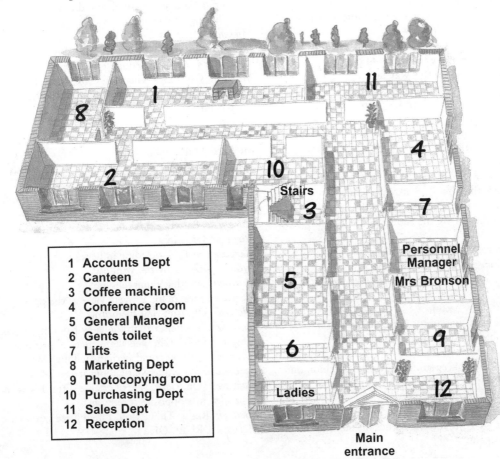

1 Accounts Dept
2 Canteen
3 Coffee machine
4 Conference room
5 General Manager
6 Gents toilet
7 Lifts
8 Marketing Dept
9 Photocopying room
10 Purchasing Dept
11 Sales Dept
12 Reception

Two extra activities

1 Here are some additional questions you can ask the students to answer. Write them up on the board perhaps before a final playing of the recording:

1 What is the name of the new man? (*Michael Hill*)
2 Where is he from? (*From our Australian branch*)
3 What is the name of the Personnel Manager? (*Mrs Bronson*)
4 When is the canteen open? (*At lunchtime and in the afternoon*)
5 Is there anything special about the office the newcomer will be working in? (*He'll have a nice view of the park from the window*)

2 Students with work experience can be asked by the others in the class about their first day at work. What is the most pleasant memory they have? What unpleasant memories do they have? What sort of office did they work in? A small or big one? What advice would they give to people on their first day in the company?
Allow time for feedback and queries.

Transcript [2 minutes 30 seconds]

Mrs Bronson: . . . Margaret, I'd like to introduce you to Michael Hill from our Australian branch.
Margaret: Hello, Michael, pleased to meet you.
Michael: How do you do?
Margaret: How's your first day going?
Michael: Oh, very well, thank you. It's…it's all very interesting.

Mrs Bronson: I was just telling Michael what the set-up here is – who's where and what's what, so to speak. I was wondering if I could hand him over to you now?
Margaret: Oh, yes, sure, fine. Um…would you like to come this way . . .
Michael: See you later, Mrs Bronson.
Mrs Bronson: Yes, sure.

5.1 Getting to know the workplace …

Michael: What was...what was that room next door to Reception? I heard a strange noise coming from it.

Margaret: Oh, right, yes, that's where the photocopier is.

Michael: Oh, I see. That's what it was.

Margaret: Yes, we've had a new one installed. It's very fast but it makes even more noise than the old one, unfortunately. Right, let's go this way now.

Michael: OK.

Margaret: Um...opposite Mrs Bronson's office just here is the General Manager's office . . .

Michael: General Manager, fine.

Margaret: I expect he'll speak to you later.

Michael: OK.

Margaret: And, um if...we go right down the corridor, on the right-hand side are the lifts.

Michael: Fine.

Margaret: And on the left are the stairs.

Michael: OK.

Margaret: So they're handy opposite each other.

Michael: Right, fine.

Margaret: And, er, in there by the stairs also is the coffee machine.

Michael: Oh, right, very useful.

Margaret: Yes, the most important thing of all. You'll meet most of the members of staff there, I should think.

Michael: Fine.

Margaret: And, er, if you keep going down the corridor, on the right-hand side, just down here, you can see the conference room.

Michael: Great.

Margaret: And, as we go round the corner on the right, here is the sales department.

Michael: Sales, OK.

Margaret: And as we come round the corner on the left is the purchasing department.

Michael: OK.

Margaret: And, if you can see, just down the end of the corridor is our marketing department.

Michael: Oh, that's where they are, right, fine.

Margaret: That's right, next to you actually, in the accounts department.

Michael: Right.

Margaret: Which is just on the right here.

Michael: Huhu.

Margaret: And on the left opposite, is the canteen.

Michael: Oh, very important.

Margaret: It's open at lunchtime and in the afternoon as well.

Michael: Oh, great.

Margaret: Between three and four.

Michael: OK, right.

Margaret: And if we come in here on the right, then. That's your desk over by the window.

Michael: Oh, that's marvellous.

Margaret: Yes. With a lovely view of the park.

Michael: Oh, isn't that beautiful?

Margaret: It's better than the view from my office.

Michael: Right. Oh, well that's marv... Just one thing, I wondered if you could perhaps tell me where the...where the gents toilet is while we're about it?

Margaret: Oh, right, yes, of course. Erm. It's at the end of the corridor just opposite reception.

Michael: Right. Thank you. I'll...I'll see you in a minute.

Margaret: Right, OK . . .

B Students work in pairs and decide which points they think are important. If you have students both with and without work experience make sure, wherever possible, that pairs are formed in which there's at least one student with experience. Then the inexperienced student can ask which points the experienced one disagrees with. After the pairs have decided which are the most important items to bear in mind, let them compare their list with another pair's. You may then ask the class as a whole to discuss which they consider the most important items to be.

C You may need to deal with items of vocabulary that come up in the students' discussion. Also allow a little time for those students who may have work experience of other countries to be questioned by the others.

D This is an integrated activity that allows students the opportunity to work through some of the standard tasks which are connected with showing someone around a company. The fax provides reading input and sets the scene. This leads into the first task which requires students to think about their own working situation. For those not in work encourage them to imagine the kind of enterprise they would like to work in and accordingly to decide what they would show a visitor.

The telephone role-play should follow the set pattern by now established.

Then, after they have written the memo they can 'send' it to another pair and 'receive' the other pair's. (Alternatively, if you're closely monitoring your students' progress you might collect this and the fax in **4** for marking purposes.) The final task can be decided by you, depending on what your students need to have more practice in: telephoning or writing.

Model memo

5.1 Getting to know the workplace ...

—————————— **MEMORANDUM** ——————————

From:	Publicity Officer	**To:**	Managing Director
Subject:	Visitor from Denmark	**Date:**	13/9/——

On 15 November Ms Anita Trosborg, Design Director of the Tivoli Design
Consortium of Copenhagen is paying a visit to our offices.
I would like to ask whether you are likely to be in that morning. If
possible I would like to bring Ms Trosborg to see you for a brief meeting,
probably ten minutes or so, just to make contact. Would 11.45 be OK?
Please let me know as soon as possible if it is inconvenient.

Thanks,

Sarah

Model fax

5.1 Getting to know the workplace ...

—————————— **Exquisite Effects** ——————————

Your address, Your Town, Your Country

Anita Trosborg
Design Director
Tivoli Design Consortium
Berstorffsgade 19,
DK-1577 Copenhagen,
Denmark
Fax: +(45) 56 39 42 38   Date

Dear Anita Trosborg,

We thank you for your enquiry concerning your prospective visit here.

I am writing to say that it would be convenient for you to visit our office
on 15 November, from 11.30. I have arranged a brief meeting with our
managing director and then a meeting and possibly lunch with our design
manager after that.

I hope you will find the time convenient.

If so, please confirm as soon as possible.

We look forward to receiving you.

Yours sincerely,

Sarah Baxter

Publicity Officer

Two extra activities

1 As an additional role-play one student can show another student, in the role of visitor, around the company they work in. Before they do this, it's advisable for them to draw up a plan of the building or site, etc. If they're not in work perhaps they could take the visitor around the college or training institution. Alternatively, they could use the floor plan in **B**.

2 Students work in groups of three or four for this activity. Ask them to design 'the perfect office' *and* give them these instructions:

Think of the office you work in (or an office you have worked in at some time). Imagine that you have the authority and the budget to reorganize the office:

- What new facilities will you introduce?
- What up-to-date equipment will you install?
- What sort of chairs will you order?
- What kind of office lighting will you put in?
- Who will be responsible for safety procedures?
- Which jobs would you prefer to do yourself without any help from machines?
- Which jobs would you be glad to leave to a machine to do?

➡ Ask the students to draw a plan of their redesigned office.
Let them show their 'perfect office' to another group for their comments.

Allow time at the end for the class to raise any queries on problems or difficulties which may have arisen while doing the activity.

5.2 Different kinds of companies

In this section various aspects of describing companies and referring to their activities are covered. It deals with types of business and occupational structure in various sectors of industry and product groups.

Vocabulary

primary	*vehicle manufacturing*	*chemicals*	*telecommunications*
secondary	*engineering*	*electronics*	*sectors of industry*
tertiary	*food processing*	*retailing*	*product groups*
	beverages	*catering*	*chart*
	aerospace	*banking*	*supply*

Procedure – *about 45 minutes*

A The task is fairly straightforward and at this stage requires little discussion about technical definitions. It may be necessary to explain some vocabulary items in the chart.

If necessary give your students some clues: 'goods-producing' companies belong to the secondary sector, 'service-producing' firms to the tertiary, etc. The companies listed have been selected to fit into these two main categories. This is the Key:

Secondary: e.g. manufacturing
Bayer   Pepsi   Saab-Scania   Ford

Tertiary: e.g. services, banking, insurance, tourism, leisure
BNP   British Airways   Sears   Hilton International

As additional help for the first discussion question, perhaps mention different criteria: one criterion could be the number of employees on the payroll, another might be physical dominance (i.e. on the landscape), a further feature might be how important they are in generating tax, etc.

To jog students' imaginations you might also take into class a copy of the yellow pages telephone directory, as a source of inspiration.

Or with a class of students who are working in different companies, you can ask them to list the companies they work for themselves and to compare them in terms of profit, turnover, quantity of products or services, etc.

Alternatively you can perhaps get students to do this as homework. A bit of personal research might be useful depending on the kind of students you're dealing with.

After the students have agreed on a list in groups, they compare another group's list. The class as a whole can also compare their lists.

B 1 When the text has been 'reconstituted', move on to step **2**.

   2 There are no correct answers to these questions, but it may be helpful to research some statistics about your students' country/countries before the lesson.

New International Business English   This document may be photocopied.

Suggested answers
5.2 Different kinds of companies

This is the completed text with the missing words **in bold type**.

> **Divisions of economic activity** Although the structure of each country is different, their economies can be shown to have similar sectors. When speaking of **business** or economic activity, commentators normally recognize three **major** 'sectors':
> - primary – agriculture, fishing, mining, construction
> - **secondary** – crafts and manufacturing
> - tertiary – **services**, including education, banking, insurance, etc.
>
> **The occupational structure** The types of activities that most **workers** are occupied in differ, sometimes dramatically, from one country to **another** and from one time to another. In **most** developing countries (and in all **countries** before the 19th century), the vast majority of the workforce **work** in the agricultural, or **primary**, sector. Their work is almost entirely manual, and most of the country's **labour** power is concentrated on the **basic** task of feeding the population. In **fully** developed countries far more of their **productive** resources are directed towards other **economic** activities. In the United States and Canada, for example, only 4 and 7 per cent, respectively, of all employed persons work in agriculture, **fishing**, and mining, compared to more than 70 **per cent** in India.

Extra activity

Make a list of five small enterprises or kinds of company you would like to work for.

5.3 Company organization

This section deals with the divisions and departments of a company and the use of job titles within the company.

Vocabulary

board of directors   *managing director*   *report to*

Procedure – *about 45 minutes*

A This activity is in part preparation for **5.5**.

1 Students work in pairs and look at the organization chart of Biopaints International. Encourage them to try and guess what the missing job titles might be. Perhaps tell the students how the names on the chart are pronounced.

2 Play the recording. This listening exercise involves listening for detail. Give everyone time to write down their answers and then play the recording a second time. Students can compare their answers in pairs.

You may need to repeat how the three missing names are pronounced:

Robert Leaf   George Harris   Chow Fung

Answers
Managing Director: **Robert Leaf***   *Finance Director:* Weimin Tan*
Marketing Manager: Rosemary Broom   *Production Manager:* **George Harris**
Personnel Manager: Deirdre Spencer   *Research and Development Manager:* Dr Tarcisius Chin
Planning Manager: **Chow Fung**   *General Manager, Singapore Factory:* Lee Boon Eng
* member of the board of directors

Transcript   [2 minutes 30 seconds]

Presenter: Today we are talking to Philip Knight about the structure of Biopaints International. Philip's the General Manager of the Perth factory. Philip, do you think you could tell us something about the way Biopaints is actually organized?

Philip Knight: Yes, certainly. Er…we employ about two thousand people in all in two different locations. Most people work here at our headquarters plant. And this is where we have the administrative departments, of course.

Presenter: Well, perhaps you could say something about the departmental structure?

Philip Knight: Yes, certainly. Well, now first of all, as you know we've got two factories, one here in Perth, Australia, and the other in Singapore. Lee Boon Eng is the other General Manager, over there in Singapore.

Presenter: And you are completely independent of each other, is that right?

Philip Knight: Oh, yes. Our two plants are fairly independent. I mean, I am responsible to George Harris, the Production Manager, and we have to co-operate closely with Rosemary Broom, the Marketing Manager.

Presenter: Mm, yeah.

Philip Knight: But otherwise, as far as day to day running is concerned, we're pretty much left alone to get on with the job. Oh, and I forgot to mention finance. The Finance Director is Weimin Tan. She's a very important woman. And her task is to make sure the money side of things is OK. The accountant and such people, they report to her directly.

Presenter: Is that all?

Philip Knight: Oh, no, no. There's Personnel too.

Presenter: Oh, yes.

Philip Knight: That's quite separate. Deirdre Spencer is Personnel Manager. And the Training Manager reports to her, of course.

Presenter: What about Research and Development? Isn't that a separate department?

Philip Knight: Well, in terms of the laboratories, there are two: one at each production plant. But it's a separate department and it has a separate head. And that's Dr Tarcisius Chin.

Presenter: Are there any other features worth mentioning?

Philip Knight: There's the planning department – Chow Fung is in charge of that. And a purchasing department – they buy in the materials for production.

Presenter: Yes, and what about the board of directors and the chairman?

Philip Knight: Yes, well they're at the top, aren't they, of course? I mean, a couple of the executives are directors themselves. The Managing Director, of course, that's Robert Leaf and then there's . . .

B Encourage the students to give reasons for their answers. Depending on the country you're working in, other parts of the company may well include the shareholders or the works council. Companies, particularly large manufacturing ones, may be divided up into divisions. Note that there are companies organized with less pyramidal structures.

Suggested answers

The Public Relations Manager reports to the Marketing Manager; the Advertising Manager too. The Works Manager probably reports to the Production Manager. The Export Manager reports to the Sales Manager. The Project Manager may well report directly to the Planning Manager.

Draw attention to the fact that some American job titles differ from British ones, which are used in the exercise. These are the equivalents:

USA	GB
President	Chairman
Chief Executive Officer (CEO)	Managing Director (MD)
Vice-President	Director
Financial Controller	Accountant
Director (e.g. Personnel Director)	Manager (e.g. Personnel Manager)

C Student A looks at File **11**, student B at **43**. They ask each other questions and complete an information-gap exercise based on the organizational diagram of a fictitious company. You may need to tell the students how some of the names are pronounced.

5.4 Company developments

This section looks at the history of two contemporary companies, and encourages students to consider the development of their own company (or, if they don't work, the company in the advertisement in File **70**).

Vocabulary

decades	*innovative*	*zest*	*limited liability company*
synonymous	*array*	*railroad*	*assets*
found	*subsidiaries*	*civil engineering*	*recommence*
link	*milestones*	*turn of the century*	*acquisition*
a fledgling firm	*maintain*	*branch offices*	*corporation*
spearhead	*production facilities*	*numerous*	*subsidiaries*
cornerstone	*fiscal year*	*proprietorship*	*versatile*
power engineering	*reliable*	*partnership*	*takeover*

Procedure – *about 45 minutes*

A **1** **Answers**

Planning and Building for over 150 years – Philipp Holzmann
Pioneering Tomorrow's Electronics – Siemens

2 **Suggested answers**

Dates	What happened?	Who did what?
1847	Siemens was founded	Werner Siemens & Johann Georg Halske
1849	Company was established in Sprendlingen	Johann Philipp Holzmann
1866	Invention of dynamo machine	Werner Siemens

Dates	What happened?	Who did what?
1882	First large foreign order begun	Holzmann Co.
1885	Workforce exceeding 5,000	Holzmann Co.
1917	Aktiengesellschaft founded	Holzmann Co.
1950	Foreign business restarted	Holzmann Co.
1979	Acquisition of J. A. Jones Construction Company	Holzmann Co.
1981	Purchase of Lockwood Greene Engineers, Inc.	Holzmann Co.
1989	Takeover of Steinmüller Group	Holzmann Co.
1992/3	Recorded annual sales of DM 82 billion	Siemens

3 Suggested answers

	HOLZMANN	SIEMENS
Locations of the company's activities	Amsterdam, Baghdad, East Africa, South America	In more than 50 countries
Activities of both companies up to 1940s	Railroad and railroad projects, all fields of building construction and civil engineering	Power engineering
Recent activities of the companies	Purchase of American companies and one of the most important German corporations	An innovative leader on electrical and electronic market

B Perhaps this activity needs to be done with a different partner to provide variety. Alternatively, if you are running out of time, students can do this for homework.

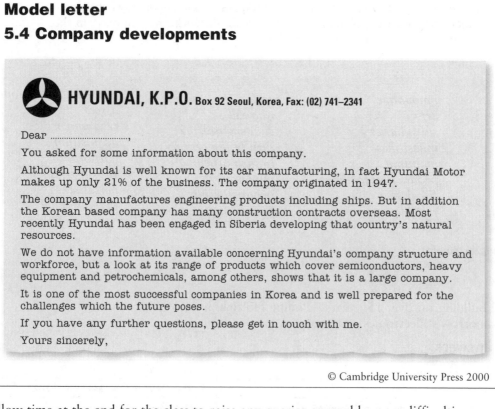

New International Business English   This document may be photocopied.

Model letter

5.4 Company developments

HYUNDAI, K.P.O. Box 92 Seoul, Korea, Fax: (02) 741–2341

Dear ....,

You asked for some information about this company.

Although Hyundai is well known for its car manufacturing, in fact Hyundai Motor makes up only 21% of the business. The company originated in 1947.

The company manufactures engineering products including ships. But in addition the Korean based company has many construction contracts overseas. Most recently Hyundai has been engaged in Siberia developing that country's natural resources.

We do not have information available concerning Hyundai's company structure and workforce, but a look at its range of products which cover semiconductors, heavy equipment and petrochemicals, among others, shows that it is a large company.

It is one of the most successful companies in Korea and is well prepared for the challenges which the future poses.

If you have any further questions, please get in touch with me.

Yours sincerely,

Allow time at the end for the class to raise any queries on problems or difficulties which may have arisen while doing the activity.

5.5 Working with others

Besides its reading and listening activities, this section deals with the functions of agreeing and disagreeing. Students have the opportunity to discuss opinions about company organization and manager-employee relations.

Vocabulary

abandon	components	dishwashers	rotate	large corporations
sites	in bulk	cooling units	rate	corporate world
expenses	share	sevenfold	consultant	parking lots
abolish	consign	debt	staff turnover	subject oneself to
rewarding	oblivion	collapse	get rid of	scrutiny
assembly line	filing cabinets	afflict	pyramid structure	corporate managers
economies of scale	confine	counsellors	concentric circles	

Procedure – *about 90 minutes*

A 1 You may feel it's necessary to explain some of the vocabulary beforehand.
Discuss which of the titles seem more suitable than others – the original article was titled **The World's Most Unusual Workplace** though others might be equally good.

2 Students read the first extract and answer the questions about it.

Suggested answers

1 Workers
2 The assembly line and economies of scale
3 A quarter of employees fix their own
4 The workers decide
5 Employees
6 Employees
7 There are no central computers
8 There are no controls over expenses and business travel
9 He makes his own

3 Students read the second extract.

Suggested answers

1 Pumps, dishwashers and cooling units
2 They have increased fivefold
3 Good, $30 million
4 23 per cent is exported
5 Free of debt

B

1 Suggested answers

- bureaucracy at work ✓
- staff promotion systems
- management elections by the workers ✓
- the design of Semco's factory buildings
- the success of large corporations ✓

2 Suggested answers

True: 2 3 5 7
False: 1 4 6 8 9 10

Transcript [5 minutes 10 seconds]

Charles: . . . Jane, I wonder if you could tell us what Ricardo Semler is trying to do?

Jane: Well, sure. Semler wants to introduce real democracy in the workplace. That's the essence of his philosophy. It's the end of the party for Henry Ford's assembly line, he would argue. He gives it at the most a hundred years. That means it still has 15 or 20 years to go. It's collapsing slowly. And the giant corporations we knew this century are coming to an end.

Charles: Robert, would you like to comment on this?

Robert: Yes, I think it needs to be stressed that autocracy is the main problem afflicting all these companies. In countries like America, Britain and Brazil people are all very proud of their democratic values in public life, and rightly so. But as Semler himself says, he has yet to see a democratic *workplace*. We are being held back by a system that doesn't allow democracy into business or into the workplace . . .

Jane: If I could just add a related point there concerning bureaucratic structures. Getting rid of seven layers of management bureaucracy is the real key to Semco's success. This went hand in hand with the introduction of genuine democracy. Managers – including Semler who is one of six 'counsellors' who rotate in the job of chief executive – are rated regularly by their employees. Every manager gets points from between one to a hundred from his staff, anonymously. This happens every six months, when a new budget is set. If managers regularly fail to come up to expectations, they give way or are pushed out. One long-serving manager, who used to score 86 out of 100, has dropped down to only 51. What will happen to him is uncertain.

Charles: Surely, this means that the workforce watches the management closely all the time, instead of getting on with their work?

Robert: Yes, but evaluating the boss was just the first step. The big break came when people were allowed to *elect* their own boss. In Semler's view managers imported from outside the company are bad news. Staff who are truly *involved* in the financial success of the factory are realistic about choosing future bosses.

Charles: Jane, can this system really work?

Jane: Absolutely! And I'll tell you why. You see, the fact that employees are free to come and go as they like, or work from home, or become a consultant, means that they don't take advantage of the situation. They recognize the responsibility that comes with controlling their own futures. And as several reports show, it appears to be a happy place to work, with very low staff turnover and a long waiting list of people applying for jobs there.

Robert: As Jane's already said, what has happened is that Semco has got rid of the old pyramid structure of bureaucrats, together with their power symbols. So secretaries and parking spaces have gone. The organization now consists of three concentric circles, an inner one of six vice-presidents (including Semler), surrounded by a second circle of up to 10 leaders of the business units, and the outer one which includes everyone else – they're called 'associates'. Just walking around the factory there's no way of distinguishing the high earners from the low earners because workers wear what they like and hardly anybody has a desk.

Charles: Of course, the major question people have been asking is whether the Semco experiment is transferable? For instance to other types of company and other countries?

Jane: Yes, that is the big question. In some parts of Europe employees already do participate actively, but in these cases there seems to be a 'special factor' to explain their success. For example, the Mondragon co-operatives in Northern Spain which are closely tied up with the Basque culture, or the benevolent former owners in employee-owned companies in several other countries.

Charles: Still Semco must be taken seriously. A company that can survive more than a decade of Brazil's inflation can't just be ignored, can it Robert?

Robert: No, no, it certainly can't. But there is one area, I believe, where this model *won't* work. Transferring the model to a large corporation like IBM or General Motors doesn't have much hope of success, as long as giving up control means bringing information out in the open. And it is precisely information, or the lack of it, which represents power in such organizations. Or as their critics would say, those are the reasons they will go to the wall!

Charles: At any rate a few smaller companies have tried to directly copy Semler's example. And if the hundreds of managers who visit Semler's shop floor are any guide, there is a considerable appetite out there for making Western capitalism more civilized. Would you agree, Jane?

Jane: That certainly appears to be the case and yet I suppose the probability of this happening quickly is very small. As the British journalist Victor Keegan puts it: 'The trouble is that the corporate world is run by people not exactly willing to lose their parking lots, let alone to subject themselves to monthly scrutiny by people whom, currently, they can hire and fire. Corporate managers don't yet look in a hurry to commit mass professional suicide!'

C Students first discuss the options listed. Remind them to use the functional exponents for agreeing and disagreeing.

> ⚠ Perhaps remind the class of the importance of choosing polite forms when one disagrees with someone in a business setting. Emphasize too that the smooth running of a relationship can be oiled by 'weakening' or toning down a disagreement. Instead of telling someone that what they have offered or said is 'rubbish' (even if you think it is!) it may often be more beneficial to your continued maintenance of good customer or client relations to say 'I don't think that is such a good idea, after all . . .'.
>
> This has nothing to do with insincerity (this is business and not a bible class) as some people claim; rather, apart from being good manners, such forms, together with a polite tone of voice are worth stressing as a useful business asset. Remind your students of the Chinese proverb:
> 'He who cannot smile should not open a shop.'

Follow-up discussion

Depending on your students, a further issue to discuss might be whether information about the firm should be given to the workforce within a company. Is it always a good thing? Students can ask each other about their own company's policy on informing the workforce about developments. You might get your students to share their views on how far they agree or disagree that having information can help employees to identify with the company.

Further related questions might include the following:
- Compare the situation at Semco with other situations or companies with which you may be familiar in your country.
- Is there a general philosophy in your country that workers and employees should be involved as much as possible?
- Do you feel that workers work better, or more willingly, if they know the objectives and the long-term plans of their managers?
- Are short-term goals or long-term goals better for companies and their workforces in your opinion?

Allow time at the end for the class to raise any queries on problems or difficulties which may have arisen during their discussions.

5.6 Women's work

Vocabulary

manual worker

Procedure *– about 45 minutes*

A For this step students work in pairs.

B Rearrange the class into groups of four. You may wish to let students discuss briefly as a class the differences agreed on and reasons given for the changes.

C It may be best to do this with the class as a whole, possibly after students have had time to discuss it in groups.

Two extra activities

1 Write up these sentences on the board and ask the students to discuss each of them in groups of three. One should support the opinion, one should oppose it, and the third should wait to be persuaded by one or the other.

Smoking should be forbidden in offices.
All offices should have flowers in them.
All companies should offer their employees free lunches.
Overtime should be obligatory if the day's work is not done.
Work is oppressive anyway; the best boss is always a tyrant.
Work and democracy cannot go together.
Democracy in civil or political life does not require democracy at work.
Efficiency is impossible in a democratic workplace.
Profits belong to the bosses not the workers.

2 If you have a class with work experience, it may be enlightening (and enjoyable) to allow the class to discuss their own experiences at work relating to some of the topics touched upon in this activity.

Here are some additional questions:

• Should the law be strengthened to protect women's rights at work?
• Are salaries and wages fairly distributed between the sexes at work?
• Is equality of opportunity between women and men something to be aimed for, or has it already been achieved?

Allow time at the end for the class to raise any queries on problems or difficulties which may have arisen while doing the activity.

Workbook contents for this unit

5.1 **Different kinds of companies**   *Background information*

5.2 **Firms at work**   *Vocabulary*

5.3 **Prefixes**   *Word-building*

5.4 **Agreeing and disagreeing**   *Functions & listening*

5.5 **Prepositions – 1**

5.6 **The eternal coffee break**   *Reading*

5.7 **Referring to the past**   *Grammar review*

6 International trade

This unit deals with the following situations connected with importing and exporting goods (or trading within the EU):

- making and answering enquiries
- making and accepting offers
- placing, acknowledging and filling orders

The functions of asking for and giving information are also covered.

In real life there would sometimes be complications. Face-to-face negotiation might take place on prices, terms of delivery, etc. In this unit we just deal with the basics and give practice dealing with overseas customers on the phone and by fax or letter. More advanced or more experienced students might like to spend longer on the finer points.

Solving problems connected with payment for goods is dealt with in Unit 7. Solving problems connected with delivery and after-sales is dealt with in Unit 8.

Background information

The Background information in the Workbook contains a summary of some of the different arrangements that have to be made in international trade. This includes the use of ICC INCOTERMS which are used to facilitate the terms of a deal, regarding the relative responsibilities of the buyer and seller as to the transportation and insurance of goods in transit.

If you or your students are unfamiliar with Incoterms, please refer to the Workbook before starting this unit.

For further background information, we recommend the illustrated booklets issued free of charge by international banks for the benefit of exporters and importers. For example, *Services for Exporters* and *Services for Importers* published by Midland Bank International, are particularly useful and attractive.

Video

Programme 6 on the *New International Business English Video* introduces the theme of this unit.

6.1 Exchanging information   *Functions*

As a warm-up, look at the photos showing different methods of distribution and ask the students to suggest what kinds of goods are more likely to be transported by sea, by air or by road (and by rail) – and to say why.

This section covers the functions of asking for and giving information or apologizing for not being able to give the required information. Apart from reminding students of the exponents, we also emphasize the importance of an appropriately friendly and helpful tone of voice – and, when face-to-face, a friendly and helpful demeanour.

The preparation in step **B**, which is not recorded, introduces the exponents. It should be prepared by the students before the lesson.

Vocabulary

exchanging	*consignment*	*available*	*conference*
supplier	*warehouse*	*confidential*	*proportion*
hostile	*truck*	*details*	*domestic*
impatient	*unload*	*delegates*	*career*

Procedure – *about 90 minutes*

⚠ If at all possible, make sure your students study step **B** at home before the lesson – otherwise it's likely to take up some valuable class time. The examples in speech balloons aren't recorded – but many of them are used in the second version of the conversation in **A**.

Before starting work on the listening exercise, ask everyone to look at the pictures and discuss these questions:

* What does each picture show?
* What kind of goods are being transported, do you think?
* What kind of goods would you expect to be carried by air, by road and by sea?

A 📼 This step looks at the importance of creating a good impression.

1 Begin by playing the first version of the conversation. Ask students to comment on the impression both speakers give. Hopefully, members of the class will identify the speakers' tone as hostile, aggressive and impatient – they sound as if they're hating every minute of the conversation.

2 Play the second version of the conversation. This time the speakers are friendly and helpful to each other – they sound as if they're enjoying talking to each other.

3 Now play the second version again and ask the class to identify how each speaker makes himself sound 'nice'.

It's a combination of their tone of voice, the way they hesitate (putting *Er...* before a request for information) and the polite forms they use (saying *Could you tell me when ...?* instead of just *When ...?*).

These polite forms are underlined in the transcript below. Students will come across them again in the preparation in step **B**.

Transcript [3 minutes]

First version of the conversation

Rusconi: Rusconi.
Garcia: Hello, this is Al Garcia.
Rusconi: At last! When can we expect the next consignment in our warehouse?
Garcia: Late Thursday or early Friday, depends on the traffic and the weather. When will you accept deliveries?
Rusconi: Up to 4 pm and from 7.30 am. Whose trucks are delivering the goods?
Garcia: Two of ours, and the others are on hire from Alpha Transport.
Rusconi: How do you spell Alpha?
Garcia: A-L-P-H-A.
Rusconi: How many trucks will be coming?
Garcia: Five.
Rusconi: Will they arrive all on the same day?
Garcia: Two will set off half a day early, so they should arrive Thursday. The other three will arrive towards midday Friday.

How long will it take to unload each truck?
Rusconi: About an hour. We can't unload more than two at a time, you know.
Garcia: I want to know what happens if one truck arrives late. Can you unload it on Saturday?
Rusconi: I don't know. Our warehouse manager would know.
Garcia: What's his name?
Rusconi: Mr Ferrari.
Garcia: What's his number?
Rusconi: 345 9800 extension 71.
Garcia: Goodbye.
Rusconi: Goodbye.

Second version of the conversation

Rusconi: Jupiter Products. Tony Rusconi speaking.
Garcia: Hello, this is Al Garcia.
Rusconi: Hello, Mr Garcia. How are you?
Garcia: Fine, thanks. I'm phoning about our delivery next week.

Rusconi: Ah, yes, good. I was just about to call you. Er...could you tell me when we can expect the consignment to arrive in our warehouse?

Garcia: Yes, as far as I know, the trucks should arrive late Thursday or early Friday, it depends on traffic and weather. Er...what time will you accept deliveries?

Rusconi: The latest time we can start unloading is 4 pm, but...but we can start as early as 7.30 am. Er...could you tell me whose trucks are delivering the goods?

Garcia: Yes, certainly. Two of them will be ours, and the others are on hire from Alpha Transport.

Rusconi: Let me just make a note of that. Er...can you tell me how you spell Alpha?

Garcia: Yes, of course. It's A-L-P-H-A.

Rusconi: Fine. A...and I'd also like to know how many trucks will be coming.

Garcia: Ah...there will be five altogether.

Rusconi: Can you tell me if they will arrive on the same day?

Garcia: I'm not entirely sure, but...er... as two will be setting off half a day early, they should arrive Thursday. Er...the other three will arrive towards midday Friday. Could you let me know how long it will take to unload each truck?

Rusconi: Yes, er...each truck will take about an hour. Er...I think you should know that we can't unload more than two trucks at a time.

Garcia: I see, well, thanks for letting me know that. Er...I wonder if you can tell me what'll happen if one of the trucks arrives later and can't be unloaded on Friday? Do you know if it can be unloaded on Saturday?

Rusconi: I'm afraid I don't know, it might have to wait till Monday. Er...you'd have to ask our warehouse manager about that.

Garcia: Could you just remind me what his name is again?

Rusconi: Yes, of course. He's...er...Mr Ferrari.

Garcia: Ah, and...er...can...can you tell me his number?

Rusconi: Yes, it's 345 9800 extension 71.

Garcia: Good. Thank you very much. It's...it's nice to talk to you. Goodbye.

Rusconi: Bye now, Mr Garcia.

B As suggested above, this step should have been prepared at home before the lesson, so that class time can be devoted to discussing the ideas rather than silently studying them.

Perhaps explain the purpose of 'probing questions', which are used to find out more detailed information. And explain how tricky questions can be fielded, and how we can hedge or delay answering questions.

Here are some more expressions that might be added to the balloons – some of these are for advanced students only:

Please tell me ...?
Do you know ...?
Do you happen to know ...?

Would you please inform us ...?

I see, fine.
Good, that's just what I wanted to know.
That's useful to know.

To the best of my knowledge ...
Well, this is off the record, you understand ...

I haven't a clue. (not polite)
I'm sorry. I'll need to check the figures on the computer. I'll e-mail you the information before lunch.

You may be interested to know that ...

Would you mind telling me something else ...?
Another thing I need to know is ...?

C Student A looks at File **12**, B looks at File **44**. Each has a partially illegible price list. They have to find out all the missing information from each other by asking polite, friendly questions.

D 🎧 This is a fairly straightforward listening exercise, reminiscent of a similar exercise in Unit 3. The emphasis is on listening carefully and concentrating hard. Students will certainly need to hear the items at least twice to get all the answers. Pause the recording between each item for them to consider the questions, compare their answers in pairs and get their breath back. You might like to play each individual item two or three times.

➡ Finally, play the recording again, pausing between each item. Ask the class to suggest what QUESTIONS they'd ask each person to CHECK that they have understood correctly or to get them to repeat the important information.

For example, for item 1 the questions might be:

Certainly. Did you say four fifty or four fifteen?

or

I'm sorry, what time did you say the flight was?

Answers

2 Mr Geoffrey
3 two seats on July 3rd
4 a double room from the 29th
5 23983 before 3 *and* 28393 after 3.30

6 a cheap party rate for delegates at a conference
7 if Mr Wilson is in room 405
8 by taxi (cab)

Transcript   [2 minutes 10 seconds]

1 Good morning. Erm...I've got to...er...I've got to fly to Rockford on Monday and I've...um...I've left my ticket in my room. I think the check-in time is 4.50, b...b...but I'm not entirely sure. Could you check this for me, please?

2 Good morning. I've tried calling Mr Geoffrey's room but there's no answer, so I suppose he's out. I've written a note for him, and I wonder if you could give this to him. It's for Mrs...Mr Geoffrey, that's Geoffrey, G-O...G-E-O-F-F-R-E-Y. OK?

3 Can you reserve theatre tickets for me for the performance on July 2nd, and charge them to my credit card? No, wait I gave you the wrong date! Ha! I need two tickets for July 3rd. OK?

4 I've booked a room for the whole of this week in the name of Sanders. The thing is on the 29th, that's the Friday, I'd like to change from a single and have a double instead if that's possible.

5 I'm expecting a call from our agent in Greece this morning. If he calls could you ask him to call me on 23983? I'll be there till about 3. After that he can get me on 28393 from about half past three.

6 Could you possibly tell me if there is a special party rate for delegates at conferences? I know I read this somewhere, but I'm not sure where.

7 I wanted to speak to Mr Wilson, he said he'd be back in his room by this afternoon. Now, it's 405, I think. Is that right?

8 I need to get to the airport by 7.30 this evening. I've probably got plenty of time but as I'll be out in the eastern suburbs I can't take the airport bus. So how long does it take by cab, would you say?

E This discussion gives students an opportunity to exchange *real* experiences and information. It's also a transitional step to the next section.

The discussion will work best if the groups are made up of students who don't usually sit together. Also, if possible, make sure that each group contains at least one student who has some experience of working for a company involved in international trade, if only in his or her work experience or in vacation work.

If you have just one or two people in the class who have practical knowledge of foreign trade, the rest of the class can 'interview' them.

Note that some students may be cagey about revealing trade secrets – a golden opportunity to use some of the 'hedging' phrases introduced.

(If your class is made up of very young students, and none of them have any work experience whatsoever, they can't really do this activity, and it should be omitted.)

➡ If you have time to spare at the end of this lesson, start work on the first step of **6.2**. Even if you don't have time to do this, ask everyone to read through the article and letter before the next lesson.

Extra activity

1 Begin with everyone working alone. They should note down some information about:
- the companies *and* the people they have worked with
- their own home town *or* another town they know quite well
- their business career *or* their education
- their family and their personal relationships

You may need to circulate round the class, helping less imaginative students to think of more information to note down. When everyone has done this, remind them that during the activity they should make an effort to avoid the easiest question forms, and maybe the use of direct Wh- questions should be banned altogether for the duration of this activity.

2 Form pairs. Get everyone to find out as much as they can about the information their partner has noted down. They should try to sound polite and helpful, and use the expressions in step **B** as they ask the questions – and when answering or avoiding answering them.

3 Students ask you for the same information they got from their partners in 2 above. While answering, you could demonstrate some hedging and delaying techniques (repeating the question, complimenting the questioner, only partly answering, etc.) so that other members of the class feel constrained to ask you supplementary probing questions.

6.2 Making enquiries   *Integrated activity*

In this integrated activity students have a series of interconnected tasks to perform. They'll be using a wide range of language skills. As they follow the steps in the activity, students develop their knowledge of the company and product.

➡ To save time in the lesson, ask everyone to read through the company description, the article in **A2** and the letter in **B** for homework beforehand – and also to note down the changes they'd make to the letter.

Vocabulary

battery-driven
vehicles
short-range
disabled people
components
stock
assembled
dealings
investigate
redundancies
plant
announcement
rationalization/rationalisation
uneconomic

order book
shares

quotations
acquaintance
specification
requirements
shipping date
samples
confirmed irrevocable letter of credit
substantial

prototypes
tooling up

range
new line
economy
output
competitive
out-performs
in good shape (financially)
sole supplier
sources of information
trade journals
associations
yellow pages

Procedure – *about 90 minutes*

Begin by making sure everyone has read the company description and is aware of the role they'll be playing. Each step is clearly explained in the Student's Book, so you should refer everyone to the instructions when making sure they all know what to do at each stage in the activity. You may need to guide them through the steps and perhaps make sure they don't spend too long on each step.

Throughout the integrated activity, students will be working in pairs (with one group of three, if you have an odd number in the class).

A 1 Once everyone has read the description of the firm, play the recording of the phone call. Ask everyone to imagine they've just come into Mr North's office and he's on the phone – they are 'Mr North's assistants'. Students may need to hear the recording twice. Perhaps ask them to guess what 'Fritz' is saying to Mr North during the call.

Transcript [1 minute]

Mr North: . . . Oh, yeah, we had a really good time up the mountain. Yeah, nice of you to take us up, nice of you. Er…I know what I wanted to ask you: have you had any dealings with Arcolite? . . . Uhuh, oh, that can't be true. Arcolite Batteries? . . . Yeah, but they've been doing real well . . . Well, if you got this from him, I guess…er…I guess there must be some truth in it . . . Yeah, we…we kind of depend on them, they've been supplying us for…for quite a long time now . . . No, they're our…er…sole suppliers. Hmm. Well, thanks for the tip. I'll…I'll…get my new assistants to investigate . . . Sure. Nice talking to you. Goodbye, Fritz.

---

2 Everyone reads the newspaper article before deciding what to tell Mr North when he returns to the office.

They'll probably decide to tell him that it may be risky continuing to depend on Arcolite – the DG's assurance may sound like a cover-up of some kind. Finding alternative suppliers might be wise.

B The letter is very friendly and informal, as befits a letter from one chum to another.

A letter to a business acquaintance would still be friendly but might not include the contractions (*I'm . . . we'd . . .*) or the friend-to-friend phrases (*. . . to see if you can help us out . . . I'd appreciate it if . . .*). And the letter might end *Give my regards to your wife and family*.

A letter to other unknown companies would need to be more serious and formal, though it would contain similar information.

NOTE If time is particularly short, and if your students don't need to practise their letter-writing skills, the letter-writing task in step **C** can be skipped without affecting the rest of the activity. But everyone should read the letter from Mr North.

C While everyone is drafting their letter, go round offering advice and suggesting corrections or improvements. Check their spelling and punctuation.

Later, the completed drafts are passed to another pair and the drafts are evaluated.

➡ For homework, after students have exchanged comments, they should write their final draft.

D In this role-play, student A has to change role and become Jim Dale. The role information is in File **13**. During the course of the conversation we discover that Dale & Sons can supply Broadway with Hercules batteries in four weeks at 10% less than Arcolite's price. At the end of the role-play, both students step back into their original roles.

Model letter

6.2 Making enquiries

BROADWAY AUTOS

444 Prince Rupert Avenue,
62008 Hentzau, Ruritania
TELEPHONE 77 1473 88999 (8 lines)
FAX +77 1473 889765
http://www.broadway.ra

Name
and address
of supplier

3 November 20—

Dear Sirs,

Lightweight batteries

We are the manufacturers of BROADWAY delivery vehicles and electric vehicles for disabled people. Our company is a subsidiary of Broadway International Inc. of Portland, Oregon. We are seeking an alternative supplier of lightweight batteries to power our vehicles. As far as we are aware you do not have a local distributor of your products in this country.

A full specification of our requirements is given on the attached sheet.
Quantity required: 4,800 units
Delivery: by 15 January 20—

Please quote us your best CIF price, giving a full specification of your product and shipping date.

We would need to have samples of the batteries to test in our laboratories before placing a firm order.

We usually deal with new suppliers on the basis of payment in our currency by confirmed 60-day irrevocable letter of credit.

If our laboratory tests are satisfactory and you can provide us with a good price and service, we will be happy to place more substantial orders on a regular basis.

We look forward to receiving an early reply to this enquiry,

Yours faithfully,

Fred North

Fred A. North
Buying Manager

Enclosed: specification and technical brochure

E The letter from Artemis describes another suitable battery. This step trains inferencing skills.

   Now the pairs should discuss the offers of Rex, Dale & Sons and Artemis and decide what action to take. Should Mr North's old chum be favoured with sole supplier status? If so, what advantages and disadvantages might there be?

6.3 Answering enquiries *Integrated activity*

This integrated activity simulates making and answering enquiries about products. Although probably none of your students are involved in industrial counter-espionage, the language used when answering enquiries is the same whatever the product!

Vocabulary

bug	*refundable*	*irrevocable letter of credit*
eavesdropping	*hands-on*	*trans-shipment*
devices	*rep (sales representative)*	*house bills*
portable	*distributor*	
scrambler	*showroom*	*inventory position (BrE: stock position)*
disguised	*exhibit*	*warehouse*
briefcase	*forthcoming*	*import license*
protector	*terms of delivery*	*specify*
workstation	*CIF (cost, insurance and freight)*	*detector*
monitor	*DDP (delivered, duty paid)*	*rechargeable*
anti-reflection	*FOB (free on board)*	*mains*
money-back warranty	*open account*	*interfere*
		voltage

Procedure *– about 90 minutes*

Step **A** is preparatory to the integrated activity. If possible, it should be prepared at home before the lesson.

A **1** First of all, make sure everyone is clear about the products described in the advertisement. Answer questions about vocabulary, especially: *bug*, *eavesdropping* and *scrambler*. All of these products are similar to products that really are on the market, by the way – they haven't been dreamed up by us!

 2 Students look at the outline for a letter answering an enquiry. As the details will vary enormously according to the product and trade practice, there are no universals here. Allow students with business experience to say what they would add or not include in the model letter. If possible, ask anyone involved in importing or exporting to bring to class an example of their own correspondence.
  The final question about additions or deletions is directed at students with experience of this kind of thing. Their answers will be based on the procedures they're familiar with. As far as we're concerned, the notes are 'complete'. So if your students answer No and No to these questions, that's OK.

 3 This document is the current stock position. Students will need to refer to this as they do the activity because they'll have to check on the availability of the products they are asked about.

⚠ Make sure there is enough time for everyone to do all the subsequent steps – and that there is sufficient time for giving feedback and discussing each step. You may well need to give some help in the early stages.
 Students will be working in pairs during this activity.

B To answer the enquiries, students will need to look at the inventory position in **A3**.
  This step involves answering Enquiries **#1** and **#2** by letter, e-mail or fax. If the class needs help with the first task, the first letter could be composed on the board or OHP with the whole class chipping in with suggestions.

When they have finished, each pair should pass their completed draft letters to another pair and ask them to comment. Have they conveyed the right information in an attractive way?

New International Business English   This document may be photocopied.

Model letters, e-mails or faxes

6.3 Answering enquiries

Enquiry #1

Dear Mr Hanson,

Thank you very much for your enquiry about AntiSpy Products.

As you requested we are sending you our latest catalog of security products. We have debited your American Express card #667589980 for the sum of $50 US. This $50 will be discounted from your first purchase from the catalog.

Do please get in touch with me if you have any queries about any of our products which are not covered in the catalog.

Sincerely,

Enquiry #2

Dear Mr Perez,

Thank you very much for your enquiry about AntiSpy Products.

I am pleased to inform you that we do supply a portable listening device detector: the AntiSpy™ CJ 4000P is a battery-driven device which will detect any eavesdropping devices within 20 feet. It is very compact, looks just like a Walkman and costs only $359. For an order of five or more items we are happy to offer you a rebate of 20%, making the price per item $287.20. All our prices include shipping by air. I can also confirm that this product is available from stock at this time.

If you would like to see a copy of our complete 120pp catalog this is available for $50 — which is refundable when you place an order. However, if you decide to order one of our CJ 4000Ps a free catalog will be included with your order.

Sincerely,

C   This step involves answering Enquiries **#3** and **#4** by letter, e-mail or fax. The recorded call requires students to alter the stock position printout in **A3**.

   The phone call also provides a MODEL for answering the enquiries on the phone in step **D** – though the tone may be rather too effusive for some people's tastes!

Transcript   [1 minute]

Speaker: AntiSpy Products, good afternoon . . . Hello, yes. Oho, Mr Saito, hi, hi, how are you? . . . Good, good . . . OK, the LR 44, yes, we've had quite a rush on those and...er...there's been a delay on supplies, I'm afraid . . . We only have nine in stock . . . Mm . . . Oh sure, eight's...eight's no problem at all. I can get them to you by the end of the week . . . Er...will you be able to pick them up at Narita, as usual?...Fine, fine. OK, that's eight items of product LR forty n...four . . . Thanks very much . . . You're very welcome. Bye now, Mr Saito.

When they have finished, each pair should pass their completed draft letters, e-mails or faxes to another pair and ask them to comment. See the questions for evaluating letters in step **B** in the Student's Book.

New International Business English   This document may be photocopied.

Model letters, e-mails or faxes
6.3 Answering enquiries

Enquiry #3

Dear Ms Graham,

Thank you very much for your enquiry about AntiSpy Products.

We do carry a telephone scrambler: the LR 44 Octopus Telephone Scrambler. The price for this is $299 including shipping by air.

I can confirm that this product is suitable for both tone dial and pulse dial and will adjust automatically to any mains voltage from 100 to 250 volts.

We have only one of these items available at this time but will have full stocks from August 15.

<u>Please let me know by fax today if you would like to purchase one at this time — I have reserved our one remaining LR 44 for you for 24 hours.</u> Please note that you would need an import license for this product.

If you would like to see a copy of our complete 120 page catalog this is available for $50 — which is refundable when you place an order. However, if you decide to order one of our LR 44s a free catalog will be included with your order.

Sincerely,

Enquiry #4

Dear Mr Ovambo,

Thank you very much for your enquiry about AntiSpy Products.

I regret that we are unable to supply our Screen Protector at this time. This is because of the import restrictions into Nigeria which are currently in force.

However, our former distributors may still have stocks and I suggest you contact them. They are: Kano Security, Independence Square, Kano.

Do please contact me if you have any further enquiries about our products.

Sincerely,

D This step involves answering two more enquiries on the PHONE.

The pairs could be rearranged at this point to give students practice in talking to someone different. There are two calls, so that each partner has a chance to speak on behalf of AntiSpy Products.

In the first call, student A (Agencia Léon) looks at File **14** and student B (AntiSpy Products) looks at File **42**. This call concerns certain details mentioned in the fax in the Student's Book. Student B calls student A with answers to the queries.

In the second call, student A (AntiSpy Products this time) looks at File **15** and student B (Agencia Léon) looks at File **45**. Here student B calls AntiSpy Products with an enquiry.

At the end, allow time for students to comment on each other's telephone performance.

E Arrange the class into groups for this follow-up discussion – or have a whole-class discussion, if you prefer.

6.4 Placing and filling orders   *Integrated activity*

This integrated activity covers the stages of dealing with an export order, with each step corresponding to a different date in the process. Additional information for each step is provided in the Files at the appropriate time.

  Each step involves deciding what to do and then writing a fax or letter. The purpose of this activity is to revise the writing of faxes by reading faxes and responding to them in kind – dealing in writing with written material.

Your students will probably find this activity quite demanding, but extremely rewarding. You'll find that it works well even with students who have no first-hand experience of international trade.

Vocabulary

stainless steel	*scheduled service*	*handbook*	*idealized*
anchors	*proforma invoice*	*exclusive*	*scenario*
container	*passage*	*distributor*	
freight forwarders	*hurricane*	*agent*	

Procedure – *about 90 to 120 minutes*

Make sure there is enough time to do justice to the whole activity – if necessary the action can be resumed in a later lesson, thus adding to the reality of time passing!

Students work in pairs – but less experienced students should perhaps do it in groups of three. The completed faxes and letters can be 'delivered' to you, so that you can check them and later provide feedback on the quality of the English. If this would take too long (in a large class), students can show their work to another pair and ask them to comment. Final drafts of some of the faxes or letters could be done as homework.

> ⚠ Begin by making sure everyone understands what they have to do.
> Be prepared to interrupt the activity from time to time to offer advice to the whole class.

A The draft fax contains some errors. First students should spot the errors and correct them. Here are extracts from the fax with the errors underlined:

```
... 179,800 (in words: one seven nine thousand eight hundred) ...
... each PB 5000 for export in a 40-foot open top container ...
... and valid for 90 (ninety) days from the date of your order ...
... Mr Richardson sends his best regards ...
```

Students may find other points they wish to change, to make the fax clearer and more friendly or polite. For example, maybe all the figures should be given both in words and numbers.

B File **15** contains an order from Costa Rica, which has to be checked against the quotation (it's OK). Then a fax has to be sent to Alpha Marine, the anchor suppliers.

New International Business English   This document may be photocopied.

Model fax

6.4B Placing and filling orders

To: Alpha Marine
From: SunWorld Powerboats

We wish to order TWO of your stainless steel anchors:
Product Number 3456: 120 kg stainless steel anchor at a price of £135 including delivery.

Please confirm by return that these are available from stock and let us know when we can expect delivery.

Yours sincerely,

© Cambridge University Press 2000

C File **46** contains a fax from Alpha Marine, answering the fax from step **B**, and a fax from the freight forwarders. Now the students have all the information needed to be able to acknowledge the Costa Rica order. They send a confirmation by fax and also a covering letter to accompany the proforma invoice which will be sent by airmail.

New International Business English   This document may be photocopied.

Model fax

6.4C Placing and filling orders

Dear Mr A__,

Thank you very much for your order for two PB 5000 vessels with stainless steel anchors. I can confirm that the total price for the two vessels will be $187,850 CIF, as stated in our quotation number 0067. This sum is payable by irrevocable Letter of Credit confirmed on a T__ bank and valid for 90 (ninety) days from the date of your order.

I can confirm that the two vessels will be shipped in 40-foot open top containers from our factory on 23 August. Passage has been reserved on m/v Caribbean Star to Puerto Limón where the containers will be unloaded on 10 or 11 September.

A proforma invoice is being sent to you by airmail today.

Again, thank you for your order. If you have any queries please contact me.

Yours sincerely,

© Cambridge University Press 2000

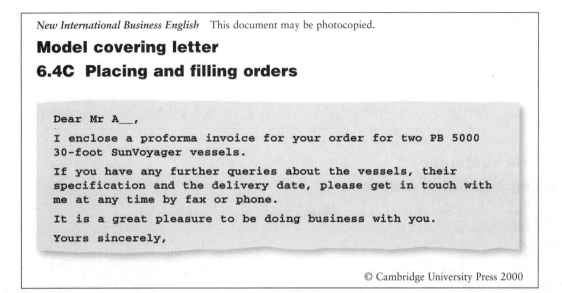

New International Business English   This document may be photocopied.

Model covering letter

6.4C Placing and filling orders

Dear Mr A___,

I enclose a proforma invoice for your order for two PB 5000
30-foot SunVoyager vessels.

If you have any further queries about the vessels, their
specification and the delivery date, please get in touch with
me at any time by fax or phone.

It is a great pleasure to be doing business with you.

Yours sincerely,

© Cambridge University Press 2000

D   Shipwreck? Disaster? File **71** contains reassuring news in a fax from Costa Rica, which must be replied to – probably again with both an immediate fax and a covering letter.

E   File **22** contains instructions from Mr Richardson to send a follow-up letter.

F   As it's nearly Christmas and it seems a good idea to maintain the excellent, friendly relationship with Naves Limón, students send a seasonal fax!

G   File **52** contains a reply to the fax sent in step **F**. Naves Limón want to be the agents in Central America – is this a good idea?

Before replying to it, students will need to discuss what action to take. Even if this only involves writing a note to Mr Richardson to ask him for a ruling, perhaps they should tell him what they think about the idea.

At this stage, before step **H**, this extra activity can be introduced, which deals with the problems of choosing an agent.

Extra activity

Tell the students that Mr Richardson says that it might well be worth appointing an agent or distributor in Central America.

Ask the students to arrange these points (which you could write up on the board or on an OHP transparency) in order of importance:

We're looking for a company ...
... who can act as our selling agent (they are paid commission)
... who can act as our distributor, selling at a marked-up price
... who can hold good quantities of our stock
... who can provide after-sales service on our behalf
... whose staff and management we get on well with
... who have a large, active sales force
... whose financial standing and growth record are good
... who are centrally placed within the territory
... who are a large, efficient firm with a big turnover
... who are a small firm who can provide the personal touch
... who have a modern showroom and good technical facilities
... whose other products don't compete with ours

➡ If they do decide to go ahead and appoint Naves Limón as their agent/distributor, what points have to be made clear in the agreement or contract?

H The follow-up discussion could be done as a whole-class activity, if preferred.

Extra activity

New International Business English   This document may be photocopied.

A letter to a customer
6.4 Placing and filling orders

Look at the letter below. Rewrite it as an individual letter to a customer who has ordered ten items at this price and not just one.
The first lines are done for you below.

Dear Customer,

We regret that your order is being returned to you due to the reason(s) checked below. Unfortunately, prices of equipment are constantly changing and these changes are often not reflected in our advertising due to the months between preparing advertising copy and its publication.

Shipping and handling are also variable, so please include the proper charges if that is the reason your order cannot be processed. It is always best to call us when more than one item is requested, to obtain exact shipping costs for your order.

From time to time items are discontinued and, though this is beyond our control, we will be happy to suggest alternative products which are suitable. Please give us a call on our enquiry line (555) 739–8723.

Thank you for your patience, and we hope to serve you when the problem with your order noted below is corrected.
(   ) Item requested is no longer available.
(   ) Item requested is not yet available.
(   ) Invalid credit card number. Please check your card.
(   ) Insufficient postage and/or handling.
     Please add $ _____ for shipping.
(✓) Price change. The new price is $ *145.75* .
(   ) Other: _____

Additional notes: *The product has been upgraded – the new version (CX 99 GT) performs better than the original version, which has been discontinued.*

Begin your letter like this:

12 April 20––

Dear Mr Stafford,

Re: Your order #767 999 for ten CX 99 processors

I am sorry to inform you that we have been unable to process this order and I am returning it to you for your attention.

© Cambridge University Press 2000

Model letter
A letter to a customer

---

12 April 20—

Dear Mr Stafford,

Re: Your order #767 999 for ten CX 99 processors

I am sorry to inform you that we have been unable to process this order and I am returning it to you for your attention.

There has recently been an upgrade of the CX99, now renamed the CX99GT, which significantly enhances its performance and reliability. Unfortunately, this upgraded product carries with it a price increase to $145.75 per item. The original version is no longer available. Prices of equipment and specifications are constantly changing and these are not always reflected in our advertisements, which are prepared some months before they appear in the press.

We consider the new product to be well worth the extra money.

Please let us know if you wish to proceed with the order at the new price. If you would like more information, do please call me.

I look forward to hearing from you,

Yours sincerely,

Workbook contents for this unit

6.1 Import and export   *Background information*

6.2 Documentation   *Vocabulary*

6.3 Making enquiries   *Speaking & writing*

6.4 Sales and delivery   *Vocabulary*

6.5 What do they want to know?   *Reading*

6.6 'J.I.T.'   *Listening*

6.7 Prepositions – 2

6.8 Looking into the future   *Grammar review*

---

7 Money matters

In business there are many occasions when people have to deal with money and talk about money. Within a company there are business situations in which receipt of money and the payment of money is the central occupation. This unit gives students the opportunity to use and practise monetary English in some of the most relevant settings. These include 'dealing with figures', 'invoicing and billing customers', 'using Letters of Credit', 'reminding a customer of non-payment' and dealing with 'credit assessment' of customers.

Background information

Draw everyone's attention to the Background information in the Workbook on accounts and foreign payments. This is important for students who have had little work experience.

Various methods of payment which may be encountered in international trade, together with the terms employed, are introduced and explained.

Video

Programme 7 on the *New International Business English Video* introduces the theme of this unit.

7.1 Dealing with figures

Vocabulary

figures	*list price*	*operating profits*	*overall group sales*
pound note	*interest*	*stroke*	*operating income*
dollar bill	*tax*	*oblique*	*marginal increase*
accounts	*annual rate of interest*	*a string of prestige brand names*	*borne the brunt*
spreadsheet	*handling charge*	*net profits*	*economic slowdown*
gross profit	*interest charges*	*downturn*	*launch*
			air waybill

Procedure – *about 45 minutes*

A This warm-up activity focuses on the importance of dealing with figures in English in business situations.

B Suggested answers

1 k   2 b   3 h   4 d   5 e   6 c   7 j   8 a   9 g

These are the items remaining:

f seventeen hundred and ninety-five   1795   i   three point six six   3.66
l one and a quarter per cent   1¼%

C 1 [recording] Before you play the recording, remind students to read through the report beforehand. Play the recording at least twice – it lasts 2 minutes. After the students have discussed their answers in pairs, discuss the answers with the class as a whole.

You will need to check through the correct figures with the students before they move on to step **2**.

Answers

The missing figures are underlined.

LVMH advances in slowing market

LVMH, the French luxury goods group which owns a string of prestige brand names ranging from Louis Vuitton luggage to Hennessy cognac, saw net profits rise by <u>7%</u> to FFr 1.29bn ($239 million) from FFr <u>1.21 billion</u> in the first half of the year in spite of the downturn in the luxury products industry.

The group saw overall group sales in the first six months of this year rise by <u>4.5%</u> to FFr <u>9.68 billion</u> from 9.26bn in the same period last year.

Operating income showed a marginal increase to FFr <u>2.35 billion</u> from 2.34bn.

Wines and spirits, which have borne the brunt of the economic slowdown, suffered a fall in sales to FFr 4.44bn from FFr <u>4.76 billion</u>, while operating profits slipped to FFr 1.26bn from 1.51bn.

Luggage and leather products were also affected by Japan's instability, but managed to increase operating profits to FFr <u>890 million</u> from 827m on sales up to FFr 2.33bn from 2.15bn.

Perfumes and cosmetics benefited from the launch of Dune, a new Christian Dior fragrance, and Amarige, under the Givenchy umbrella.

Sales rose to FFr 2.54bn from <u>2.05 billion</u> and operating profits to FFr 330m from <u>321 million</u>.

LVMH earlier this week relaunched Miss Dior, one of its classic scents.

2 This activity gives more practice in using figures and numbers in English. It is not important to get the arithmetic right but these are the answers to the subtraction sums:

Suggested answers

a) to FFr 1.29bn from FFr 1.21bn = FFr 0.08bn (*or* nought/zero point nought/zero eight billion French Francs)

b) to FFr 9.68bn from FFr 9.26bn = FFr 0.42bn (*or* nought/zero point four two billion French Francs)

c) to FFr 4.44bn from FFr 4.76bn = FFr 0.32bn (*or* nought/zero point three two billion French Francs)

d) to FFr 890m from FFr 827m = FFr 63m (*or* sixty-three million French Francs)

e) to FFr 2.54bn from FFr 2.05bn = FFr 0.49bn (*or* nought/zero point four nine billion French Francs)

D Student A looks at File **17** and student B at File **47**. Each student has a copy of an air waybill in which some of the figures are missing. This is an information-gap activity in which they have to help each other complete the correct figures.

7.2 Cash flow

This section covers the general issue of cash flow by means of a reading comprehension activity. The relevant vocabulary and focus of the later sections is presented and, in particular, the way is prepared for the treatment of payments which follows in **7.5**.

Vocabulary

owe	*bank references*	*factoring*
credit control	*pay-by date*	*face value*
assess	*interest charges*	*negotiate*
assign a credit limit	*recovered*	*bottom of the pile*

Procedure – *about 45 minutes*

1 The first question about the article is to get the students thinking about the gist. Arguably, the article is aimed at small business people.

  If you have students with experience of dealing with accounts, you should ensure that they are asked by the others to respond to the questions. Alternatively, you can ask the students to think about their individual situations and how they ensure they have money regularly coming in and the consequences when this is not the case.

Answers

We make sure we are paid by our customers. There are a number of possible courses of action (they are dealt with in **2**).

2 Suggested answers

   a 5   b 3   c 8   d 10   e 1   f 4   g 9   h 6   i 2   j 7

Follow-up discussion

• How are such problems solved in your students' country?
• Make an overhead transparency of the following 'snippet' as a focusing text for this discussion – or write the paragraph on the board – and ask students for their views on it.

> Introducing a legal right to interest on overdue bills is a seductive idea. But it could be counter-productive, according to the British Federation of Small Businesses, which represents nearly 50,000 self-employed people and small firms. Strengthening the legal remedies for pursuing debts through the courts might turn out to be a better bet.

7.3 Changing prices: Dealing with invoicing errors   *Integrated activity*

In this section we have an integrated activity which involves billing and invoicing. It includes a number of complications. The first step involves completing the invoice according to the price list given and the information contained in the customer file. The second step, the role-play, then introduces numerous complications in the form of additional information and snags. In all there are four pieces of information which are listed below in step **B** for clarification purposes.

Before they begin this section, you can ask the students who do not have much experience of dealing with accounts to look at the Background information in the Workbook, where there is a summary giving some idea of the multitude of dealings with money which go on in an accounts department.

Vocabulary

bill	*merchandise*	*delivery note*
invoice	*Irrevocable Letter of Credit*	*acknowledgement*
quotation	*draft sight*	*remittance*
gross (144)	*on presentation*	

Procedure – *about 90 minutes*

A Remind everyone to look first at the various documents before they begin to fill in the invoice. Be prepared to explain any vocabulary items which students may have problems with as they read through the documents.

Remind the students that *gross* is a unit of quantity equivalent to 12 dozen in this context (i.e. 144). Essentially, the nub of the first step is simply completing the invoice.

After everyone has had time to consult the documents and to complete the invoice, items filled in may be compared with another pair or else as a class.

Note: At this stage you do not need to tell the students that the model invoice has been completed according to a different price list than that in force at the time the quotation was made. This will become significant in step **B**.

B Student A looks at File **18** and rings up the customer, student B looks at File **48** and plays the role of Julio Martinez.

The role-play introduces some complications in the form of additional information and snags. In all there are four pieces of new information. They are listed here to make it easier for you to follow the development and to explain to students should they fail to work out the solution themselves:

1. There has been a change of price since the quotation was given to Julio Martinez and the order was taken. The A6D was quoted at $1.60, but Frigorifico Ameglio S.A. have been charged at $1.80.
2. Payment of last month's account has not yet been received by FINNTEC.
3. FINNTEC have only delivered 25 gross switches, instead of the 35 gross ordered. But they have billed 35 gross.
4. The Accounts Department of Frigorifico Ameglio S.A. have paid for the 25 gross at the old price, i.e. $1.60 each.

Frigorifico Ameglio S.A. have received 25 gross (=144) A6D switches and have paid the old price of $1.60 x 25 gross = $5,760.00 minus 10% discount, total $5,184.00. FINNTEC have, however, billed them for 35 gross A6D switches at the new price of $1.80, i.e. x 35 gross = $9,072.00 minus 10% discount, total $8,164.80. (The invoice they sent, according to Julio Martinez later on, had the decimal point in the wrong place: $81,648.00!)

The correct price for 25 gross at the new price of $1.80 x 25 gross = $6,480 minus 10% discount, total $5,832.00. This means that the difference between the amount due ($5,832.00) and the amount paid ($5,184.00) is $648.00.

Model invoice

7.3A Changing prices: Dealing with invoicing errors

Seller (name, address, VAT reg. no.)	INVOICE RECHNUNG FACTURE FACTURA فاتـــورة
FINNTEC P.O. Box 325 SF – 33200 TAMPERE FINLAND	**Invoice number** 04276

© SITPRO 1992

Invoice date (tax point) 1 February 20 __	**Seller's reference** LS 43352/91
Buyer's reference 645	**Other reference**

U N I C

Consignee VAT no.	Buyer (if not consignee) VAT no.
N/A	Frigorifico Ameglio S.A. Colonia 1023 Montevideo URUGUAY

	Country of origin of goods FINLAND	Country of destination URUGUAY

Terms of delivery and payment

FOB HELSINKI

Payment against **sight draft** accompanied by documents through Rabobank

Vessel/flight no. and date MS JUPITER	Port/airport of loading HELSINKI
Port/airport of discharge MONTEVIDEO	Place of delivery MONTEVIDEO

Shipping marks: container number	No. and kind of packages: description of goods	Commodity code	Total gross wt (Kg)	Total cube (m3)
UU LS 433			Total net wt (Kg)	

Item/packages	Gross/net/cube	Description	Quantity	Unit price	Amount
1		Sensor switches Type A6D	35 gross	US $ 1.80 less 10% discount	$ 9072.00 -907.20
				Invoice total	$8164.80

C Students read the letter in File **85** and draft an appropriate answer. After they have drafted their letters, students look at another pair's letter and comment on tone and form.

Model letter or fax

7.3C Changing prices: Dealing with invoicing errors

FINNTEC
P. O. Box 325
SF–33200 Tampere
FINLAND

Frigorifico Ameglio S.A.
Colonia 1023
Montevideo
Uruguay
20 February 20__

Ref: Customer No: 645

Dear Mr Martinez,

Account No. 645/A6D/03764 Invoice No. 04276

We refer to your letter of 14 February 20——, concerning the payment of Invoice No. 04276.

As you state in your letter, the sum of $81,648.00 was incorrectly entered into the invoice.

Since our accounts department has recently received new computing equipment we can only conclude that the error occurred before the program had been fully tested.

The correct amount due for the 25 gross actually delivered is $5,832.00. This means the difference now due is $648.00.

We apologize for any inconvenience we may have caused you and look forward to doing further business with you in the future.

Yours sincerely,

G. Aaltio

G. Aaltio
Accounts Department

D Students look at File **72** for the fax from Julio Martinez. They work in pairs and draft the acknowledgement which Mr Martinez has requested. If you wish you can collect this in and correct it. Alternatively, this step can be done individually for homework.

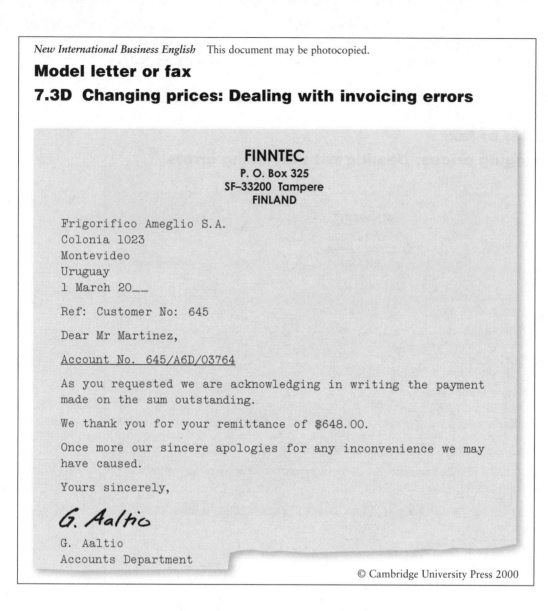

New International Business English   This document may be photocopied.

Model letter or fax

7.3D Changing prices: Dealing with invoicing errors

FINNTEC
P. O. Box 325
SF–33200 Tampere
FINLAND

Frigorifico Ameglio S.A.
Colonia 1023
Montevideo
Uruguay
1 March 20__

Ref: Customer No: 645

Dear Mr Martinez,

<u>Account No. 645/A6D/03764</u>

As you requested we are acknowledging in writing the payment
made on the sum outstanding.

We thank you for your remittance of $648.00.

Once more our sincere apologies for any inconvenience we may
have caused.

Yours sincerely,

G. Aaltio

G. Aaltio
Accounts Department

7.4 Letters of Credit

This section deals with the most commonly used method of payment for imports, the Irrevocable Letter of Credit. See below for further information.

Vocabulary – see below for a partial glossary

shipment	*irrevocable*	*transhipments*	*the bills of exchange are to be drawn*	*stipulated*
revocable	*partshipments*	*port of discharge*	*of a particular tenor*	*inconsistent*

Procedure – *about 90 minutes*

A This is a reading task which involves both scanning skills, gist reading and comprehension of detail.

There may be a number of items of terminology which you can go through with the whole class before letting them loose on the pair work phase. It may help to introduce briefly the method of payment dealt with here. See the following:

Further methods of payment are dealt with in the Workbook, and you may want to suggest that students do particular exercises there.

Alternatively, you can start them on the pair work and deal with the vocabulary questions on an individual basis. This exercise gives the opportunity to revise abbreviations such as FOB, CIF, etc. which were used in Unit 6.

A partial glossary of some of the technical terms:

revocable = a letter of credit, etc. which can be cancelled

bills of exchange = documents containing an instruction, usually to a bank, to pay a stated sum of money at a specified future date or on demand

drawn at sight = a bill of exchange, payable when the beneficiary presents it at the bank, is said to be 'drawn at sight'

of a particular tenor = according to stated terms or in a specified manner or at a specified time

port of discharge = the port at which the cargo is unloaded, etc.

Answers

This is the correct numbered order. It is also given in File **73** in the Student's Book.

1 The name and address of the exporter
2 The expiry date
3 Precise instructions as to the documents against which payment is to be made
4 The terms of contract and shipment (i.e. whether 'EXW', 'FOB', 'CIF', etc.)
5 The type of credit (revocable or irrevocable)
6 The amount of the credit, in sterling or a foreign currency
7 The name and address of the importer
8 The name of the party on whom the bills of exchange are to be drawn, and whether they are to be at sight or of a particular tenor
9 A brief description of the goods covered by the credit
10 Whether the credit is available for one or several partshipments
11 Shipping details, including whether partshipments and/or transhipments are allowed. Also recorded should be the latest date for shipment and the names of the ports of shipment and discharge. (It may be in the best interest of the exporter for shipment to be allowed 'from any UK port' so that a choice is available if, for example, some ports are affected by strikes. The same applies for the port of discharge.)

B 🔊 This is an exercise in listening for detail. First, give the students time to read through the summary before hearing the recording. Then play the recording in which a banker discusses problems encountered in using letter of credit documentation. Play the recording at least twice with sufficient time in between for students to think about what they are reading.

Transcript [2 minutes]

Speaker: . . . So now, on the…on the subject of letters of credit, now you'd be surprised at the kind of mistakes people make when using letter of credit documentation. Er…these errors can often lead to rejection o…on the first presentation. The research department of our bank found that 25% of the documents were rejected. Yup, and the main reasons were things like the fact that the letter of credit had expired, or the documents were presented after the period stated by the letter of credit or, of course, the shipment was late.

Now, if you think about it, it's quite amazing really. But I can't stress enough the need for consistency between the different documents. I mean, for instance, our bank study found out that spelling inconsistencies or mistakes are part of the problem. That is, the description or spelling of goods on invoices was different from that in the letter of credit. Or the weights were different on the export documents. And then the amounts of money value shown on the invoice and the bill of exchange differed too. Even the marks and numbers were found to be different. Then, now, another thing we found was that the amount of money mentioned on the letter of credit was smaller than the value of the order. Or the shipment was short.

Then you might even find that some documents were missing which were called for in the documentary letter of credit. And we even had cases where signatures had not been witnessed as required for certain documents presented. Or else facsimile signatures were used when they're not allowed. And this is by no means the end of the list, which goes on and on – I won't bore you any more.

So, you see that many of the documents presented along with letters of credit were rejected on their first presentation and this meant sometimes long delays in payment with all the complications that can involve. And I don't need to tell you that . . .

Suggested answers

1 expired	5 weights	9 shipment
2 after	6 money value	10 were missing
3 late	7 marks and numbers	11 signatures had not been witnessed
4 spelling	8 smaller than	12 facsimile signatures

C Before the more general discussion, let everyone compare their answers to **B** in pairs.

Follow-up discussion

At least one member of each group should be working or have had work experience for this discussion to work most effectively. Rearrange the groups if necessary to take this factor into account. If there are just a couple of people in the class who have encountered problems with such documents, the rest of the class can 'interview' them. A class entirely without work experience (or commercial training) cannot do this activity. If your students have had work experience, the following set of questions might be discussed, preferably after having read the Background information in the Workbook.

- What are your own experiences with making foreign payments?
- Are there any standard practices which are different from the methods of payment mentioned? What are they? Are they preferable? Why?
- What method(s) do you use in your firm?
- What method(s) do you never use and why?
- What method(s) would you advise small companies in your country to use? Why?
- What are your own personal experiences with discrepancies?
- What other problems have you had or seen?
- In what ways are foreign payments similar to or different from home trade or doing business with established and known customers?

Finally, as this step deals with quite a lot of 'difficult' vocabulary, give the students a chance to go back over the activities they have been engaged in and to raise any queries they may have.

7.5 Chasing payment   *Integrated activity*

This section deals with the problems of cash flow from both sides of the fence: people who have to make apologies for non-payment and people who are insistent on receiving their rightful payments. It consists of an integrated activity. After step **A** the main skill practised in this section is that of writing.

Vocabulary

credit controller	*unsettled debts*	*rectify*
overdraw our account	*enclose*	*liquidation*

Procedure – *about 90 minutes*

A

1 This is an exercise in listening for gist. Students should compare their answers in pairs.

Answers

True: 4   6
False: 1   2   3   5

2 Play the recording a second time and allow the students to complete the notes with the reasons (or excuses) that the customer gives for the late payment.

Suggested answers

1st reason: **money is very tight** (request for an extension of credit)
2nd reason: company **has a considerable overdraft**
Another reason: our **overheads** have to be considered
Major problem: **our own customers having difficulties** – number of outstanding
   accounts ourselves
Our bank **may allow** us to overdraw our account
We have given a major client who owes us a lot of money **an extra two weeks' credit**
Another customer who owes us a lot of money has **just gone bankrupt**

Transcript   [2 minutes 40 seconds]

Becker: Hello. Becker here.
Santinelli: Good morning, Mr Becker! This is Valentina Santinelli. I'm sorry to ring you like this.
Becker: Ah, that's all right.
Santinelli: Did you receive our January shipment?
Becker: Yes, we did.
Santinelli: When did it arrive?
Becker: Er...it arrived on the...25th of January.
Santinelli: Are all the things you ordered included?
Becker: Yes, thank you, yes.
Santinelli: Did you get the invoice as well?

Becker: Yes...yes.
Santinelli: And, er, have you paid the invoice for the last shipment yet?
Becker: I'm afraid we haven't managed . . .
Santinelli: Because I haven't a record of the payment and our department was just getting a bit worried about it.
Becker: Yes, money is very tight at the moment, you see.
Santinelli: Of course.
Becker: I'd like to ask for an extension of credit.
Santinelli: Ah.
Becker: You see, we have a considerable overdraft.

Santinelli: Mmhmm.	money.
Becker: And our overheads have to be thought about.	*Santinelli:* Yes, I think I know what you mean. We have a similar problem.
Santinelli: I see.	*Becker:* They've just gone bankrupt.
Becker: A major problem is that our own customers are going through a difficult period too.	*Santinelli:* Oh dear.

Santinelli: Mmhmm.
Becker: And our overheads have to be thought about.
Santinelli: I see.
Becker: A major problem is that our own customers are going through a difficult period too.
Santinelli: Yes, I know how that is.
Becker: We have a number of outstanding accounts ourselves, so we know exactly how you feel.
Santinelli: Hm, yes.
Becker: We're hoping that our bank will show us some generosity and allow us to overdraw our account.
Santinelli: Well, I hope so as well . . .
Becker: And, er, what's more we have just guaranteed one of our major clients an extra two weeks' credit and…er… they've accepted our offer.
Santinelli: Really?
Becker: And as if that isn't enough, we have a large crisis on our hands with another customer who owes us a lot of money.
Santinelli: Yes, I think I know what you mean. We have a similar problem.
Becker: They've just gone bankrupt.
Santinelli: Oh dear.
Becker: Yes, so what do you suggest we do about the money we owe you?
Santinelli: Well, please try and send the cheque before the end of the month. That's one more week. Our accounts department is considering changing the conditions of payment for future orders otherwise.
Becker: Yes, we…we will do our best.
Santinelli: I hope we can continue to co-operate together.
Becker: Oh, I hope so too.
Santinelli: And we hope to keep you as a regular customer despite any troubles you may be having.
Becker: Thank you very much for being so understanding. Goodbye.

B The model first reminder can be handed out when students have completed their first draft.

New International Business English   This document may be photocopied.

Model first reminder
7.5B Chasing payment

Dear Mr Becker,

According to our records, payment of our invoice, no. 35823, sent to you last March, has not yet been made.

As specified on all our estimates and invoices our terms of business are 30 days net. Your invoice has now been outstanding for 90 days. In the case of unsettled debts of this duration it is our company policy to take legal action.

We would naturally prefer not to have to go so far. Would you please send us a cheque by return? In case you have lost/mislaid the original I am enclosing a copy of our invoice.

We look forward to receiving your payment by return.

Yours sincerely,

Valentina Santinelli

Valentina Santinelli
(Credit Controller)

C Students read the letter. The particular mode of communication chosen at this point will clearly reflect your perceptions of what your students need to practise. If you feel they should concentrate on spoken telephone communication, then at this point the students should make a phone call. Otherwise, they should draft a letter.

If the telephoning option is chosen, student A plays the role of the credit controller and looks at File **19** and makes the phone call. Student B looks at File **27** and plays the customer.

Students who draft a letter, e-mail or fax to the customer, can be given the model second reminder when they have completed their draft.

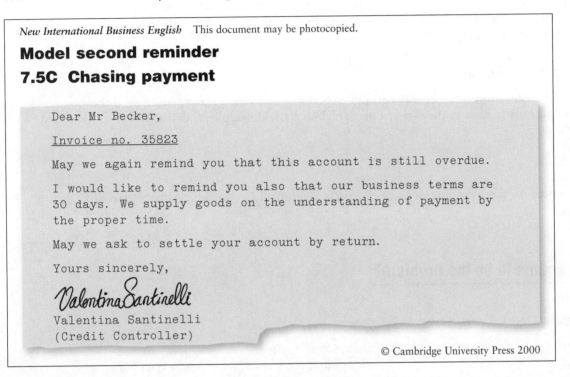

New International Business English   This document may be photocopied.

Model second reminder
7.5C Chasing payment

Dear Mr Becker,

Invoice no. 35823

May we again remind you that this account is still overdue.

I would like to remind you also that our business terms are 30 days. We supply goods on the understanding of payment by the proper time.

May we ask to settle your account by return.

Yours sincerely,

Valentina Santinelli

Valentina Santinelli
(Credit Controller)

© Cambridge University Press 2000

D Students discuss their reactions to the letter in File **74**.

➡ Finally, allow time for the class to raise any questions concerning problems or difficulties they may have had doing the activities, which haven't been dealt with while you've been circulating around the class. These may be of a more general nature and hence of relevance to most of the class.

Workbook contents for this unit

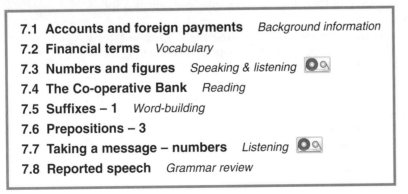

Dealing with problems

This unit looks at some of the problems that may arise between customers and suppliers. There are a series of integrated activities and case studies where students have to resolve a variety of problems connected with delivery and after-sales. The functions of complaining and apologizing are also covered.

Background information

Before they begin this unit, students without experience of foreign trade should read the Background information in the Workbook, which deals with suppliers, delivery and after-sales.

Video

Programme 8 on the *New International Business English Video* introduces the theme of this unit.

8.1 What seems to be the problem?

Vocabulary

damaged	*documentation*	*inadequate*	*service engineer*
replaced	*invoiced*	*withholding payment*	*faulty circuit board*
credited	*consignment*	*design fault*	*personnel*
faulty	*packages*	*feed roller mechanism*	*purchasing*
repaired	*packaging*	*jammed*	

Procedure – *about 45 minutes*

A We start with a warm-up discussion on 'problems'. Encourage everyone to speculate what the people are saying – and maybe even role-play conversations where they discuss what to do.

B Besides giving students practice in careful listening, this exercise introduces a lot of vocabulary connected with problems.

Make sure everyone understands how the exercise works – pause the recording after the examples to check that everyone does. It's probably best to pause the recording between each pair of sentences (at the places marked ★★ in the Transcript) so that students can make their decisions under less pressure. Maybe, for a change, tell everyone that you're only going to play the recording once, so they'll have to listen extra carefully – but if necessary be ready to play it again.

Get everyone to compare answers – which they could do whenever you pause the recording or at the very end – before you reveal the correct answers. There may be some discussion about what was correct.

Answers

3 f   4 e   5 g   6 i   7 l   8 k

C This discussion sets the scene for the next section, as well as for **8.3**.

Transcript   [4 minutes]

1 The agreement was that you'd let us have three sets of documentation, but we only seem to have been sent one. Could you do something about this right away, please?

2 We asked you to send us all the necessary documentation, but we've been invoiced for three sets. As far as I can tell we only need one set, and there should be no charge for this, according to your letter.

★★

3 Hello. Listen I'm terribly sorry, but I thought I'd be able to make it in good time for our meeting this afternoon. The trouble is that there's been a terrible hold-up on the motorway. I've been sitting in a queue for two hours so I don't think I'll be able to get to you till quarter to two. Will you still be available then?

4 Sorry about this but, there's been a problem with air traffic control and my flight has been re-timed to quarter to two. This means that it won't arrive in time for our lunch appointment. I'm terribly sorry about this. Will you still be in the office later in the afternoon, say about quarter to five? I know this is very late, but I won't be able to make it till then.

★★

5 The thing is that there are some scratches on the front panel of 15 of the consignment. Now I realize this won't affect the operation of the units but obviously we can't sell them to our customers unless they're in perfect condition, so what we want you to do is to include an extra 15 in next month's order and we'll send the faulty ones back to you. Is that agreeable? Oh, and if in the meantime we discover any more with the same fault, we'll let you know and perhaps we can have our money back on those.

6 We examined the packages when they were delivered and they seemed to be in good order, but when we opened the packages, we discovered that 15 out of 20 packages were water-stained on the inside. Some of this water seems to have soaked through the inner packaging and the contents are wet inside. They've obviously been left out in the rain in transit and your inner packaging was…was inadequate. Anyway, I've been asked to tell you that we'll be withholding payment on the entire consignment until you arrange to have the faulty items collected and replaced.

★★

7 Look, the blessed thing has broken down again. And yes, we have switched it off so that it can cool down. Yes, I suppose it is a quite warm day, but this machine is supposed to be capable of operating 24 hours a day. No, I want you to get someone out here today to look at it and put things right. Assuming it's not a design fault, there must be something an engineer can do to stop this happening every time the temperature rises over 25 degrees!

8 Yes, it's happened again. The feed roller mechanism has jammed again. I called the service engineer, but he says we've been using the wrong grade of paper and that we should be using 60 gram. Well, we can't replace our entire stock of 85 gram just to make it work in one machine. Now I'd like you to know that we want the complete feed and transport mechanism replaced straight away. The last time the engineer serviced it he informed us that the problem was caused by a faulty circuit board, even though this was obviously not what was wrong with it. Anyway, he replaced it and we were charged for this, and by the way, we'd like a refund for this charge, too.

8.2 We all make mistakes – sometimes!   *Integrated activity*

The purpose of this activity is to make students aware of the difficulties of dealing with a big mistake that has been made – particularly when people may be upset or disgruntled. The work they have done in Units 6 and 7 will have prepared them for this activity. The theme of dealing with mistakes is continued in **8.4** and **8.5**. Students should discuss various solutions to the problem, the best of which will result in nobody feeling as if they have 'lost' in the deal.

Vocabulary

reels	*repeat order*
cable	*misunderstanding*
SpA = Società per Azioni	*mix-up*
s.r.l. = società responsabilità limitata	

Procedure – *about 45 to 90 minutes*

Arrange the class into an even number of pairs or groups of three. Students who have little or no work experience should be placed with a more experienced colleague. If most of the class have no work experience, then groups of three or four may be more effective. The groups will be rearranged at step **C** for the role-play.

A Students should read the notes and form their own impressions of what has happened. (Young Max has confused the two companies and placed a big order with the wrong company – Uniplex instead of UNIFLEX.) Don't spend very long on this step.

B 1 🔲 After step **A**, *without* discussing the problem with the class, play the recorded telephone message: 'There's a message on the answerphone, we'd better listen to it' …

Transcript [40 seconds]

Lucia Donato: This is Lucia Donato at UNIFLEX in La Spezia. We've been expecting your order this month and it hasn't arrived yet. And…um…I must admit that I'm a bit surprised by this but…er…I'm assuming that you want to repeat last month's quantities.

If you want to make any changes, you'd better let me know. We'll be loading tomorrow afternoon, so could you contact me first thing tomorrow, please?

2 Then tell everyone to look at File **75**, where they will discover that Mr Conti of Uniplex in Pisa is delighted to have received this unexpectedly large order. Just to make it quite clear what has gone wrong, they also see their own files about Uniflex and Uniplex.

3 While the groups are deciding what to do by discussing the questions, go round giving advice and hints. There are no 'correct answers' to these questions, though members of the class may have strong feelings about what should be done!

If necessary, point out that as the order has been placed with Uniplex by Zenith, there is now a binding contract between the companies which can only be revoked by mutual agreement.

Get an impression of how far the groups have progressed in making their decision, so that you can tell everyone to begin step **C** at the same time.

C Rearrange the groups so that the conversations take place between students who haven't been together so far. The conversations may be on the phone or face-to-face.

Here are some points to bear in mind:
- Point out that there are two role-plays: one conversation between the Zenith buyer and Piero Conti and another between the Zenith buyer and Lucia Donato.
- Remind everyone to make notes before the call, because the situations are delicate: both Conti and Donato may be disgruntled or indignant.
- The third person, if there is one, should listen to the call as an 'observer' and make notes of what the speakers might have done differently or better.
- Make sure *both* partners have a turn at being the Zenith person, so that no one has to play the role of both Mr Conti and Ms Donato.
- If there's time, the third person can replay one of the roles, with the benefit of his/her experience and observations.

D The original pairs or groups should reassemble to draft their faxes or e-mails. The model versions may give some ideas to less imaginative or less experienced groups – but point out that these documents may not represent the wisest decisions!

More experienced groups may well disapprove of the way the situation has been handled in the model versions.

➡ Collect the completed drafts and 'deliver' them to another group for comments.

Model faxes

8.2D We all make mistakes – sometimes!

```
To: Piero Conti, Uniplex srl, Pisa
From: Zenith International

Dear Mr Conti,

Re: Our order for MCL88 cable

We regret that we shall have to cancel this order. Unfortunately, a
temporary member of our staff placed the order by mistake while I was on
holiday.

However, we are still very interested in your products. We do hope that we
may be able to do business with you in future. Perhaps you could contact
us to discuss this soon?

We are very sorry about the inconvenience this may have caused.

Regards,

Zenith International
```

```
To: Lucia Donato, Uniflex SpA, La Spezia
From: Zenith International

Dear Ms Donato,

MCL88 Cable

We are very sorry about the confusion about our order this month. There
was a slip-up in our buying department during the holidays, which resulted
in a number of errors.

Page 2 of this fax is a copy of the order that should have been sent to
you. As you will see, this is exactly the same as last month's order. I
hope that you will be able to fill the order in spite of our delay.

I apologize again for the inconvenience caused. Thank you for drawing our
attention to the situation and for your patience.

Looking forward to seeing you next time you are in _____.

Best wishes,

Zenith International
```

© Cambridge University Press 2000

E   Reassemble the class and ask each group to report on what they did. Encourage the others to ask questions, particularly on their reasons for making their decision.

F   The report can be started in class and then completed as homework. Suggest that each group makes notes together first. They should decide how the facts may need to be 'slanted' so as not to cast too bad a light on Max. (He is your boss's favourite son, who is perhaps being groomed to take over his father's job?! Neither do you want to take the blame for the mistakes that happened because you didn't brief Max adequately before you went on holiday.)

[There's no model report here – there are so many ways of dealing with the problems that have arisen in this activity that it wouldn't be very helpful.]

➡ Before you collect the homework, encourage students to read each other's reports.

Follow-up discussion

Ask the class what they learned from doing this activity:

- How important is it to apologize for mistakes?
- Why is it desirable to establish a friendly relationship with your suppliers?
- Why should suppliers be treated with politeness and consideration, if they're just out to make a profit by selling you things? (See the Background information in the Workbook.)

8.3 Complaining and apologizing   *Functions*

As the style of complaining is different in other cultures and languages, it's important for students to realize that a cool, direct criticism may be interpreted by British or American people as aggressive or even insulting. In some cultures, a direct complaint may be even more hurtful. As the purpose of complaining is often to get someone to change or improve things (and not simply to apologize humbly), it is counter-productive to antagonize them, even if they have made a stupid mistake.

Vocabulary

slipped your mind	*branch*	*warehouse*	*shortage*
threaten	*refund*	*inefficient*	*pressure of work*
solicitors/attorneys	*colour negatives*	*clumsy*	
A4 paper		*careless*	

Procedure – *about 90 minutes*

Preparation If possible, students should study this section *before* they come to class. This will give them a better chance of remembering the expressions, will save time in class and will lead to a more informed and interesting discussion of the topic in class. If this isn't feasible, begin by getting the class to look at the examples.

Ask them to spot any expressions that mean the same as each other. (*I think you may have forgotten* and *It may have slipped your mind* are the only ones that mean exactly the same.)

In class discuss any points arising from the section.

Do a quick repetition exercise with the expressions, emphasizing the *tone of voice* that should be used: a polite, slightly tentative tone is preferable to a cold, unfriendly or angry one. Ask the class to suggest how the incomplete sentences might continue.

A Play the recording. It may be best to pause between each conversation so that partners can discuss their notes as they go, while they can still remember what happened in each part. Point out that they only have to make brief notes – the first one is partly completed as an example.

If you anticipate having to play the recording several times, perhaps get students to note down only the PROBLEMS on the first listening, and then the ACTION to be taken on the second listening.

Find out if any members of the class have been in similar situations. Was the outcome different for them?

➡ Afterwards play the recording again: with no questions to answer, students can sit back and enjoy listening to the conversations again. They will be receptive to the language used in the conversations and will be in the right mood to assimilate useful expressions – in particular, they will be able to notice how the speakers complain and apologize.

Suggested answers

PROBLEM	ACTION to be taken
1 Wrong size paper — wrongly labelled box	refund: £11.95
2 forgot to send in Eastern region order	telex the order to Compass International
3 wrong quality delivered (not A1 quality)	charge 20% less for the order
	AND ship load of A1 quality tomorrow morning
4 colour negatives not sent	Mr Patel will collect them tomorrow personally

Transcript [4 minutes 40 seconds]

1 *Customer:* Er…good morning. Er…I bought this box of computer paper last week but it's not the right size – it should be A4.
Assistant: Oh, sorry about that. Um…it says A4 on the box.
Customer: Oh, yes I know, but…here…if you look inside you'll see: it's a smaller size.
Assistant: Oh, yeah, so it is. I'm very sorry…er…I'll get you another box.
Customer: Oh, right, thanks.
Assistant: Er…I'm very sorry but we haven't got another box in stock.
Customer: Oh, no!
Assistant: Yeah, I am sorry about that. Er…if you like, I'll just call our other branch to see if they have any.
Customer: Oh, no…er…don't bother. Um…I'd prefer a refund.
Assistant: Of course. That's 11.95…Here you are. Sorry about that.
Customer: Oh, that's all right, thanks anyway. Bye.
Assistant: Bye.

2 *Mr South:* I'm…er…I'm sorry to bother you, Mrs West.
Mrs West: Yes, Mr South?
Mr South: Er…it may have slipped your mind, but you told me last week that…that *you*'d send in the orders to Compass International.
Mrs West: Yes, that's right, yes, I did send in the order. Er…on Friday afternoon.
Mr South: Well, the…the thing is, did…did you realize there were two separate orders: o…one for northern region and another for eastern region?
Mrs West: Oh dear! Jeez, I'm sorry. I didn't realize the eastern region had…had to be done too.
Mr South: Oh, it really doesn't matter, there's still just time.
Mrs West: Well, I'll phone Compass and explain, shall I?
Mr South: Er…no, no, I think it'd be best to send the order by telex, don't…don't you?
Mrs West: Yeah, yeah, all right. I'll do that right away. Sorry again!
Mr South: Oh…oh, that's all right.

3 *Mr Joiner:* Good morning. Carpenter and Sons, can I help you?
Miss Zimmermann: Hello, this is Heidi Zimmermann of Schreiner International.

Mr Joiner: Hello, Miss Zimmermann. This is Ted Joiner. What can I do for you?
Miss Zimmermann: Well, I think there may have been some…a misunderstanding about our last order.
Mr Joiner: Oh dear, what seems to be the problem?
Miss Zimmermann: We've just started unloading the truck and the quality of the goods doesn't appear to be Class A1, which is what we ordered.
Mr Joiner: Oh dear, I'm very sorry. Let me just check this on the computer . . . Er…oh dear, yes, I'm afraid there has been a slip-up in our shipping department. I'm very sorry, it's certainly our fault. Wh…what would you like us to do about it?
Miss Zimmermann: Well, we can keep the goods and…and use them for another order of ours, *if* you will charge us 20% less for the load and ship us a load of Class A1 right away.
Mr Joiner: That sounds fair enough. Let me just check the stock position . . . Yes, we can ship tomorrow morning, if that's all right?
Miss Zimmermann: Oh yes, that will be fine.
Mr Joiner: Oh, good. Er…thank you very much, Miss Zimmermann. I'm very sorry that this happened.
Miss Zimmermann: That's quite all right. Goodbye.

4 *Telephonist:* Good afternoon. Windsor Products.
Mr Wong: May I speak with Tina Castle in marketing, please?
Telephonist: Tina Castle, certainly. One moment, please.
Miss Castle: Tina Castle.
Mr Wong: Hello, this is Henry Wong of ArrowPrint.
Miss Castle: Hi, Mr Wong. What can I do for you?
Mr Wong: It's about the order for your new packaging. I think you may have forgotten to send us the colour negatives.
Miss Castle: I sent the complete set of negatives by airmail on the 14th, I remember packing them up myself. They should have arrived by now.
Mr Wong: Yes, well we did get a package from you on the 18th, but the problem is that the *colour* negatives were missing.
Miss Castle: Are you sure?
Mr Wong: Yes, we only got the black and white ones.
Miss Castle: . . . Oh dear, I've just been through my out-tray and I've found them here. I'm very sorry, it's my fault. I'll send them by courier at once.

Mr Wong: No, no, no, that's not necessary. My assistant, Mr Patel is coming to your office tomorrow, so you can give them to him and he can bring them back.

Miss Castle: Right. I'll make sure he gets them. I'm sorry this happened.

Mr Wong: It's perfectly all right, Miss Castle. Goodbye.

B After the pairs have completed the sentences, it might be wise to check their work. Then get them to work out how they would reply to each letter.

Suggested completions and replies – all of which are open to discussion

we are concerned that the order we placed by letter on 8 June may have got lost in the post. Could you please

. . . confirm that you have received the order and that you have the goods in stock?

REPLY: . . . Please accept our apologies for not having confirmed your order. The reason is that we have been understaffed this month as there has been a flu epidemic here. We can confirm that the order has been received and will be shipped to you tomorrow, in accordance with your instructions.

the order has not yet arrived at our warehouse, even though we received advice of shipping from you ten days ago. Would you

. . . please look into this matter? We can only assume that this shipping note was sent in error and that the goods have not been dispatched.

REPLY: . . . We are very sorry for this mistake. Our dispatch manager discovered at the last moment that your order was incomplete and he delayed the shipment until the missing parts had been found. Unfortunately, the shipping advice had already been posted and we failed to inform you of the delay.
I am pleased to inform you that the missing parts have now been packed and left our works yesterday . . .

according to your scale of charges the price of a single room with bath is $55 including tax. However, on checking my account later I discovered that I was charged $69.50 per night. Will you please

. . . refund the difference, which I calculate to be $72.50 for five nights.

REPLY: . . . We wish to apologize for our mistake in overcharging you for your room. I have looked into the matter and discover that you were charged at the double room rate by mistake. I have refunded the sum of $72.50 to your MasterCard account and enclose the refund slip.
In view of our error and in the hope that you will stay with us again, may I offer you a special discount of 15% for your next stay at our hotel?

our order was for 80 boxes containing 144 items each. Each box we have opened so far contains only 100 items. Will you please

. . . arrange for the missing items to be shipped to us at once?

REPLY: . . . Please accept our apologies for this mistake. Since your order was placed, we have begun using new boxes which contain 100 items. Your order was short by 3,520 items. A further 36 boxes are on their way to you now.

C In this activity the same situations are dealt with on the phone. Students, working in pairs, should sit back-to-back as usual so that they only use their voices to communicate. Tell them that each call must be continued until both parties are satisfied.

D Here are some more excuses that may be used to cover up for a mistake:
a typing error   a keyboard error   a misunderstanding   a bad telephone line
pressure of work   temporary staff   bad weather delaying delivery
your suppliers letting you down   sabotage by a disgruntled employee
a clumsy employee dropping something fragile

Unit 8   Dealing with problems

E For this freer practice, student A should look at File **20** and student B at File **51**. They should imagine that they're colleagues, working in the same office. In each file there are some things they should apologize for doing (or for forgetting to do) and some things they want to criticize their colleague for doing (or for forgetting to do).

Point out that the expressions in the speech balloon may help them to *start* a complaint or apology but that they must use their own ideas to continue.

These are just short exchanges. Between each one, students could pretend to go away and come back again. Or they could have an extended conversation, exchanging a whole series of complaints and apologies in a friendly way.

Follow-up discussion

- How is the British/US behaviour in making complaints and apologies different from that in your students' country – and in other countries they know?
- Why is complaining sometimes rather risky? (See the first paragraph of this section above.)

Finally, perhaps ...

Tell the class the story about the man who was travelling years ago in a sleeping car on an American railway train. He found a bed bug in his bunk. He was furious and complained to the company.

He got back a long, beautifully typed letter saying that this was the first time anything like this had ever happened, they would be doing a thorough check of every sleeping car in their trains, they were truly sorry, they were really grateful to the man for bringing this to their attention, and so on for a whole page. As he was reading the letter, a little slip of paper fell out of the envelope and onto the floor.

He picked it up and on it he read the words: *Send this bum the bug letter.*

8.4 Friday afternoon: Delivery problems

These case studies will give students a chance to exchange ideas and experiences in dealing with problems. Students with little or no experience should work in groups of three or four, rather than pairs.

➡ If your students work on Saturdays, you may have to point out that the staff at Ocean View and Arctic Refrigeration *don't* work on Saturdays!

Vocabulary

distributing wholesaler
alloy
screw adaptors (whatever they may be – just some sort of component, we assume)
anticipated
inconvenience
refrigeration

Procedure *– about 45 minutes*

A If you anticipate that your students will have difficulty with the listening and reading, perhaps check that everyone has understood exactly what the problem is before they discuss how to solve it. You could ask: 'So what exactly has gone wrong in this situation?'

(The company has received the wrong components and if they aren't replaced fast, the production line will have to stop.)

1   🔲🔍 Play the recording of a telephone message from Mr Robinson, the production manager. This contains a lot of information and will need to be heard at least twice.

Transcript   [1 minute 10 seconds]

Ted Robinson: This is Ted Robinson. Um…it's about these new alloy components. Now, when the components were unpacked and inspected, we found that although most of the parts are OK, the screw adaptors don't meet our specifications. Now, they…the ones that you sent us are GJ 501s and we need JG 507s. I'll say that again – JG 507s. Now I've checked your order and that was correct and so was the proforma the suppliers sent, so it seems to be the fault of the supplier's export packing department.

Now, the problem is: if the right parts don't arrive by next Wednesday, part of the production line will have to stop. And in all 5,000 screw adaptors have to be replaced, of which 500 are needed for next week's production. So, can you do something about this and let me know what you propose to do? OK? Goodbye.

Suggested notes

Screw adaptors don't meet our specifications
Need JG 507s, not GJ 501s
If right parts don't arrive by next Wednesday, part of production line will have to stop
5,000 screw adaptors to be replaced – 500 needed for next week's production

2 & 3   The fax from 1999 can be used as a MODEL for the 'complaining fax' in this step, and the letter can be used as a MODEL for the 'apologetic letter' in **B**.

(In the fax delivery was promised for 30 May; in the letter the reason given was a late delivery by Ocean View's suppliers.)

4 & 5   You may feel it advisable to direct your students towards one of the options (letter, fax, e-mail or phone call) depending which one they need more practice in.

If there's time (and if this is what they've decided to do), they could role-play the phone calls, with one student acting for Pacific International, one for Ocean View, and the other(s) eavesdropping as 'Observers'.

At the end, perhaps ask one or two groups to report their solutions to the whole class and ask them to justify the action they took.

Suggested solution

Phone Ocean View and ask for all or part of the order to be air-freighted or shipped at once. Or maybe find another supplier locally who can deliver more quickly?

➡ Be prepared for members of the class to argue with this. It may be best to preface it with '*Do you think it might be a good idea if . . .?*' if you're asked what you would do – after all you're an English language expert, not an experienced business person.

B   Again, it may be necessary to check that everyone has understood what the problem is before they start deciding what to do.

(The goods are damaged, but it's not clear who is responsible for this – so the students must decide whether or not to accept responsibility and agree to Arctic Refrigeration's demand for credit.)

To write an apologetic letter, students may have to refer back to Mr Duvall's letter in step **A3**, which they can use as a model.

You may feel it advisable to direct your students towards one of the options (letter, fax, e-mail or phone call) depending which one they need more practice in.

If there's time (and if this is what they've decided to do), they could role-play the phone calls, with one student acting for Atlantic International, one for Arctic Refrigeration, and the other(s) eavesdropping as 'Observers'.

Suggested solution

Either placate Arctic Refrigeration by accepting responsibility (if you think $535/585 isn't a sum worth bothering about), but find out if the correct amount to credit is $535 or $585, preferably by checking with your delivery manager.

Or (if you think it's a significant sum and that Arctic really are trying it on this time and are likely to do so again) fax a letter to Arctic disclaiming responsibility and implying that they can whistle for their money.

C At the end, ask the class what they learned from the activities. Is it best to tell the whole truth, to tell part of the truth, to lie or to tell a white lie?

Finally, give students a chance to talk about their bad experiences. Even students without work experience may have been on the receiving end of a delivery problem, by mail order perhaps.

Two extra activities

These are probably of most interest to students with some business experience, which is why there are no suggested solutions to them here.

New International Business English   This document may be photocopied.

8.4 Friday afternoon: Delivery problems

1 'Not on Friday'

You are a distributing wholesaler. You have been waiting for an order to arrive and you receive this letter about it:

> Dear Ms S____,
>
> <u>Your order ref. 57/BEH</u>
>
> I am writing to apologize for the late delivery of this order.
>
> We normally pride ourselves on keeping to our delivery dates, but in this case the order was more complex and time-consuming than we had anticipated.
>
> Our revised delivery date is now Friday, November 22. Our truck will arrive at your warehouse after lunch and unloading will take approximately one hour.
>
> We hope that this revised date and time is suitable and we greatly regret any inconvenience that may have been caused.
>
> Yours sincerely,
>
> *Joe Lorenzini*
>
> J. Lorenzini
> Export Sales Director, Medco Industries

The problem is that Friday afternoon is an extremely busy time in the warehouse. However, the sooner you get the goods from Medco, the sooner you can supply your own customers.

❶ *Work in pairs* Decide together what you are going to do this time. How will you solve this problem? What will you say or write to Medco?

❷ Draft a letter, e-mail or fax to Medco – or make notes for the phone call you will make.

8.4 Friday afternoon: Delivery problems
2 'Two to three weeks delay'

You are a supplier. You are going to have to delay your delivery to Florida Imports of Miami by two to three weeks. This is due to staff shortages in your warehouse and to a late change that the customer made to the order, which required a lot of extra work. The order will arrive in Miami some time during the second half of February.

1 *Work in pairs* Decide together what you are going to do this time. Will you inform Florida Imports of the delay? What will you say or write?

2 Draft a letter, e-mail or fax – or write notes for the phone call you will make.

3 You are about to get in touch with Florida Imports when this fax arrives:

> Dear Mr B___,
>
> Our order ref. 4498
>
> I am writing to you regarding your delay in shipping this order.
>
> As you will appreciate, we have commitments to our own customers who are depending on these goods. We require this order to arrive in our warehouse by February 14 at the latest. If you are unable to keep to this date we will deduct 5% from your invoice for each week of delay that we experience.
>
> If we do not receive confirmation of this revised shipping date by return, we will be obliged to cancel this order and will seek another supplier.
>
> Please acknowledge that you have received and understood this letter.
>
> Sincerely,
>
> *Felipe Castro*
>
> Felipe Castro
> Florida Imports

➡ Write the letter, e-mail or fax you would send to Mr Castro (if you didn't want to phone him).

8.5 Only the best is good enough …

This section provides a foretaste of Unit 10 Marketing.

Vocabulary

board	cost-effective	format	graphics	user interfaces
defects	eliminate	spreadsheets	one-stop shopping	cross-platform software products
mass-produce	line managers	databases	no fuss	productivity
rejects	established	utilities		customer loyalty
random		dedicated		

Procedure – *about 45 minutes*

A This is a warm-up for the listening exercise in step **B**.

B 🔲🔍 Allow everyone time to read the task through before they hear the recording. They might even like to guess some of the mistakes and underline them lightly in pencil.

Suggested answers – some variations are possible

2 With 'Zero Defects' the company aims to produce goods that are <u>mostly</u> perfect.   absolutely/all

3 In the past, customers expected some faults – they could be corrected by <u>apologizing</u> to the supplier, who would replace the faulty goods.   complaining

4 Putting mistakes right is labour-intensive and <u>inexpensive</u> and it's more cost-effective to produce a perfect product with no defects.   costly

5 If your competitors can produce perfect products, your customers will prefer <u>yours</u>.   theirs

6 A service has to be so good that there is no dissatisfaction and there are <u>few</u> complaints from your clients.   no

7 A manufacturer can change suppliers to get materials of the highest quality, even if this means paying <u>less</u>.   more

8 The extra cost is justified if the quality of your own production <u>deteriorates</u>.   improves

9 To introduce Quality you must sell the idea to everyone in the company: <u>most</u> of the staff have to believe in quality.   all

10 It's <u>easier</u> to sell new ideas to established staff.   harder

---

Transcript   [4 minutes 40 seconds]

Interviewer: Sarah Lockhart is the Quality Director of AP Management Consultants. Sarah, how is Quality with a capital Q different from what's always been known as 'quality control'?

Ms Lockhart: The idea of Quality is a concept that is coming to be the driving force of many parts of industry today. The interesting thing is that it can be applied to both the service sector and the manufacturing sector. We can talk about Quality of manufacturing and quality of service. Quality is something that affects all the functions of the company and all the staff from board level down to line managers and employees.

Interviewer: So how would this be applied to manufacturing?

Ms Lockhart: Well, the key idea here is 'Zero Defects' – the company should be aiming to produce goods that are perfect. So that customers are entirely satisfied and they don't discover any faults at all after delivery has taken place.

Interviewer: Yes, but surely nobody's perfect. We all make mistakes sometimes.

Ms Lockhart: Well, yes, people make mistakes, but we believe that everybody wants to be perfect and they want their product to be perfect and to have no eff…defects.

Interviewer: Ah, I see.

Ms Lockhart: In the past it was considered impossible to mass-produce goods to a very high standard. There would always be rejects and some faulty goods would inevitably get through to the customer, because carrying out a quality control of every manufactured item would be too expensive and therefore unprofitable. Quality control usually consisted of random checks – operating rather like Customs officers in the green channel at an airport. Customers came to expect there to be some faults in the goods – and it was just a fact of life in manufacturing. Anything that was wrong could always be put right later by complaining to the supplier and getting him to repair or replace the faulty goods.

Well, the Quality revolution, if I can call it that, turns these views on their head. There are several reasons for this. First, putting mistakes right – fixing a faulty machine or collecting it and replacing it – are labour-intensive and costly and it's more cost-effective to eliminate the need for this by producing a perfect product with zero defects in the first place. Second, if your competitors are able to produce goods with zero defects, then clearly customers will prefer those. So in order to survive, you have to keep ahead of your competitors. Obviously this applies to services too – your service has to be so good that there is no dissatisfaction and hence no complaints from clients. Complaints usually mean that there are defects in your product or in your service – and even your accounts department is providing a service to you and your suppliers and customers.

Interviewer: The big problem about all this is the other links in the chain. I mean, you're dependent on the quality of materials supplied to you as a manufacturer that you will then transform in your factory. How does this fit in?

Ms Lockhart: Yes, I agree, this is one of the problems. You normally don't have a direct control over your supplier's processes, but you can change suppliers in order to obtain the materials of the highest quality. This will normally mean paying more, but the extra cost can be easily justified if your own production quality improves. If, however, you're obtaining poor quality materials from a single source, you may have to start looking for alternative suppliers, or impose your own quality control on all incoming supplies before you accept them.

Interviewer: All right, suppose a company wants to introduce Quality as part of its business philosophy, how easy is it to set about doing this?

Ms Lockhart: First of all you have to sell the concept to everyone in the company: at board level, to senior management, to line managers and to the employees. Everyone has to believe in Quality for it to succeed – it won't work if you have a group of people somewhere in the company who are working against you – that may mean production staff who are careless or office staff who don't provide a good service to customers and to other members of their own company. New staff can be trained relatively easily, but established staff tend to be much harder to persuade about new ideas. The major arguments we use in our seminars are to do with taking a pride in your work – well, you know, everyone likes to feel they're doing a good job, and we say 'If your competitors are successfully doing this, can you afford not to?' If we can't sell our service or product, we'll lose business and people will lose jobs.

Interviewer: Sarah, thanks very much.

Ms Lockhart: Thank you.

C **1** Students who have strong feelings about whether marketing should or should not pervade every corner of business life will find plenty to say in this discussion.

It may be necessary to reassure everyone that they don't have to understand computer jargon in the documents to discuss the questions.

2 This may be best done as homework, but prepared in class in pairs.

Get the students to show their completed work to each other.

New International Business English   This document may be photocopied.

Extra discussion activity

Companies, customers and the community

Many large companies publish 'Corporate Objectives', explaining their principles to the public.

How do you react to these quotes?

1 From Hewlett-Packard corporate objectives:
'Objective #2: To provide products and services of the greatest possible value to our customers, thereby gaining and holding their respect and loyalty.'

2 From ICI corporate objectives:
'ICI's principal objective is to improve the effectiveness of wealth creation within the group and hence its financial performance, to the benefit of shareholders, employees, customers and the communities in which it operates.'

3 From the Chairman's Statement, Marks and Spencer:
'We recognize our social responsibilities and help the communities in which our customers and staff live. We shall make progress so long as we pay attention to people and continue to be sensitive to the needs of our customers.'

4 Well-known saying (first coined as a slogan by the founder of Selfridges department store in London):
'The customer is always right.'

5 Professor Theodore Levitt, Harvard Business School:
'The customer is king.'

Discuss these questions:

• Do companies have a social responsibility to the community in which they operate?

• Do companies have responsibility for the health and welfare of their workers and their families?

• Should Ethics be taught as part of a management course (as it is in some business schools in the USA)? Or is 'dog eat dog' or 'survival of the fittest' the name of the game in business life?

8.6 Monday morning: After-sales problems

These case studies will give students a chance to exchange ideas and experiences in dealing with problems, both as customers and suppliers.

In business, customers are sometimes dissatisfied with a product or service after it has been delivered and paid for – maybe because they have unreasonable expectations, maybe because the service really is bad. Often, it's six of one and half a dozen of the other, though!

Vocabulary

tooling and cutting machine   *a.s.a.p. = as soon as possible*   *maintenance*
vibration   *installed*

Procedure – *about 45 minutes*

There are no suggested solutions to these problems – it's up to the groups to justify their own solutions to the others.

In each problem, if students have decided to make notes for a phone call, allow time for them to role-play the call – possibly with another group listening in as 'Observers'.

A   If you anticipate that your students will have difficulty with the reading, perhaps check that everyone has understood exactly what the problem is before they discuss how to solve it. You could ask, for example: 'So what exactly has gone wrong in this situation?'

(Fox Industries' after-sales service has deteriorated and you have already complained about this – but received no reply. Now a new machine has gone wrong, possibly as a result of incompetent servicing by Fox's engineer.)

In step **5**, students look at File **76**, where they will see an unexpectedly apologetic, placatory fax from Mr Reynard, which they must read, discuss and respond to.

Before they begin step **B**, perhaps ask one or two groups to report their solutions to the whole class and ask them to justify any action they took.

B   If time is short, half the groups could deal with a different problem and then report their solutions to the others at the end. Again, before they start work, you could ask, for example: 'So what exactly has gone wrong in these situations?'

(In the first case, the customer has been supplied with goods that don't work properly, in spite of being assured that they would work. In the second case, the customer has been sent a handbook which has missing pages.)

If necessary, allow time for any phone calls to be role-played. In groups of three, the third member can listen in as 'Observer'.

C   This follow-up discussion rounds off the unit. Encourage students without business experience to draw on their own experiences of buying goods from shops or by mail order – and their experience as consumers of services in banks, travel agents, restaurants, on public transport and so on.

Workbook contents for this unit

Three extra activities

New International Business English   This document may be photocopied.

1   A serious bug

'Six weeks ago, you ordered a computer software package from ACME Inc. by mail order. It arrived promptly but now you have discovered that there is a serious bug in the program. You have written to ACME and got no reply. You have tried telephoning ACME, but they don't answer the phone.'

1   What action are you going to take?
2   Draft a suitable letter, e-mail or fax – or notes for the phone call you will make.
3   Role-play the phone call (if you decided to make one).
4   Decide what you would do if you were marketing manager of ACME Inc. and you found out what had happened.
5   Draft a suitable letter, e-mail or fax – or notes for a phone call.

2   Under guarantee

'Last week the service person repaired a faulty connection in your Volpone 337 binding machine and now it's broken down again. The service department of Volpone SpA has been faxed, but they say that your guarantee has run out and you'll not get any further service without paying for a full service contract. You check your records and discover that the guarantee ran out just one day after the service call.'

1   Decide what action you're going to take.
2   Draft a suitable letter, e-mail or fax – or notes for a phone call.

3 I am writing to you to explain . . .

1 Imagine that you work for a company that has been receiving a lot of complaints from customers recently . . .

Read these extracts from correspondence your company has received this month:

Your service has been very poor.

We have twice received incomplete consignments.

I have sent you two letters and a fax, but received no reply.

I have tried calling you several times but not been able to get through.

Your products are excellent but your service is terrible.

We used to be able to rely on you to supply us promptly.

2 Your boss, who is away on a trip this week, has left you these notes to deal with while he is away:

Please draft a letter that we can send to all our customers with the new catalogue.

POINTS TO BE MADE IN THE LETTER

1 Apologize for poor service (mention typical customer complaints):
   a) ten phone lines, always manned, but once overloaded we can do nothing
   b) correspondence staff working all hours to catch up

2 Reason: Rapid expansion from small family firm to sizeable business. Working procedures haven't kept pace with expansion.

3 Last year old computer replaced with new hardware + software. We were told this would solve our problems but speed of processing orders slowed down. Last month new version of software supplied: system speeded up, catching up with backlog of orders. By end of month we'll be up to date.

4 Promise: orders will be delivered promptly + correctly; enquiries answered courteously + efficiently.

5 Actions speak louder than words:
   a) more staff now
   b) new warehouse acquired
   c) heavy investment in computer systems

6 End on positive note:
   We enclose latest catalogue, new product range more attractive + better value than before. Working hard to continue to improve service. Hope to count on your support in future.

3 Draft a letter to your customers, beginning like this:

Dear Customer,

I am writing to you to explain the reasons for the very poor service we have given over the past few months.

9 Visitors and travellers

This unit covers many of the situations in which students may find themselves if they are dealing with visitors from abroad (or if they are themselves travelling abroad on business): making travel arrangements, arranging accommodation and dealing with hotels, looking after visitors and having a meal with an English-speaking person. We also deal with the situation of organizing a small conference or symposium and the function of narrating.

We don't assume that members of your class are globe-trotting executives. But if anyone in the class has travelled on business, then they should have some interesting experiences to contribute.

Video

Programme 9 on the *New International Business English Video* introduces the theme of this unit.

9.1 Did you have a good journey?

Please note that in this section 'looking after a visitor' also involves 'being a visitor', and both roles are considered. Students are encouraged to imagine what it might be like to receive visitors, even though they may not have actually done so. They should be urged to draw on their own experiences of travelling abroad, however limited, or travelling in their own country.

Vocabulary

trolley	*reconfirm*	*track*	*connection*
engine failure	*business class*	*gate*	*physical contact*
traffic jam	*economy class*	*itinerary*	*belongings*
exhausting	*platform*	*chain smoker*	*traveller's cheques*

Procedure – *about 90 minutes*

A This warm-up discussion will help students to empathize with the situation of being a newcomer to a strange country.

B The recorded conversation illustrates some of the phrases in the speech balloons being used in a typical situation. Play the recording and ask for questions.

Allow time for everyone to study the phrases silently for a few moments, highlight the most useful exponents, and then ask any questions they wish to.

Transcript [1 minute]

Sandra: Hello, are...are you Mr Brown?
Mr Brown: Yeah.
Sandra: Oh, I'm Sandra Ellis.
Mr Brown: Hi, Sandra.
Sandra: I...er...welcome to Manchester.
Mr Brown: Well, I'm sorry I'm so late. You see, there was fog at Amsterdam and we were delayed there. I hope you haven't been waiting too long.
Sandra: No, no, it's OK. I was able to catch up on some of my notes.
Mr Brown: Oh, good.
Sandra: Well, it's a great pleasure to meet you, Mr Brown.
Mr Brown: Yeah, I've been looking forward to meeting you too, Sandra.
Sandra: How was your flight?

Mr Brown: Well, not too bad, thanks.
Sandra: Oh, good, well I think the best thing is we'll go to your hotel first if that's OK. My car's just outside.
Mr Brown: Terrific.
Sandra: Can I take one of your bags?
Mr Brown: Oh thanks, yeah, here you are Sandra.
Sandra: Right now, is there anything you'd like to do before we set off?
Mr Brown: Well, I'd just like to make a quick phone call, if...er...that's all right.
Sandra: Yes, sure. Look, there are some phone booths over there. Um...would you like to have a drink or something to eat before we go into town or . . .?
Mr Brown: Well, er...maybe just a coffee if we've got time.

C For this role-play students should be in pairs – if possible there should be an even number of pairs (pairs of pairs).

1 Allow everyone enough time to decide who they are and why they are where they are.
2 For the role-play, where they are enacting an 'arrival at the airport', everyone should STAND UP and move around realistically.
3 Rearrange the pairs so that students who 'arrived' previously can now be the ones who are 'waiting'. This is quite straightforward if there are pairs of pairs.

D Students work in pairs as they decide who they'd speak to and what they might say. The speech balloon gives some clues and useful expressions.

After a while, get the pairs to compare ideas and discuss this as a class.

Suggested answers – many variations are possible

1 To airport information clerk: *Can you tell me what time flight BZ 431 is going to depart? I've heard there's going to be a delay.*
2 To ticket office clerk: *A second class return to Manchester, please, I'll be coming back on Friday morning.*
3 To travel agent or clerk in airline office: *I'd like to reconfirm my reservation on flight TR 998 on Monday evening. The number on the ticket is . . .*
4 To travel agent: *I'd like to fly to Bangkok on the 18th of next month. Can you tell me what the cheapest fare is, and when the best flights are?*
5 To taxi driver: *I've got to get to the airport as quickly as possible. How long do you think it'll take?*
6 To person at check-in desk: *I know I'm quite early, but can I check in for the . . . flight now?*
7 To anyone in a uniform: *What platform does the train to . . . leave from?*
8 To clerk in information office: *I've heard that the 17.55 has been cancelled. When is the next train from here to . . .?*

E Now rearrange the class as groups. If time is limited, different groups can be assigned different problems to discuss.

Allow a little time for each group to report on its discussion to the rest of the class.

Suggested answers – many variations are possible

2 To member of airline ground staff: *I was supposed to be on flight . . . to . . . but I've missed it. The problem is that some people are meeting me there. Is there any way I can get a message to them?*

3 To flight attendant: *Excuse me. I wanted to get a non-smoking seat, but this was the only one available. Is there any chance of finding me a seat in the non-smoking section?*

4 To information clerk: *I have to get to . . . in the city centre. What's the best way of getting there and how long do you think it will take?*

5 To your host, having found a public phone: *Hello, this is . . . . I've missed my connection at . . . . This means I'm going to be an hour late. Sorry about this. Must rush or I'll miss the train. Bye.*

6 To the visitor: *I'm afraid the airline's on strike. We'll have to see if you can get onto another flight. Let's go over to the Daedalus Airlines desk and see if they have a spare seat.*

Extra activity

Here are some more similar problems, which your students might be interested in solving, if they have enjoyed the six in the Student's Book.

New International Business English   This document may be photocopied.

9.1 Did you have a good journey?

1 You're seeing off a visitor. He/she wants to get home before the weekend. The only flight tonight is on an airline with a bad reputation. The safer airline has no flight until Sunday.

2 You are all alone for the weekend as a foreign visitor to your own town or city. It's Friday evening now: what are you going to do?

3 You arrive at Melbourne Airport, Australia, for a one-week visit. The immigration officer tells you that you may not enter the country because you have no vaccination certificate.

4 You are driving a rented car down a country road in an English-speaking country. You hear a bang and stop at once to find that you have a flat tyre. You open the boot but there is no spare. In the distance, you can see a car approaching . . .

5 You are on your way by car to give a presentation to which people from ten different firms have been invited. 50 km from your destination you stop to fill up with petrol. You pay and drive off, but 200 metres down the road the car stops and you realize that you have filled up with diesel fuel.

6 You are on a business trip to India. You have a meeting tomorrow morning in another city. Will you take the overnight train or the plane at 6 am? They both arrive at 8 am.

7 You land at an airport and find out that you need a visa to enter the country. The cost of a visa is $60 but you only want to stay in the country for 24 hours while you wait for a connecting flight.

© Cambridge University Press 2000

F Still looking at things that can go wrong – but this time considering ways of preventing them from happening!

If time is short, it might be a good idea to return to this step later in the unit, rather than rush through it.

More advice that could be added to the list

General

Carry medications, documents, glasses, change of clothes, and other important items with you on the plane, don't put them in the suitcase that you check in.

Don't carry unnecessary items. Carry your handbag under your arm. Keep your wallet in your jacket or a side pocket.

Keep up to date with what is happening in the world and don't travel to unsafe locations.

Use non-stop or direct flights. The fewer stops you make, the fewer chances of security breaches.

Travelling locally

Be wary of excessively friendly strangers.

Know how to get to your destination before you leave.

Leave word with someone about your destination and your expected time of return. Give them a telephone number where you can be reached.

In hotels

Make sure you know where the emergency exits for your floor are.

Don't meet strangers in your hotel room. Don't give out your room number casually.

Don't loiter or discuss your plans in hotel lobbies.

Extra activity

Begin by writing these notes on the board:

Picking a visitor up at the airport or station　　*Helping to fill in forms in your language*
Accompanying the visitor to his or her hotel　　*Translating or interpreting for a visitor*

And announce to the class:

'Here are some things you might have to do when looking after a visitor from abroad. Work in pairs and add some more things to the list.'

Then later, after the pairs have had long enough:

'When you're ready, join another pair. Compare your lists and find out about your partners' experiences.'

Some more activities that might be added

Explaining to a visitor how to get somewhere　　*Spending an evening with a visitor*
Accompanying a visitor on part of his or her journey　　*Helping a visitor with problems*
Showing a visitor round your office or factory　　*Showing a visitor the sights and tourist attractions*
Introducing a visitor to your colleagues and superiors　　*Explaining the economy and industry of your area*
Having a meal with a visitor　　*Helping a visitor with shopping*
Explaining how to use the public transport system　　*Seeing a visitor off at the airport*
Explaining local customs and habits

➡ At the end you could ask the students to role-play some of the activities in pairs.

9.2 Hotels and accommodation

This section deals with making hotel bookings and discussing accommodation facilities. Students who haven't actually ever travelled abroad on business may well have experience of travelling abroad for pleasure and should draw on this experience.

Vocabulary

single room   accessible   single occupancy
overlooking   conference room   minibar
balcony   business trip   buffet-style breakfast
wheelchair   twin beds   domestic flights

Procedure – *about 45 minutes*

A   After looking at the fax, play the recording.

The recording shows a fairly typical phone call to a hotel. Students may need to hear the recording more than once: first to get the gist of the conversation and again to note down their answers. Point out that the notes that the students are making simulate the kind of notes Vera Müller would make, in order to relay the information to her boss.

Vera Müller phones because she has special requirements – one of the people she's booking for is unable to climb stairs – and she needs the information very urgently.

The relevant information she gets from the hotel (which the students should note down) is underlined in the transcript below.

Transcript   [3 minutes]

Receptionist: Hotel Concorde.
Vera Müller: Good morning. My name's Vera Müller. I'd like to book some accommodation for tomorrow for five nights.
Receptionist: April 1st to 5th. Just one moment, madam. We are rather full at the moment, because of the trade fair. What kind of rooms would you like?
Vera Müller: I'd like three single rooms, all on the same floor.
Receptionist: I have three double rooms but not three singles available, sorry.
Vera Müller: What's the difference in price?
Receptionist: <u>Single rooms are 400 francs, doubles are 700 francs.</u>
Vera Müller: I see, um…what kind of rooms are the double rooms?
Receptionist: Very nice rooms, madam. I can give you three doubles on the sixth floor overlooking the city. They have balconies and bathrooms.
Vera Müller: Now, one of the guests is in a wheelchair. Are these rooms accessible by wheelchair?
Receptionist: Ah, no, madam. The lift goes to the fifth floor only. In this case <u>you could have three rooms on the ground floor, one single and two doubles. No view of the city, but close to the garden.</u>

Vera Müller: And do you have a small conference room I can reserve for April 3rd all day?
Receptionist: Er…yes, <u>we have a nice quiet room that will take about 12 people</u>, would that be suitable?
Vera Müller: Yes, that will be fine. And…um…are the public rooms all accessible without having to go up or down steps?
Receptionist: <u>Yes, madam. The restaurant is on the first floor – there's a lift. Otherwise everything, including the conference room is on the ground floor.</u>
Vera Müller: All right, fine. Um…then I'd like to book the three rooms on the ground floor for Acme International. The guests' names are: Mr H. Meier, Miss A. Schwarz and Mr D. Negri.
Receptionist: Thank you, so that's three rooms on the ground floor arriving on April 1st and departing on April 6th. And the conference room all day on April 3rd.
Vera Müller: Right.
Receptionist: OK. Can I have your telephone number, please?
Vera Müller: Yes, it's 41 (that's Switzerland) 22 34 89 23. And I'm Vera Müller.
Receptionist: Fine, thank you, Ms Müller. Goodbye.
Vera Müller: Goodbye.
   . . . It's OK, Mr Meier. I've booked the rooms in Toulouse.
Mr Meier: Great. Thanks, Vera.

B   If the likelihood of a business trip to South America is pretty remote for your students, encourage them to daydream a little here!

1   Student A calls the hotel to book rooms, and his or her requirements are given in File **21**; student B is Reservations Manager and has all the necessary information in File **50**. Make sure both partners read their information through BEFORE they begin the call.

2   Same again, but with reversed roles. In this case, make it clear to the students that the other hotel should be phoned.

3 Both partners work together to draft a letter, e-mail or fax to one of the hotels, confirming what was agreed on the phone. This task can be set as homework.

C This activity creates a link with Unit 10 on Marketing. It is NOT necessary to have experience of business travel to do this activity. It works well with students who have stayed in a hotel a few times (but might be beyond the imaginations of students who have never spent a single night away from home).

It may be necessary to arrange the groups so that there is at least one reasonably well-travelled person in each. This person needn't have travelled abroad but at least stayed in hotels in their own country.

9.3 Local knowledge: You are the expert!

Vocabulary

back street	*local dishes*	*historical figures*
lake	*public transport*	*TV personalities*
museum	*briefed*	*entertainers*
art gallery	*politicians*	*big names*

Procedure – *about 90 minutes*

A 1 [recording icon] Three recorded conversations illustrate the words in the speech balloons being used in typical situations. Play the recording and allow time for everyone to ask questions, highlight the useful phrases and discuss the situations:

- Who are the people speaking?
- What is their relationship?

It may be necessary to spend a little time revising 'giving directions' in English before students take part in the role-play in step **A2**.

Transcript   [2 minutes 30 seconds]

Man: Um, can you tell me how to get to the restaurant for the meal tonight?

Woman: Well, it's a bit complicated…um…I'd better show you on the map. It'll take about 20 minutes on foot.

Man: Oh, that's OK, I've got enough time and it's a lovely evening.

Woman: Right then. Now let's see, um…well, first of all you go to the right as you leave this building, OK? And then you turn left when you get to the town hall.

Man: Right.

Woman: Mm, then you keep straight on and you just cross the river. Er…oh, you'll see the railway station on your right, got it?

Man: Yeah.

Woman: OK, now you continue along that road for about three blocks till you come to a church. Um…and opposite the church there's a big square. Now, the restaurant is down a little back street on the other side of the square. It's called the Black Bear – it's just there on the map.

Man: Oh, I see. Yes.

Woman: Do you see?

Man: Yes, that's fine, no problem. Thanks very much.

Woman: You're very welcome. Enjoy your evening.

Man: Thanks.

Woman: Can you tell me how to get to the restaurant where the lunch is being held?

Man: Oh, yes, sure. Well, er…you can take a taxi or you can take the tram, that's the best idea, yes.

Woman: Oh, wow, yeah!

Man: It's the number 89 which says 'Zoo' on the front.

Woman: 89–'Zoo'. Mmm.

Man: Right, you'll need to get a ticket from the machine before you get on. Right now, at the fifth stop you get off, cross the road, walk on for about 100 metres.

Woman: OK.

Man: OK, now…now, the restaurant on the left. And you can't miss it because it's called the Black Eagle.

Woman: Black Eagle. OK fine, thanks very much.

Man: That's all right, not at all. Enjoy your lunch!

Woman: Thanks.

Woman: Can you tell me how to get to the restaurant where we're meeting tomorrow?

Man: Certainly. When you come out of the car park, turn left, OK?

Woman: Left. Right, fine.

Man: Drive straight on until you see the blue signs that say 'City'. Now, follow these signs as far as the lake and then turn right and drive along the lake for about five kilometres. Now, the restaurant is on the right just after the first village, you can't miss it. It's called the White Swan.

Woman: Oh, fine. OK, I'll see you there tomorrow at about 11 then.

Man: At 11, fine.

---

2   As preparation for the role-play, it might be helpful to draw on the board or OHP a rough street plan of the town or city your class are studying in – with their assistance, as they call out suggestions. Then they can use this as the basis of their role-play. Write up a list of the important tourist sights and commercial sites in the town. Or you could try to get enough copies of a real street plan for each pair to have one.

Alternatively, as suggested in the Student's Book, get the 'Host' to actually draw a rough map as he or she is giving directions – this is more challenging but a very realistic demand of this type of situation.

B   Although these activities come last, please don't omit them – an essential element of looking after visitors is putting yourself in their shoes!

Point out that many of the things you take for granted about your own country and home town are unfamiliar to foreigners. The names of people and products that are 'household names' in your country may be a closed book to other nationalities. By contrast, paradoxically, what a visitor may need to know about (museums, bus routes, renting a car, etc.) may be unknown territory for someone who actually lives in a place.

Divide the class into an even number of pairs, so that pairs of pairs can form groups of four (or five) when necessary.

1   If your class all come from different places, you may need to agree on a single place to discuss for this activity. Maybe, instead of doing this in pairs, go through the 'What do you know about your own city?' questions with the whole class contributing ideas.

2   During the preparatory discussion in pairs, go round offering advice and encouragement.

Each pair joins another pair. One pair plays the role of 'foreigners', the other the role of 'residents'. Later the roles are reversed.

3   When entertaining a visitor you may often be called on to explain aspects of local culture – this is also part of 'local knowledge'.

If you have different nationalities in class, rearrange the pairs to have the same nationalities working together.

Finally, each pair joins another pair – or they can form larger groups. Make it clear to everyone that the idea of this activity is to explain to 'foreigners' what each of the 'household names' listed represents. These are some of the points that may come up:

- What are the people famous for?
- What kind of image do they have?
- Are they admired or regarded with affection?
- Are they feared or considered to be comical?

9.4 Eating, socializing and telling stories

As one essential task that students will probably have to perform when eating with a foreigner is explaining dishes on the menu, it makes more sense if these are national dishes of their own country.

➡ So encourage students to get hold of menus from restaurants that they frequent, to add a local flavour to this section. If they can't or won't do this, perhaps you could supply these for them – most restaurants are delighted to allow customers to advertise for them!

Vocabulary

dessert
Pecan Pie = a sweet pie made with pecan nuts
Mississippi Mud Pie = a very chocolatey, fudgy pie
Pumpkin Pie = a sweet pie made with pumpkin
starters (BrE) / appetizers (AmE)
main courses (BrE) / entrees (AmE)
speciality (BrE) / specialty (AmE)

soaked
extended business trip
sightseeing
leaflets
security check
manifesto
compensated

knocking back
screwdriver
flap
landing gear
exaggerate
jet lag

Procedure – *about 90 minutes*

⚠ The **Preparation** in step **B** must be done by students before the lesson. If they can't be relied upon to do this, it could be done by students working together in class (not alone) – but you'll need more time to fit this in.

A **1** 🔊 The useful expressions are illustrated in a recorded conversation, which takes place in a restaurant in the USA. Students may need to hear this more than once. John decides to have Zabaglione – what would you order?

Transcript [1 minute 20 seconds]

Man: Mmm, that was delicious!
Woman: Mmm, would you like a dessert?
Man: Yes, please. Can you...um...help me with the menu?
Woman: Yes, certainly. These are starters, and these are main courses and these are desserts. See?
Man: Ah, yes, um...hmm, can you tell me what Boston Indian Pudding is?
Woman: Yes, it's a specialty of this region. It's a sort of...mm...dark cake which contains dried fruit soaked in tea.
Man: Tea?
Woman: It's hot and you have it with ice cream. Very nice.
Man: I see. And...um...what's Hot Fudge Sundae?
Woman: That's something rather special. It's a kind of ice cream with a hot sticky sauce over the top – very sweet and fattening!
Man: I don't really like the sound of that. What about Zabaglione?
Woman: Well, that's difficult to explain, it's a bit like a warm mousse. It's made of egg yolks, sugar and Marsala wine. It's an Italian specialty.
Man: That sounds very nice, I'll have that, please.
Waitress: Are you ready to order your desserts?
Woman: Yes, John?
Man: I'd like to have the Zabaglione and a large black coffee, please.
Woman: Just an iced tea for me, please.

2 For this role-play, the pairs should use the menus they have gathered or which you have provided.
You may like to begin this step by composing (with the help of the class) a typical menu of national dishes from your students' country on the board – then they can refer to this, as if it was a menu on a chalkboard in the restaurant.

In case it isn't feasible to use local menus, there are two menus on the next page which could be used instead. The first one is a traditional English Christmas menu and the second one is a lighter international one.

9.4A Eating, socializing and telling stories

Christmas Lunch Menu

Citrus and Avocado Salad
oranges, grapefruit and clementines with sliced avocado

Melon with Parma Ham

Cream of Tomato and Apple Soup

Roast Turkey with all the trimmings
Prime Norfolk turkey with sausages, chestnut stuffing and cranberry sauce

Pan-fried Trout with Almonds

Grilled Scotch Fillet Steak in a Creamy Pepper Sauce

all served with a selection of seasonal vegetables and roast or steamed potatoes

Christmas Pudding
served with brandy sauce or cream

Apple Pie
served with cream or vanilla sauce

Chocolate Mousse

Coffee and Mince Pies

≈ LUNCH MENU ≈

STARTERS

Fresh Asparagus with Lemon Butter Sauce

Six Oysters served with Vinaigrette

Soup of the Day

MAIN COURSES
served with vegetables of the day or a side salad, new potatoes or French fries

Lamb Cutlets with Redcurrant and Red Wine Sauce

Fried Calves Liver with Onions, Bacon and Wine

Grilled Fish of the Day
on baby leaves with a lime and olive oil dressing

Vegetarian dish of the day

Pasta of the day

DESSERTS

Profiteroles with Chocolate Sauce

Fresh Fruit Salad

Baked Bread and Butter Pudding with Vanilla Sauce

Vanilla, Chocolate, Strawberry or Coffee Ice Cream

ENJOY YOUR MEAL!

© Cambridge University Press 2000

Extra activity

To participate in the discussion in the activity at the top of the page opposite, students need only have experience of travelling abroad on holiday – or they can use their imaginations.

Here are some more tips which might come up in the discussion:

- It's essential to organize everything before you travel.
- Take a Walkman and plenty of batteries.
- Arrive a day early to give yourself time to adjust and acclimatize.
- Foreign customs are difficult to get used to: you should only do what you feel comfortable doing.
- Don't get involved in a political discussion.

9.4 Eating, socializing and telling stories

Work in small groups Imagine you're a foreign visitor and his or her hosts. Look at the menu you used in step **A2**. Discuss what you're going to order.

   While you're waiting for your order to be taken and for the food to be served, keep talking to each other, as if you're really having lunch or dinner together. Find out what your partners think about these aspects of travelling abroad by discussing the questions below:

Staying in a hotel	Driving a car in another country
Visiting new places	Living out of a suitcase
Jet lag	Eating in restaurants
Delays and waiting	Not being able to speak the language
Weekends and evenings away from home	

- Which aspects of travelling do you find are enjoyable, or exciting? Why?
- Which aspects do you think are stressful, annoying or depressing? Why?
- What difference does it make if you're travelling for pleasure, rather than on business? Why?

B **Preparation** This must be done before the lesson. As a variation, students might be asked to think of some true stories and some invented ones. These stories will be the basis of what the students do in step **E**.

Answer any queries about the expressions in the speech balloons. Some of these are demonstrated in the stories that will be heard in step **C**.

C 〔🔊〕 The stories should be played with a break between them, so that students can discuss their answers after each story. Suitable places for pausing are marked with ★★★ in the Transcript.

Correct arrangement of the pictures

1 a d c e b
2 c a b
3 d b c a
4 e a c d b

Transcript   [5 minutes 20 seconds]

Man: . . . anyway, I felt pretty upset, I can tell you!

Woman: Haha. Well, something even worse happened to some friends of a colleague of mine in New York. The husband was on...on an extended business trip and the idea was that his wife would come over in the middle of it to spend a long weekend with him. He was flying in from Boston, and the wife from Europe and they were going to meet up on the Friday evening and stay the weekend together at one of those very big hotels near Central Park.

Well, the hotel computer had got the first letter of their name wrong – their name began with a B (I think it was Berry) but it was spelt on the computer with a P. So the wife arrived at the hotel, gave her name and asked 'Has my husband arrived yet?' and the reception clerk looked her up on the computer and said 'No, not yet' and so she said she'd wait in their room and she was shown to the room. So she turned on the TV and, you know, started waiting.

Well, then about half an hour later the husband arrived

and gave his name and spelt it out very carefully to the reception clerk and asked 'Has my wife arrived yet?' and she looked up the name on the computer and said 'No, not yet', so he said he'd wait in the room and the clerk promised to send his wife up to him when she arrived and he was shown up to a different room. So he turned on the TV and started waiting.

Well, they both waited for a couple of hours and then the wife called reception, was told her husband still hadn't arrived so she went down to the restaurant and had a meal and then, being tired, you know, she went to bed. The husband was now quite hungry so, after calling reception and being told his wife still hadn't arrived, he went down to have his dinner, and then went to bed.

Well, the next day, they narrowly missed each other at breakfast, so they decided there was no point in sitting around waiting so they both went out shopping or sightseeing, missed each other again that evening and didn't finally meet up again till the next afternoon. By this time the husband had to fly off to Washington for a meeting first thing on Monday!

Man: Oh, that's amazing! ★★★ It's always strange in a new city. I…I remember once I was going to a conference in Norway. I landed at Oslo Airport and as I didn't know the city I picked up a whole lot of leaflets and a street map at the airport before catching the bus into town. Well, one of the leaflets was quite fat, about 100 pages long and it was called 'Where to eat in Oslo', so I started looking at it to find a nice restaurant to go to that evening – I always prefer to eat out rather than in my hotel. And I soon realized that the same restaurant was being described again, I looked all the way through the leaflet and every page was a description of the same restaurant! There were no others in there! 100 pages all about the same restaurant.

Woman: What was the name of the restaurant?

Man: I can't remember!

Woman: Haha! ★★★ Oh, that reminds me. Ha! A colleague of mine was in Sweden. He was at the end of a tough series of meetings in Stockholm and about to fly back home to London. Well, he checked his suitcase in and went through to the departure lounge, had a drink and caught his plane back to Heathrow. Unfortunately, the check-in clerk had put the wrong label on his case and it had the tag for a different flight on it . . .

Man: So he went to London and his luggage went somewhere else?

Woman: No, no, no, no, worse than that. They did a security check on all the luggage that was being loaded onto the other flight and found that there was no passenger name with that manifesto to match the particular suitcase. So they very carefully took the case off to the far corner of the airport and security police blew it up! Haha. Luckily it only contained dirty clothes and a toothbrush and stuff like that. And he got fully compensated by the airline. ★★★

Man: I remember my boss telling me about something that happened a few years ago. There was a long delay at the airport, which apparently was quite common then, and then there came an announcement over the loudspeaker: 'We are sorry but the plane is sick, we will find a new one.' So they all settled down for a long wait, feeling reassured that they weren't having to fly in a faulty plane.

Two hours later there was another announcement: 'We have found a new plane. But the new plane is more sick than the first one, so we will take the first one.' And they were all escorted to the first plane and it took off but they all felt very nervous and everyone started knocking back the gin and the whisky.

Anyway eventually they arrived at their destination and by this time everyone had managed to forget that the plane was 'sick' but instead of landing the plane kept circling round and round and round. Everyone started to get worried again. Mhm. And then a man in uniform came out of the little door leading to the flight deck with a screwdriver. He walked half way down the aisle, stopped and lifted up the carpet. Then he raised a metal flap and reached inside with the screwdriver. There was a loud click and then they heard the landing gear going down. The man in uniform went back to the flight deck. The plane made its final approach and landed safely. As they all came down the steps he said you could literally see everyone still shaking with fear.

D The picture story is deliberately enigmatic, including ambiguous clocks and baffling icons, so as to provoke discussion in pairs and different versions of the story. (There is no 'model story'.)

E This is where the students sit in groups and exchange the stories they prepared earlier. (Using the variation suggested in **B**, they would also have to guess which stories were true or invented.)

To start things off, why not tell them one that you've prepared earlier? This could be true or fictional, and would probably contain EXAGGERATIONS!

The groups should be arranged at 'tables' – and, if you feel like it, you could go from table to table taking orders for coffee. It may help to set the scene by saying that one member of the group has just arrived in the country after a long, eventful journey …

➡ If, horror of horrors, nobody has prepared a story this step should be postponed to the next lesson.

Vocabulary

provisionally	*delegates*	*refund*	*fee*
simultaneous	*venue*	*APEX ticket*	*four-star hotel*
seminars	*sole occupancy*	*overhead projector (OHP)*	
firm bookings	*full board*	*self-catering*	

Procedure – *about 90 minutes*

This integrated activity involves resolving problems, making arrangements, and drafting correspondence with speakers: here students will be practising their letter-, e-mail- and fax-writing skills. The three steps could be done on different days – then the passage of time may seem more realistic.

The groups should consist of three or four members. A more advanced or experienced class may be able to do the activity in pairs. There should be an EVEN number of groups.

All the necessary instructions for the integrated activity are given in the Student's Book, but a few additional pieces of information are given below. Note that students should show their draft correspondence to another group for comments – and you should also check some of this as you move from group to group.

First of all the groups should agree on what kind of arrangements need to be made. Even if no one has organized a conference or a weekend course, some students may have participated in them. The arrangements being made would be fairly similar if you were organizing a sales conference or a training course. If necessary, this could become a whole-class discussion.

March 16

A final draft letter could be done as homework.

March 30

Three of the speakers have replied in writing, the fourth has left a recorded message on the answerphone. The important point is <u>underlined</u> here:

Transcript   [Time: 30 seconds]

Speaker: Er...this is Madeleine Tennant. Um...I'm calling about the conference in May. Um...I'd like to have my <u>expenses paid in cash in dollars</u>, not by cheque in your currency. Um...I haven't had time to book a flight yet so I don't know how much the tickets'll cost, but...um...I'll let you know the amount when I arrive for the conference.

Step **3** may take a very long time unless each member of the group drafts a different letter. Alternatively, all the letters, e-mails or faxes could be written as homework.

April 13

In this case, step **2** may take a very long time unless the group decides on a template that will be suitable for all four speakers, and which can be 'individualized' as necessary. Again, the final draft could be written as homework.

Follow-up discussion

Here are some more questions to keep the discussion going:

• What tasks did you find difficult in doing the activity?
• How similar were the tasks to the ones you really have to do in your work?
• If you could do the whole thing again, what would you do differently?
• Which of the tasks should the organizer of a small conference or weekend course delegate or perform personally?

Workbook contents for this unit

9.1 **Going abroad**   *Vocabulary*

9.2 **Air travel in the USA**   *Reading & listening*

9.3 **Travelling**   *Functions*

9.4 **Negative prefixes**   *Word-building*

9.5 **Prepositions – 5**

9.6 **What the clever traveller knows**   *Listening*

9.7 ***To be* or not *to be* ... or *be-ing*?**   *Grammar review*

Extra activity: Flying down to Rio

Procedure *– about 90 minutes*

This challenging but very enjoyable activity begins with a problem-solving task, involving a considerable amount of discussion about dates and times – saying times, dates and numbers aloud is a skill that even more advanced students need to practise frequently – and continues with letters and faxes to write.

There should be an even number of groups, with about three students in each group. If you have a large wall map of South America that you can pin or stick up in class, this will make the task more realistic and appealing. Dealing with maps and timetables is a process that some people find intimidating – while others relish it. If possible, try to mix both these 'types' up in different groups.

The procedure is fully explained in the documents for photocopying which follow. Don't get too worried if no one seems to be producing a perfect solution – it's the PROCESS of discussing that is the point of the exercise as far as language practice is concerned.

If a group is having a lot of trouble with the schedules, you can whisper this clue to one member of the group:

'If you arrange all the people in alphabetical order, you can get the meetings to come out right!'

Solution

The following schedule will work out OK, but it's just a suggestion and your students may be able to do the whole thing differently and/or better. If the people are seen in alphabetical order there are no 'wasted' free days.

AUGUST

16 Getting over the flight and confirming meetings by phone
17 Meeting in Rio with Anna Almeida
18 Meeting in Rio with Bruno Baena
19 Flight to Lima at 11.00
20 Meeting in Lima with Carla Castro
21 Flight to Rio at 11.50
22 Shuttle flight to São Paulo, meeting with Doris Dias and back to Rio
23 Meeting in Rio with Edison Echevarria
24 Flight to Florianopolis at 07.00: trade exhibition begins in the afternoon
25 Trade exhibition in Florianopolis
26 Trade exhibition in Florianopolis
27 Trade exhibition in Florianopolis
28 Taxi to Blumenau for meeting with Flora Fischer
29 Flight from Florianopolis to Montevideo at 10.15
30 Meeting in Montevideo with Gregorio Garcia and flight to Buenos Aires at 16.20
31 Meeting in Buenos Aires with Hector Hudson and flight to Iguaçu Falls at 18.00

SEPTEMBER

 1 Sightseeing in Iguaçu – the Falls are incredible and it'd be a shame to have to miss them out!
 2 Flight to Rio at 17.30
 3 Shuttle flight to Brasilia for meeting with Ivan Itaparica and back to Rio
 4 Flight to Belo Horizonte at 08.00 for meeting with João Jardim and back to Rio afterwards
 5 Flight to Bogota at 12.00
 6 Meeting in Bogota with Klaus König and flight at 21.40 to Santiago via Rio
 7 12.50 arrival in Santiago
 8 Meeting in Santiago with Lucia Lluch
 9 Flight to Rio at 14.15
10 Shuttle to São Paulo, meeting with Maria Martin and back to Rio
11 Meeting in Rio with Nelson Neves and flight home at 22.30

New International Business English   This document may be photocopied.

Flying down to Rio

Ⓐ *Work in groups* Use the information below to arrange a business trip around South America. Decide on the itinerary to take, taking in all the cities shown in ❷ below. The trip should be as short as possible, and there should be a meeting or a flight every day. Your outward flight arrives in Rio on Thursday 16 August at 05.00 and it's best not to arrange a meeting for that day. Imagine that *you* are the traveller.

❶ You have already booked a stand at the trade exhibition in Florianopolis: this starts in the afternoon on August 24 and ends on August 27. The rest of the time you will be based in Rio and will need to make day trips to other cities within Brazil. Trips outside Brazil will require at least one overnight stay. Flights back home are at 22.30 on Tuesdays and Saturdays.

❷ You have to meet the following people, and you will need the best part of a day with each one of them. Don't arrange meetings on public holidays or Sundays.

City	Name	Availability
Belo Horizonte	João Jardim	Tuesdays only
Blumenau	Flora Fischer	August only
Brasilia	Ivan Itaparica	Sept 3 onwards
Rio de Janeiro	Anna Almeida	Thursdays or Fridays only
	Bruno Baena	Saturdays only
	Edison Echevarria	any day
	Nelson Neves	second week of Sept
São Paulo	Doris Dias	August only
	Maria Martin	any day
Bogota, Colombia	Klaus König	Sept only
Buenos Aires, Argentina	Hector Hudson	end of August
Lima, Peru	Carla Castro	August only
Montevideo, Uruguay	Gregorio Garcia	any time
Santiago de Chile	Lucia Lluch	Sept only

Also fit in a weekend break at the Iguaçu Falls, if possible.

❸ Refer to the calendar, map and airline timetable which follow.

August

S	M	T	W	T	F	S
			1	2	3	4
5	6	7	8	9	10	11
12	13	14	15	16	17	18
19	20	21	22	23	24	25
26	27	28	29	30	31	

September

S	M	T	W	T	F	S
						1
2	3	4	5	6	7	8
9	10	11	12	13	14	15
16	17	18	19	20	21	22
23	24	25	26	27	28	29
30						

PUBLIC HOLIDAYS

Argentina: Aug 17

Brazil: Sept 7

Chile: Sept 18 – 19

Peru: Aug 30

Uruguay: Aug 25

Venezuela: Aug 15

Unit 9   Visitors and travellers

Rio to/from SÃO PAULO

Every 30 mins to/from Rio de Janeiro, Santos Dumont Airport
(first flight 06.30, last flight 22.30, duration 1 hour)

To and from RIO DE JANEIRO, Galeão Airport

Rio to/from BRASILIA	Every 90 mins *(first flight 06.00, last flight 22.00, duration 1 hour)*
Rio to BELO HORIZONTE **Belo Horizonte to Rio**	06.00 08.00 10.30 14.30 17.15 18.00 *(duration 1 hour)* 07.00 09.00 13.15 14.30 18.00 20.30 *(duration 1 hour)*
Rio to FLORIANOPOLIS **Florianopolis to Rio** **Florianopolis to Montevideo**	07.00–09.50 14.00–18.00 08.40–12.15 20.30–23.15 10.15–14.00 *(Wed only)*
Rio to IGUAÇU FALLS **Iguaçu Falls to Rio** **Buenos Aires to Iguaçu Falls**	09.15–12.30 11.00–14.15 16.00–21.25 15.30–18.45 17.30–20.45 20.30–23.30 18.00–19.45
Rio to BLUMENAU* **Blumenau to Rio**	12.00–15.50 08.55–12.55
Rio to BUENOS AIRES **Buenos Aires to Rio**	08.45–11.55 16.15–20.45 08.30–13.00 16.00–21.15 18.00–20.50
Rio to MONTEVIDEO **Montevideo to Rio** **Montevideo to Buenos Aires**	08.45–13.50 16.20–20.50 16.20–17.10
Rio to SANTIAGO DE CHILE **Santiago to Rio**	08.00–12.50 14.15–20.30
Rio to LIMA **Lima to Rio**	11.00–14.15 *(Sun)* 22.00–01.00 *(Wed)* 17.30–22.00 *(Sat)* 12.50–20.15 *(Mon)* 11.50–17.25 *(Tues, Fri)* 14.40–20.15 *(Sat)*
Rio to BOGOTA **Bogota to Rio**	12.00–16.05 *(Sun)* 12.00–17.35 *(Wed)* 21.40–05.40 *(Mon)* 21.40–07.05 *(Thu)* *[both connect with 08.00 to Santiago]*

* Blumenau is about 2 hours by taxi from Florianopolis.

B *Work in small groups* When you have decided on your routes:

❶ Draft a letter, e-mail or fax to one of the people, arranging a meeting on the day you've decided.

❷ And, if you have been unable to fit anyone into the itinerary, write to them explaining why they have been left out.

❸ Draft a fax or e-mail to the Hotel Cambridge in Santiago, booking a room for one or two nights.

❹ Join another group and ask them about the itinerary they have worked out. Get them to explain why they've made the decisions they've made.

© Cambridge University Press 2000

Marketing

This unit deals with various aspects of marketing: market research, applying marketing principles, promotion and advertising.

Section **10.4** covers the notions of expressing degrees of certainty, possibility and probability.

Background information

Before starting work on this unit, students should read the Background information in the Workbook. This is particularly important for students without business experience.

Video

Programme 10 of the *New International Business English Video* introduces the theme of this unit. It deals with Swatch AG.

10.1 The marketing mix

This section introduces the topic of marketing, including some crucial concepts and vocabulary, and encourages students to look at some familiar products and how they are marketed.

Vocabulary

brand	promotion	outlets	tastes
image	publicity	hire purchase	buying habits
design	P.R. = public relations	opportunities	
labels	distribution	threats	
posters	end-users	demand	

Procedure – *about 90 minutes*

Begin by looking at the illustrations in the Student's Book: these show some local products and services from Melbourne and Victoria. Ask the students to identify the products which are shown there.

A Students should think of specific examples of local products and services, including the brand name and the producer or provider of the service.

B This discussion sets the scene for the unit. Students will be discussing how all kinds of products and services are actively marketed these days, even public services and monopolies that have captive customers.

To start everyone off you could discuss with the class just one of the items listed – a particular local cinema, for example:

• What competition does the local cinema face from other cinemas, from other leisure industry products, from non-leisure related products?

- Does it have an up-market or a down-market image?
- Where do customers receive their information about its product?
- Is promotional material generated by the owner of the cinema or by the distributors of the films shown?
- Are its customers regular customers or one-time customers?
- If you were running the cinema, would you market it more strongly and if so how?

After the group discussions, ask each group to report to the class on the most interesting product they have discussed.

C IF POSSIBLE, THIS EXERCISE SHOULD BE DONE AS HOMEWORK BEFORE THE LESSON – or, if the worst comes to the worst, after the lesson. It could also be done in class by students working together in pairs, but that might take up too much time.

Suggested answers

1 product   price   promotion   place
2 satisfy   image   design
3 competes   rival
4 commercials   radio spots   newspaper advertisements   posters   labels   materials   public relations
5 distribution   end-users   outlets   hire purchase   mail order
6 strengths   weaknesses   opportunities   threats

D This step leads on from the last question in step **C**.
   If your class contains some students with business experience, arrange the groups so that they are distributed among the class. (Students who are working may prefer to concentrate on talking about their own company – or perhaps *avoid* talking about it!)
   To start the ball rolling it may be necessary to brainstorm the names of some of the main local industries and write them on the board. Some preparation may be needed for this discussion, but presumably students will discuss the firms they talked about in **A** earlier.

10.2 Advertisements and commercials

Make sure everyone does the preparation before the lesson. If they don't, this section could be postponed till a later time when they *have* had time to do this.

Vocabulary

USP = Unique Selling Proposition	nostalgic	cross-referenced
AIDA = Attention, Interest, Desire, Action	desirable	package
features	rate	tense nervous headaches
benefits	updated	commercials

Procedure – *about 90 minutes*

Preparation The members of the class have to seek out some of their own favourite advertisements and bring them to class. These ads may be in English and/or in their own language.
   Depending on the time available, and how much interest you think this section will generate, you might ask the students to include a dreadful ad in their selection.

➡ Take to class your own selection of large, colourful, up-to-date magazine ads in English. The text should be readable from a distance if you're planning to display them in the classroom. Maybe include some ads that are terrible or tasteless as well.

A 🔲 This is a lead-in to steps **B** and **C**. The speakers are talking about the ad for Michelin Maps and Guides but we don't hear them dealing with the last two questions. Encourage the students to continue looking at the same ad and discuss the remaining questions.

Transcript [2 minutes]

Man: What do you think of this advertisement?

Woman: Mm, I quite like it.

Man: Yes, yes, so do I. It makes the product seem sort of likeable, doesn't it?

Woman: Mm, well, it's an advertisement for *three* products really: hotel and restaurant guides, guide books of places to see and maps.

Man: Mm, I like the way the nice pale colours catch your attention – and the smiling Michelin man looking straight at you makes you want to step into the countryside – even though it's only a drawing. It has a nostalgic, old-fashioned look and that makes you interested in reading the text.

Woman: That's right yes, and when you read the text you find the selling points of each of the three products. It makes them all seem very desirable.

Man: The message is "Make sure it's a Michelin", which means next time you're thinking of buying a map or a guide book, you should think of Michelin products.

Woman: What kind of people is this message directed at, do you think?

Man: Well, I suppose motorists and tourists, people who stay in hotels or eat in restaurants.

Woman: Yes, and what seems to be the Unique Selling Proposition of the products, according to the ad?

Man: It's actually different for each product. Er…the red guides list more hotels and restaurants than their competitors. Er…the green guides use a star system to rate places of interest. And the maps are updated every year – u…unlike their competitors, we are supposed to think.

Woman: Yes, but it also says that the three products are cross-referenced, which means they can be used together easily. They're a sort of package. I'd say that was the USP!

Man: Yeah, yes, you're right.

B The ads in the Student's Book should be treated as 'starters'. Your own selection of large, colourful, up-to-date magazine ads in English may be more motivating.

It will be particularly revealing to compare different national styles and conventions in advertisements. For example, the use of visual or verbal humour in different countries. Also the use of 'knocking copy' in Britain and the USA – in some countries criticizing competing products is illegal or considered to be unsporting.

The ads in the Student's Book show the following products:

First Choice Holidays – the first poster is a 'teaser' which arouses the public's interest by apparently advertising a mystery product. The last poster on the page is the 'reveal' ad which makes sense of the 'teaser', while still keeping the comic image alive in the public's minds.

Ben & Jerry's Ice Cream – an interesting combination of cartoon-style drawing and real photograph of Ben Cohen and Jerry Greenfield, whose luxury ice cream ranks second to Häagen-Dazs in the USA. Their 'product mission' is to make the finest all-natural ice cream in innovative flavours from Vermont dairy products. Their factory is Vermont's number one tourist spot.

Michelin Maps and Guides – as described in the recording – Michelin's main business is making tyres, but their maps and guides are an important part of their income.

United Colors of Benetton – one of a series of posters on the theme of 'black and white' promoting racial harmony. These posters don't show any Benetton products, but promote the brand name and its positive image.

C This is where everyone presents their ads to the other members of their group. Students may need a little help before doing this.

There are some suitable opening gambits in the Student's Book.

Extra activity – if you have video available

Tape some British or American TV commercials and show them to the class. Use the questions in step **B** as the basis of an analysis and discussion of them.

10.3 Promoting products and brands

Vocabulary

brochures	*showrooms*	*comic*	*manure*
leaflets	*stands*	*portable*	*trend*
direct mail	*trade fairs*	*brand name*	*global brands*
point of sale displays	*sponsorship*	*bubble gum*	*luxury brands*
press releases	*word of mouth*	*liqueur*	

Procedure – *about 45 to 90 minutes*

The box at the beginning reminds students what is meant by the term 'Total Product'.

A The discussion gives everyone a chance to use the vocabulary introduced in the illustrations.

Some students may need a little help before doing this. Here are some suitable gambits, which could be written on the board:

That wouldn't be suitable because …   *One good way of promoting … is …*
If you rely too heavily on …   *It's not a good idea to …*
The best way to promote … is …   *One disadvantage of … is …*

B 🔘 We now hear part of a lecture. After completing the task, students are encouraged to suggest some foreign brand names that are unsuitable in their country – in this case, maybe, British or American brands.

Answers

Portable radios: Party Center ✓   Concert Boy ✓   Party Boy ✓   Yacht Boy ✓
Drinks: Irish Cream liqueur ✓   Irish Mist liqueur ✓
Food: Häagen-Dazs ice cream ✓
Cars: Bluebird ✓   Applause ✓   Accord ✓   Carina ✓   Previa ✓   Micra ✓
Corolla ✓   Primera ✓   Shogun ✓   Mondeo ✓   Celica ✓   Xantia ✓   Vauxhall ✓
Astra ✓   Corsa ✓   Golf ✓
Computer software: PageMaker ✓   WordPerfect ✓   QuarkXPress ✓   Microsoft
Word ✓

Transcript   [5 minutes 20 seconds]

Lecturer: … Now, on the subject of brand names: English names are often used in foreign countries to make products sound more 'international'. But this doesn't always work. Take, for example, portable radios. There's the *Party Center*, the *Concert Boy*, the *Party Boy* and the *Yacht Boy* – these are all marketed in the UK under those names, but they do sound a bit silly to British ears, don't they?

Um…many foreign brand names just don't sound quite right in Britain. Here are a few examples of brand names which would have to be changed if they wanted to sell the products…um…on the British market. *Pocari Sweat* – that's a drink for sports people, and…er…*Calpis*, *Pschitt* and *Sic* – these are drinks which sound quite disgusting in English. *Bum* – that's a…a brand of bubble gum. There's *Mother*, a brand of biscuits. *Bimbo*, and that's a brand of bread.

Um…another strange name is *Häagen-Dazs* ice cream. This brand name was invented in the USA – um…it's supposed to have a European 'quality' sound and look, but it doesn't actually mean anything in any language. Still, it's the most popular luxury brand in Britain despite the fact that no one can spell it correctly!

Um … Oh, and not all British brands sound right in other countries. Um…there are two Irish whiskey liqueurs you can buy in the UK: *Irish Cream* and *Irish Mist*. The latter wouldn't sell in Germany, where the word *Mist* means 'manure'.

And…er…h…how about the Nissan cars: *Cedric* and *Gloria*? Those English first names sound so unglamorous that neither of them could be sold in the UK under those brand names. But, having said that, er…a good product can succeed even if the name does sound a tiny bit strange. Look at Japanese cars: you've got the Nissan *Bluebird*, the Daihatsu *Applause*, the Honda *Accord*, the To…Toyota *Carina* – all very successful in the UK.

Oh, er…by the way, I've always been puzzled by how many Japanese cars have an R or L in their name: there's the Toyota *Previa*, the Nissan *Micra*, the Toyota *Corolla*, the Nissan *Primera* – um…most Japanese cars I can think of have a…an R or a…a…an L in their name, even though many Japanese people pronounce the sounds 'r' and 'l' the same. A…an exception is the four-wheel drive Mitsubishi *Shogun* (a…as it's called in the UK), but…er…in most countries it's called the *Pajero* – er…except in Spanish-speaking countries where that word is very rude indeed. There the same car is the *Ranchero*.

Er…many international car names have been invented specially. They don't mean anything in any language but they're just supposed to sound attractive – most of the brands I've already mentioned are invented words. Some more examples of these on sale in the UK are the Ford *Mondeo*, the Toyota *Celica* and the Citroën *Xantia*.

But sometimes they may have to change the brand name to make it acceptable in different countries. In Europe, General Motors cars are marketed under the *Opel* brand name. In Britain, these cars are *Vauxhalls* – a name that most Europeans find very hard to pronounce. But there's a definite trend to create European brands: um…the *Opel Kadett* used to be called the *Astra* in the UK, now it's the *Astra* all over Europe. And here in Britain the *Vauxhall*

Nova has taken on the European brand name *Corsa* – in Spanish and Italian *No va* means 'it doesn't go', which wouldn't have been a suitable name for a reliable small car! And in the USA they have a car called the *Rabbit* – a sort of light-hearted, amusing image, hasn't it? That's what we call the VW *Golf*, because consumers here seem to prefer a more serious sporty image.

A fashionable product like…er…computer software has to have a marketable, and a…a memorable brand name. And as more products are developed increasingly meaningless new names have to be invented, which nobody else has thought of before.

Computer software products on sale in the UK often have brand names consisting of two words without a space between them. So instead of being called *Page Maker*, the product is called *PageMaker* with a capital M in the middle. Then…um…there's *WordPerfect* (with a capital P in the middle) and *QuarkXPress* (with capital X and capital P in the middle). Um…but *Microsoft Word* is two words and…er…there are no capitals in the middle anywhere.

Now, having said all that, what I'd like you to do is to think of some…er…foreign brand names that you think are unsuitable for the market in your country. Get together with a colleague and you've got three minutes to make notes. OK? . . .

C **1** Some competing brands are:

Pepsi-Cola *Post or Weetabix* *Burger King* *Fuji* *Benson & Hedges* *Apple (Macintosh)* *Diner's Club* *Philips* *BMW* *Maxwell House*

– but these may vary from country to country. Not all the competing brands are brand leaders in every country.

Some other famous global brands are:

Toyota *Mitsubishi* *Sanyo* *JVC* *Hilton* *Sheraton* *Levis* *Heinz* *Hoover* *Mars* *Kleenex* *Benetton* *Body Shop*

2 The luxury brands are famous for, among other products:

cigarettes & lighters   luggage   jewellery & watches   fountain pens
shirts & leisure wear

3 Of course, everyone will claim that brand names aren't important for them, but it's worth discussing the 'image' of various brands of, for example, cars. Most (?) people buy a new car because of its image as well as its price and performance.

Write up some of these, and maybe other, makes of car on the board:

Volvo *Rolls Royce* *Hyundai* *Cadillac* *Honda* *Skoda* *VW* *Porsche* *Citroën* *Renault* *Nissan* *Mazda* *Daihatsu*

– and ask the class to explain what their images are in their country.

This is a rather grammatical Functions section! Many different structures are used in English to describe degrees of certainty. To save time in the lesson, ask everyone to look at the box at the beginning and the phrases in **B** before the lesson.

Vocabulary

degree of probability	*break into*	*sales literature*
sales forecast	*over-optimistic*	*sales-wise*
sales figures	*prediction*	

Procedure – *about 45 to 60 minutes*

Before playing the recording for step **A**, allow everyone time to read through the box at the beginning. Answer any questions arising.

A ▢ This recording introduces the idea of 'talking about degrees of probability'. Pause the recording between each conversation (marked with ★★★ in the Transcript) to give everyone time to write in their answers and discuss them with a partner.

Answers

2 certain (100%)	likely (75%)	possible (50%)	unlikely (25%)	impossible (0%)
Betty – and Eric doesn't know	*no one*	Diana	Alan	Christian

3 certain (100%)	likely (75%)	possible (50%)	unlikely (25%)	impossible (0%)
Alan	Eric	Betty	Christian	Diana

4 certain (100%)	likely (75%)	possible (50%)	unlikely (25%)	impossible (0%)
Alan	Eric	Christian & Diana	*no one*	Betty

Transcript [3 minutes]

Narrator: You'll hear Mrs Frost finding out from her staff about a sales campaign in Canada. Notice how certain each member of staff is about each of the points she raises. I'll explain how the first is done for you as an example.

Mrs Frost: First of all. What about the sales literature we said we'd send to Toronto? Alan?

Alan: I'm not altogether sure whether the literature has been sent yet.

Narrator: So Alan wasn't sure – according to him it was possible.

Mrs Frost: Betty?

Betty: The literature must have been sent on Friday afternoon.

Narrator: Betty was sure – according to her it was certain.

Mrs Frost: Christian?

Christian: I very much doubt if the literature was sent at all.

Narrator: Christian was doubtful – according to him it was unlikely.

Mrs Frost: Diana?

Diana: I wouldn't be surprised if it was all sent on Friday without Christian noticing.

Mrs Frost: Eric?

Eric: It couldn't possibly have been sent, we didn't get it from the printers till Thursday.

Narrator: And Diana thought it was likely and Eric thought it was impossible. Now do the same yourself. Ready?

★★★

Mrs Frost: Now, how about our new sales drive in Canada? Is it going to succeed? Alan, what do you think?

Alan: Well, in my opinion, it probably isn't going to go well.

Mrs Frost: Betty?

Betty: Oh, I'm absolutely certain it'll work.

Mrs Frost: Christian?

Christian: It couldn't possibly succeed, we haven't done enough field work.

Mrs Frost: Diana?

Diana: There's a chance it'll succeed – it may or it may not, hard to tell really.

Mrs Frost: Eric?

Eric: Hmm, I don't really know. It's not really my area.

★★★

Mrs Frost: Now about the new product range – will it make a big impact on the Canadian market? Alan?

Alan: I'm quite sure it will, we've got a really exciting new product here.

Mrs Frost: Betty?

Betty: It may well have a big impact, but only if we manage to get enough repeat customers.

Mrs Frost: Christian?

Christian: I doubt if it'll make that big an impact – last year's figures suggest that Canada is becoming very slow sales-wise.

Mrs Frost: Diana?

Diana: It can't possibly have much impact, not after last year's consumer tests.

Mrs Frost: Eric?

Eric: Well, I'm not so sure. I wouldn't be at all surprised if it made quite a big impact.

★★★

Mrs Frost: Were the sales forecasts for Canada encouraging? Alan?

Alan: They must have been encouraging, that's why CJ's so keen on Canada this season.

Mrs Frost: Betty?

Betty: Well, I had a quick look and it seemed to me that they couldn't possibly have been encouraging.

Mrs Frost: Christian?

Christian: They may have been encouraging.

Mrs Frost: Diana?

Diana: It's quite possible they were encouraging, CJ didn't let me see them though.

Mrs Frost: Eric?

Eric: I expect they were encouraging. CJ can't have made a mistake, can he, Mrs Frost?

Mrs Frost: Ah…no he couldn't possibly have made a mistake – I just wanted your views, that's all. Thanks everyone.

All: That's all right, Mrs Frost.

B   🔊 Play the recording which shows the phrases being used in a sales meeting. It lasts 1 minute 30 seconds.

Answer any questions that may arise and, in a more advanced class, maybe consider shades of meaning and emphasis among the recorded examples.

> ⚠ Students sometimes get confused between the concepts involved: for example, *I'm not certain that it is true* doesn't mean *I'm certain that it is not true*!

C   🔊 We hear some predictions about future events. Encourage everyone to experiment with the new phrases that were introduced earlier.

Pause the recording after each statement (or each pair of statements) for students to discuss it.

Transcript   [1 minute 20 seconds]

Interviewer: What do you think might happen in the business world in the next 20 years or so?

Woman: I think robots will replace production workers.

Woman: There'll be less need for transport, as people will work from home.

Woman: Well, business travel will be replaced by live video meetings, there won't be any need to go to see the client any more.

Man: Er…in a few years' time we'll all have video phones instead of ordinary phones. Everyone will be able to see the person they're calling.

Woman: There won't be any people in offices. Well, there'll just be computers doing all the work.

Man: Jobs will change so quickly that we'll have to retrain for new job skills every few years.

Woman: Offices won't use paper any more. All communications will be electronic, even letters and faxes will just be sent from screen to screen.

Man: Um…I don't know, there'll be much higher unemployment. I mean, half the working population may be out of work.

Extra activity

Write one sentence to give your view on each prediction.

D   Finally, groups of three look into their crystal balls and try to foresee trends in marketing the products listed. To start everyone off, a couple of the products can be discussed as a class.

Depending on how much time you want to spend on this, you could specify how many items should be picked. You might like to add fruit, telephones, cigarettes and publishing to the list.

Extra activity

In this activity, students evaluate the 'truth value' of the trivial facts given. Encourage them to experiment with the expressions presented earlier and not just to say 'Probably true' or 'Maybe true'.

New International Business English   This document may be photocopied.

10.4 Possibility, probability and certainty

Work in small groups   Some of the information given here is true and some is untrue. Use the expressions in **B** to say how PROBABLE it is that each of these statements is true.

1. The world's biggest spenders on advertising are the Danes.
2. The world's greatest consumers of coffee are the Swedes.
3. The world's largest employer is a French company.
4. 99% of all businesses in Japan and Switzerland employ an average of 15 people.
5. The world's biggest manufacturer of motor vehicles is the USA.
6. Over $100 billion a year is spent on advertising in the USA.
7. The world's largest airport is Dallas – Fort Worth, Texas.
8. Families in the USA spend less on food and drink and more on health than any other nation in the world.
9. The airport that handles the second largest number of international passengers in the world is JFK, New York.
10. The average person over 15 smokes 1,750 cigarettes annually.
11. The world's no. 1 exporting country is Japan.
12. It cost Esso $200 million to change its name to Exxon in 1972.
13. The world's biggest restaurant chain, McDonald's, serves about 1.5 million hamburgers a day at its 9,000 restaurants.
14. The world's largest food company is Swiss.
15. The world's busiest port is New York.
16. The world's greatest beer drinkers are the Germans.

Examples: *I wouldn't be surprised if the first statement is true.*
             The first statement couldn't possibly be true.

© Cambridge University Press 2000

Answers

All the odd-numbered facts are untrue.
All the even-numbered facts are true.

Further information about each statement

1. The Swiss spend more per head on advertising than the Danes, followed by the Americans, the Finns and the Canadians.
2. – eight kilos per person per year
3. Indian National Railways, with two million employees, is the world's biggest employer. In most countries, the state is the largest employer of both civilian staff and military personnel.
4. – and in Italy 99% of businesses have an average of eight employees
5. Not any more – it's Japan
6. – and a quarter of this is spent by the top 100 national advertisers

7 It's Jeddah (by area) or Chicago (by number of passengers)
8 – this may be partly because of their larger disposable incomes; No. 2 in health spending are the Egyptians and No. 2 lowest spenders on food and drink are the Canadians.
9 It's Gatwick (No. 1 is Heathrow)
10 – state monopolies make over half the world's cigarettes, most of the others are manufactured by six multinational companies
11 It's Germany
12 – company name consultants in the USA make $40 million a year
13 It's actually 15 million a day
14 – Nestlé
(A Nestlé executive was once looking for companies to acquire in Italy and began negotiations with a pasta manufacturer, only to find that Nestlé already owned it!)
15 It's actually Rotterdam, in terms of tonnage handled
16 – of course: 150 litres per head per year!

10.5 Marketing your own region   *Integrated activity*

In this integrated activity, students will be considering the different stages of marketing a product: analysing statistics, conducting market research, devising a questionnaire and carrying out a market survey, considering the strengths and weaknesses of the product, devising a marketing strategy and drafting an advertisement. In real life, of course, all these processes would take a lot more time and require more specialized skills than may be available in class.

One has to have an enormous amount of information about a product to market it. This is why we have chosen a product that everyone is familiar with – even students with no business experience can participate actively in this simulation.

Vocabulary

questionnaire	*hospitality*	*outside agencies*
misconceptions	*wilderness*	*consultants*
gloomy	*landscape*	
package tours	*specialist skills*	

Procedure – *about 90 minutes*

Begin by asking students to read and comment on the advertisements shown in the Student's Book. This makes it clear that even a country or a region is a 'product'.

Decide with the class exactly what 'product' everyone will be marketing. If several regions are represented in the class, agree on just one as the 'product' for the activity – or the whole country might be considered as a single product.

In a multinational class, the class could be divided into several groups, each dealing with a different country, but not too many, or the activity will become unwieldy.

Make sure everyone is clear what they will have to do, perhaps by briefly previewing what will happen in steps **A** and **B**.

⚠ If you feel that the activity may take too long to do in the time you have available, decide in advance which parts you can skip – or which you can set as homework (for example, step **7**).

A Students working in pairs consider what kind of information they need to obtain in order to carry out the tasks in **B**. After a while, ask the pairs to report to the class and pool everyone's ideas.

B The three groups each have different information to obtain by devising and later administering their questionnaire.

File **23**: Group A's questionnaire will find out what factors people take into account when choosing a holiday destination for both a main holiday and a second holiday.

File **53**: Group B's questionnaire will find out people's attitudes to the unattractive features of five competing countries or regions as well as to the unattractive features of the region under consideration.

File **77**: Group C's questionnaire will find out people's attitudes to the region and also their attitudes to competing countries or regions.

From now on, follow steps 1 to 7 in the Student's Book. Here are some additional ideas and comments:

1 First the groups discuss what to do (this may take a few minutes) and then get down to drafting their questionnaire.

2 Make sure everyone is involved here. Point out that it's up to each person to find members of other groups to interview – the ideal is for everyone to be interviewed twice.

   For the sake of realism, each encounter should end with a 'Thank you for helping me' not 'Now it's my turn to ask you some questions'.

   If students are getting involved in the activity and have invested a lot of time in devising their questionnaires, the interviews could be continued out of class with neighbours, colleagues and friends (in their own language).

3 The results are collated and tabulated before being evaluated in step **4**.

4 In a small class, this can be a whole-class discussion. In a larger class, form groups of three (one member from each original group).

5 Another change-round: groups of three, with members drawn from each original group, as in step **4**, perhaps.

6 Having considered the questions in step **5**, a small class or two groups of a larger class (or even more groups of a huge class) devise a marketing strategy. A class with little business experience should skip this step and go on to step **7**.

7 Make sure there's time for everyone to discuss this before they draft an advertisement (maybe based on the ones at the beginning of the section). If time is short, this could be done as homework.

Extra written work

Ask everyone to draft a report summarizing their group's findings, including a table or chart. This could be prepared in class and then finished as homework.

C Make sure there is enough time for the follow-up discussion – if necessary postpone it until the next lesson and ask everyone to prepare their answers to the questions.

For students who are currently in employment, here are some extra questions:

- How is marketing your own company's product different from marketing a tourist destination?
- What is similar about marketing your firm's product?
- How is export marketing handled differently from domestic marketing in your own firm?

Extra activity

The purpose of the activity is to provoke discussion and encourage students to apply some of the ideas about marketing which they have encountered during this unit. Different groups could deal with different cases. There are no 'correct answers' – the best solutions, in reality, would depend on many other factors than the ones outlined here.

As homework, students could be asked to select one of the cases and 'write up' their explanation of what they would do.

New International Business English   This document may be photocopied.

What would you do?   *Case studies*

Work in groups Imagine that YOU work in marketing for these firms. What are you going to do?

Dentallo is a medium-sized firm making toothpaste and toothbrushes. Your Dazzle toothpaste and Protect toothbrushes are market leaders in the home market, but due to heavy competition from multinational companies with big advertising budgets you are no longer able to reach your export sales targets.

Market research shows that a large proportion of consumers abroad find your product image is old-fashioned and dull, though your prices are still competitive.

Elysium Sport is a company that produces clothing for cycling clubs, athletics and football clubs. In the home market, you have so far managed to hold your own against cheaper competition from overseas, because your customers appreciate the quality of your products and because you can produce short runs of customized garments (using a patented printing process) with their logo or badge.

At present, you only export a small amount, but you would like to find a gap in the overseas market where your kind of product would sell well.

© Cambridge University Press 2000

Workbook contents for this unit

11 Meetings

Most business people spend a lot of their time attending meetings. This unit revises some of the skills that are required when participating in meetings of different kinds and sizes. Students will be considering some of the issues involved in taking part in both formal and informal meetings. The relationships and behaviour at meetings where many people are involved (as in a committee) or where just two people are involved (as in one-to-one meetings) are discussed and practised.

We have deliberately avoided the use of the term 'interview' for one-to-one meetings and have reserved this term to describe job interviews, progress interviews and promotion interviews (see Unit 13).

Background information

Before starting on this unit, draw your students' attention to the Background information in the Workbook. This covers some of the basic rules of meetings of different sizes and the importance of planning, agendas and good chairpersonship.

Video

Programme 11 on the *New International Business English Video* introduces the theme of this unit.

11.1 Taking part in a meeting

This section introduces the idea of meetings and ends with a full-scale committee meeting. Don't be surprised if this turns out to be less than perfect. The idea is for students to discover what they need to improve – there are plenty of opportunities in later sections for further practice.

Vocabulary

proposal	*responsibilities*	*majority*	*full-time*
flexible working hours (flexitime)	*cover*	*to and fro*	*credited*
core times	*vote*	*stipulations*	*part-time*
agenda	*opt out*	*designated*	*chair*

Procedure – *about 90 minutes*

A This warm-up discussion encourages students to remember meetings they have attended themselves. Students who have never attended a meeting won't have much to say about the last two questions.

B 1 The only points NOT mentioned are:

The staff canteen must be open longer at lunchtime – say from 11.30 to 2.30.
Flexible hours should only be worked on Mondays and Fridays.
Staff should be allowed to work all through the lunch hour and not have a lunch break.

2 This is quite a formal meeting, and the chairman does a pretty good job, though Mr Johnson doesn't get a chance to say anything. The way he chairs the meeting can be used as a 'model' for the chairperson in the meeting in step **C**.

3 To begin with, it would be a good idea to refer students back to the expressions presented in **5.5C**.

4 🔊 Play the recording for **B1** again and ask everyone to listen out for the expressions they've highlighted in the Student's Book.

Transcript [3 minutes 40 seconds]

All: . . . yes...it took an hour and a half for my bags to come through...yes, but it...it's always the same...the last time I saw you I . . .

Chair (Mr Brown): Er...OK, it's ten o'clock, everybody, so I think we'll...er...make a start. Now, the first item on the agenda is a discussion of the management's proposals on flexitime. Now, you've all discussed the proposals within your departments, haven't you?

All: Yes. We have, yes.

Chair: Good. Er...Miss Garcia, would you like to start, then?

Anna Maria: OK, well, most of my people are perfectly happy with the present non-flexible system. They think a change would be dangerous.

Carla: I'm sorry, I'm not quite with you. Dangerous?

Anna Maria: Well, they feel more flexible hours would make it difficult to cover for each other. We all have quite clearly defined responsibilities. Some people would benefit more than others.

Enzo: It seems to me that your people can just agree together to go on working from nine to five, they don't have to work later.

Anna Maria: Yes, but the problem is that if one or two people opt for the new system, the others will have to cover for them when they're not there.

Chair: Ah, Mr Bergman, what are your views on this?

Alex: Well...um...the thing is that...er...

Carla: Look, I'm really sorry to interrupt. I'd just like to say that any department can vote to opt out. They can just vote on it and the majority wins.

Chair: Thank you, Mrs Baldini. Ah...Ms Legrand, yes.

Tina: Um...could I make a suggestion? Wouldn't it be...um...be best to hear what each member has to say about the proposals...er...from the point of view of his or her department?

Chair: Yes, all right. Er...Ms Legrand, wh...what are your views?

Tina: Well, the main problem is...is the decision about...about basic core times.

Enzo: I'm sorry, I didn't catch what you said.

Tina: I'm talking about core times – that's...er...the basic hours that would not be flexible. It's been suggested that these be ten to three, but this seems much too restricted, don't you agree, Carla?

Carla: Absolutely. In fact I'd say that there should be flexible days.

Anna Maria: Sorry, I'm not quite with you.

Carla: Well, staff should be allowed to build up a credit of hours to entitle them to take whole days off, not just fewer hours on other days.

Chair: Ah...Mr Rossini, what do you think about this?

Enzo: Yes, I'd go along with that. As for cover, in my own case it's no problem, there are three of us in the Export Department and we work as a team, so it's easy for us to cover for each other as long as there are still two of us in the office.

Alex: Er...Mr Brown?

Chair: Yes, Mr Bergman?

Alex: Er...If I could just make a point here...er...in our case, we do a lot of dealing on the phone with the States and...er...sending messages to and fro by fax in the afternoon. Er...if we had anyone off then we wouldn't be able to manage. That means our core times would have to be one to five. Maybe each department should set its own core times.

Chair: Mm...er...yeah, Mrs Baldini?

Carla: That's all very well, Alex, but then no one in any other department would know who was in at what time, I mean there'd be chaos. There has to be a standard for all departments.

Chair: Er...yes, Mr Rossini?

Enzo: Yes, coming back to the flexible days idea, this just wouldn't work. People phoning the company or visiting would get terribly confused.

Tina: No, no, that...that's not true, Enzo. I mean, when people take holiday or...or when people are sick, cover arrangements are made. Well, with flexible days, exactly the same kind of arrangements would be made.

Chair: Well, any other points?

All: No . . . Don't think so . . . Covered it all . . .

Chair: Have you got all this down, Mr Johnson?

Ron: Yes.

Chair: Then I think we'll move on to the next item on the agenda . . .

C **1** In **B** we heard the meeting of departmental representatives. Now follow-up meetings within each department are to be held.

Arrange the class into an even number of groups so that they can combine later. Four or five in a group would be a good number. Tell everyone how long they have for this – real-life meetings go on longer than you can allow in this lesson!

As we said earlier, don't be dismayed if the students' performance is less than perfect. In fact, if the meetings are very chaotic, perhaps stop everyone and discuss what's going wrong. Then start everyone off again, maybe with new chairpersons.

2   In this discussion, students evaluate their performance in the meetings.

D   This discussion should be in smaller groups than **C2** – or it could be a whole-class activity.

Here are some suggestions for 'golden rules', which you could write on the board for the class to evaluate and then add to:

Start on time
Be punctual
Make sure everyone has a chance to contribute
Don't let anyone dominate
Stick to the agenda
Don't insist on everyone addressing the chair

➡ And this might be a good time to raise this question:

• What are the qualities of a good chairperson?

Here are some (perhaps contradictory) qualities of a good chairperson:

A good chairperson is someone who … listens carefully, interrupts people when necessary, keeps to the agenda, allows everyone to have their say, asks non-speakers to speak, keeps to the time limit …

11.2 One-to-one meetings

Vocabulary

buffet lunch	*pre-lunch*	*pro-rata*	*wedding reception*	*venue*
overdoing it	*snack*	*flap-over desk tops*	*banqueting*	*premises*

Procedure – *about 90 minutes*

A   🔊 We begin by listening to a one-to-one meeting between a customer and a supplier. You may need to play this twice. Not only does this show some of the exponents in the speech balloons being used in context, but it also sets the mood for the role-plays that follow in **B**.

This recording is illustrative: the actual content of the meeting is not really important, so there's no need for any detailed comprehension questions. However, if you feel it's necessary to play it through twice at this stage, the first two questions can be considered as 'first listening questions' and the second two as 'second listening questions'.

Transcript   [3 minutes]

Paul: Ah, good morning, Ms Ross, do come in.

Pam: Hello, Mr Fisher. Nice to see you.

Paul: Nice to see you – face-to-face instead of on the phone, what? How are you?

Pam: Fine, thanks, very well.

Paul: Oh, do sit down. Would you like some coffee?

Pam: Oh, yes, please – black.

Paul: Mmm. Here you are.

Pam: Thanks. Well, how's it all going?

Paul: Oh, not too bad, we're just about to open a branch in New Zealand.

Pam: Oh, will you be going there on your travels?

Paul: Oh…I'm hoping to – if I can justify it to the marketing director! How's your little boy, has he started school yet?

Pam: Oh, yes, he's in the second year now.

Paul: What, already? Doesn't time fly! Is he enjoying it?

Pam: Very much, it's much more fun than being at home!

Paul: Haha. Well, I suppose we'd better make a start. Shall we get down to business?

Pam: Right. First of all can I confirm the time and date of the presentation? It's Saturday 24 October in the morning. What time exactly?

Paul: Well, on the invitations we've sent out we've said that the presentation itself will start at 11 and go on till 12.30.

Pam: So you'll need the room from about 10 till 2. Would you like us to serve coffee beforehand?

Paul: Yes, yes – and drinks and snacks at the end.

Pam: Better to have buffet lunch?

Paul: No. People who are invited won't be expecting a free lunch, they might think that's overdoing it. They'll want to get back to their families, as it's Saturday.

Pam: All right, the normal pre-lunch snack buffet will be what you need – that's basically the same as what you had last February.

Paul: Oh, that'll be fine.

Pam: OK, well, we'll charge for the room, coffee and snack buffet at the standard rate less 15%, as we agreed. And we'll charge for the drinks served on a pro-rata basis.

Paul: Fine, fine, yes.

Pam: What type of...um...equipment, furniture would you like?

Paul: Well, let's have...um...four...no, no...five tables for our display. Er...we'll bring our own stands.

Pam: Right.

Paul: Now, there's an overhead projector and sound system already in the room, I believe? Can you get someone to check that, you know before we come, so that it's working?

Pam: Oh, of course, the technician will be with you when you're setting everything up.

Paul: Oh, well.

Pam: Oh, the seats in that room have flap-over desk tops, will that be all right?

Paul: Yes, yes, that's fine, sure.

Pam: You say you've sent out the invitations, any idea how many people there'll be? Um...I think you know there's...the capacity for the room is about 50, but 40 is ideal.

Paul: Yes, ah...the problem is that we won't know exactly how many there'll be until shortly before.

Pam: Can you let me know definitely by the Thursday?

Paul: Mm...no. But I'll have a rough idea and we'll budget for the number I give you then. We've sent out a hundred invitations . . .

Pam: A hundred?!

Paul: Yes, well, in theory that means that there could be two hundred people.

Pam: Yes, but the room won't . . .

Paul: But of course...haha...I don't expect more than about thirty to come.

Pam: But what if they do? This is the only room we have that day – there's a wedding reception in the banqueting rooms, so we . . .

Paul: Well, in that case, I suppose we could . . .

B   In this integrated activity students prepare and simulate a series of one-to-one meetings. The class should be arranged into an even number of pairs (pairs of pairs: Pair A and Pair B). To make the numbers match, there can be some 'pairs' of three.

The procedure is explained in the Student's Book, but here is an overview and some extra comments:

1   The two pairs decide who will play each role. Pair A will be the suppliers (supplying the services of their educational institution), while Pair B will be the customers (looking for a venue for their conference).

2   Pair A consider their facilities while Pair B make a list of requirements.

3   One partner from Pair B phones a member of Pair A: meanwhile the non-participating partners eavesdrop and make notes and comments afterwards.

   Alternatively, both partners could make simultaneous phone calls to their counterparts, so that everyone participates.

4   Pair A draft an agenda while Pair B list the actual questions they'll ask at the meeting in the next step. Maybe remind students of different kinds of questions they might ask or have to answer: open questions, probing questions, leading questions, etc.

5   Now we come to the climax of the activity: one member of each pair meets his or her counterpart in the other pair. The 'Observers' sit in on the meeting and make notes on their partner's performance.

   Make sure everyone knows how long the meeting should last and draw their attention to the expressions in the speech balloons in **A**.

6   Still in groups of four, the 'Observers' give their feedback. Then the two sets of notes that the client and salesperson made are compared.

7   Finally, everyone changes roles so that the 'Observers' have a chance to be client or salesperson (redoing steps **5** and **6**).

➡   Finish by asking the class what they learned from this activity – how different was the process to what might really happen?

11.3 Different kinds of meetings

This section deals with some of the differences between formal and informal meetings, and between larger and smaller meetings.

Vocabulary

on our behalf	economy class (AmE coach class)	influential	crockery
arising	club class (= business class)	safety rules	cutlery
advance	long-haul	cautious	
on-the-spot expenses	short-haul	verbal warnings	
contacts		leaking information	
sauna		territories	
		boundaries	

Procedure – *about 90 minutes*

A 🔊 As this conversation is quite long, it'll be helpful to PAUSE the recording at suitable places (marked with ★★★ in the Transcript). Give everyone time to compare their notes during each pause.

Note that the answers don't come in the same sequence as the agenda – people in one-to-one meetings may have an agenda but they don't always stick to it.

Suggested answers

Advance to cover anticipated expenses:
* How much should the advance be?
  Estimated expenses plus £200 for emergencies
* When should it be paid?
  At least ten days before date of travel
* How should they pay their on-the-spot expenses when abroad?
  Traveller's cheques and/or cash (– not with company credit card)

Air travel:
* Who should book & pay for the tickets?
  The company
* Who should check dates & times?
  The traveller him/herself
* What class: club or economy?
  Long-haul club (business) class (short-haul economy class)

Itinerary:
* Who should have copies of it?
  Everyone involved – especially the local contacts (in the foreign country)
* What details should be on it?
  Full names of everyone involved (not just initials) Their addresses and phone numbers

Accommodation:
* What kind of accommodation should we book?
  Somewhere central, comfortable and secure – not normally the most expensive hotel in town

---

Transcript [6 minutes 20 seconds]

Kate: David, thanks for coming.
David: You're welcome.
Kate: OK, I've sketched out a rough agenda, here.
David: Er...fine, yes, yes, that looks as if it covers everything. And I agree that we...we've simply got to sort out a procedure for preventing this kind of thing happening again. We...we do need some guidelines.
Kate: I think the basic problem is one of communication. None of the things that went wrong are really any single person's fault.

David: Right, now let's talk about J.L.'s report on the trip to Germany. As you know, J.L.'s self-employed, he isn't a member of our staff. But he was travelling on our behalf and we were supposed to make all the arrangements.
Kate: The first problem is about finance. He didn't ask us to give him an advance.
David: I know, yeah.
Kate: And then he complained later that he'd had to pay his expenses out of his own pocket.
David: Well, if he was supposed to pay for himself and

um…and then claim expenses later, the…the arrangement should have been explained to him.

Kate: We agreed that anyone who travels on our behalf, for whom we're making the arrangements, should receive an advance.

David: I wonder, should they have a…a company credit card, as our own salespeople do?

Kate: Oh, I don't think that's necessary. Traveller's cheques and some local currency in cash can easily be arranged. They can pick 'em up from a local bank – because, remember, some of these people live out in the country.

David: Yes, well now, how much should they get as an advance?

Kate: We need to estimate how much they'll need and add, say, I don't know, £100 for emergencies.

David: Well, I'd say £200 would be more realistic.

Kate: OK, whatever we estimate plus £200 in traveller's cheques. And we'll be responsible for booking and paying for the air tickets. Yes?

★★★

David: Yes. Now, right the next problem: no one met him at the airport – he had to make his own way to the hotel.

Kate: Well, he wasn't expecting to be met. It's easy enough to get from the airport to the centre of Frankfurt.

David: And…and the local rep was just as much in the dark – she hadn't been told his hotel address.

Kate: When he did finally meet up with the local rep, everything went smoothly I gather.

David: Well, that's fine, yeah, but he had to phone me and get me to phone them in Germany. He wasn't…he wasn't given a contact number in Frankfurt, only the address and the time of the presentation. I mean…he needed photocopies made. Luckily he speaks the language.

Kate: Well, he could have done all this without all this panic. Why didn't he just find somewhere to make the copies and then turn up at the arranged time? I don't understand.

David: He needed…he needed 300 copies and quite rightly he knew that would be expensive. He claimed that he couldn't find the room where the presentation was being held. He had the address, but it wasn't easy to find. He says he…well, he says he needed directions.

Kate: Maybe, but look, if he'd met up with the local rep, she could have done the copies at her office and then taken him to the venue. I just don't think we need to draw up town plans.

David: Anyway, how can we…how can we prevent this kind of thing happening again? That's the point.

Kate: Well, what we should do is to make sure everyone involved has a copy of the itinerary.

David: Yes, I agree.

Kate: And the names and addresses and phone numbers of the various contacts en route must be copied to everyone involved too.

David: Um, yes, yes, there's one point I'd like to make here. It's…it's about initials and first names. Now, I don't think it's clear to some people in the firm that although they know who D.J.P. and D.L.P. are, there isn't…this isn't at all obvious to an outsider or a new employee.

Kate: That's true.

David: Similarly, there are several Davids working for us – everyone needs to know whether 'David' means David Peterson or David Potts or David Adams, you know that's…I mean that needs to be made clear.

Kate: Yes, I agree with that. OK, full names should be used. Right.

★★★

David: Right, now then shall we move on to…heavens, F.E.'s problems in Japan?

Kate: Well, he did get an advance, but instead of getting traveller's cheques, the accounts department sent him a cheque two days before he was due to travel – he had to go off and buy the currency then.

David: Right, so we must make sure that the advance arrives some time before the date of travel. Um…um…ten days seem OK?

Kate: Mmm, yeah, that seems fine.

David: So, he was…he…in Japan he was met all right at the airport but the hotel he was taken to was somehow unsatisfactory: the room – what does it say here? – the room was too small, overheated.

Kate: Well, that's just bad luck. There's nothing we can do about that. Personally, I think he was just being fussy. But, I don't know, maybe we can issue some guidelines about accommodation, something along these lines: 'we won't pay for the very best hotel in town, but the one we do book should be good and central'.

David: I think that's fair.

Kate: That's very important. Because it wouldn't normally be the Hilton or the Holiday Inn, would it?

David: Well, well, it could be in some places – it depends. I mean, if you're in a very hot or dangerous place you need to be in a very comfortable, air-conditioned, international-style hotel.

Kate: All right. How many stars?

David: Oh, well, that's hard to say. I mean, the standards vary so much from country to country. I don't think we can define the standard in a realistic way.

Kate: OK. Now, you'd agree about the need for the accommodation to be central?

David: Yes, I would um…and preferably near the railway station. And it should be good enough for them to feel comfortable and secure. Swimming pool and sauna not essential!

★★★

Kate: Haha. We haven't talked about the other problem that J.L. had. Apparently his flight back had the wrong date on it, the 24th.

David: Oh, that's right.

Kate: He didn't notice this till the 25th, the day he was due to fly. Luckily, the flight wasn't full and they accepted the ticket with no extra charge.

David: Well, I mean, he should have checked the ticket, so that's…that's really his own fault.

Kate: But this needs to be made clear. I don't know, maybe a covering note when we send the tickets saying 'Please check that the times and dates of these flights are correct.' I don't know.

David: Yes, simple. Very, very good idea. We'll do that. And someone in your department must double-check this. Do we need to make it clear that flights would normally be economy class by the cheapest route? F.E. seems to have the…idea…F.E. seems to have the idea that he…he should have flown club class.

Kate: Well, actually, normally we would book club class on a long-haul flight. I think we should make this clear in the guidelines too.

David: Oh, well, I didn't...I didn't even know that!

Kate: Right, anything else?

David: Er...no, I don't think so, but let's meet again when we've circulated a report on this meeting and...and we've got some feedback.

Kate: OK. Can you just switch off the tape recorder?

David: Sure, I press this one, do I? Like this?

Kate: Yes. That's right.

B Draw everyone's attention to the suggested 'If ...' sentences at the end of this step. There are no 'correct answers' as the practice tends to vary from country to country and from firm to firm. In some countries decisions tend to be reached by consensus, while in others managers are more autocratic.

In general, it may be better to meet individuals if the problems aren't shared by or relevant to anyone else, or if the problem is too delicate for a public airing.

Ask each group to suggest which members of staff should be involved to solve each of the eight problems.

C The groups should consist of four or more people. Everyone is a member of the Staff Committee.

Before the meeting starts, the chairperson should look at the tips on how to conduct the meeting in File **80**, while the others see the points they will have to make in Files **24**, **54** or **78**. In a larger group two members can share a file.

The meetings take place. The group's proposals will be the basis of the meeting that follows in step **D**. Once completed, the proposals should be delivered to the group sitting on the left (anti-clockwise).

D The theme is the same, but now everyone has a different role. They are members of the Management Committee.

Again, before the meeting, the chairperson (who should be a different student this time) reads the tips in File **80**, while the others discover the costs of carrying out any proposals suggested by the Staff Committee by looking at Files **25**, **55** or **79**. The meetings are held.

Extra written work

Ask the groups to draft a short memo to the staff, explaining what action they intend to take on the proposals.

Once completed, the memo is delivered to the group sitting on the right (clockwise) and this is the management's reply to the proposals they sent in step **C**.

E Now in pairs, the roles change again with one partner playing the role of staff rep and the other the role of manager. The management's reactions to the proposals (and the memo if one has been drafted) are discussed.

Follow-up discussion

Discuss these questions as a class, or write them on the board for discussion in groups:
* What did you find most difficult in the various meetings?
* How well did the people in the chair control the meetings? Did everyone have a chance to put forward their points of view?
* If you were going to do the activity again, what would you do differently?
* How is the situation of staff vis-à-vis management in your firm similar to the simulation in this activity?
* Would such matters be dealt with in meetings or simply decided by a benevolent, paternalistic manager?

11.4 We need to have a meeting …

Vocabulary

duration
adjourn
decision-making

Procedure – *about 90 minutes*

A 🔲🔍 First a discussion, based on these recorded opinions and experiences. Pause the recording at the points marked with ★★★, so that the pairs don't have to try and remember all of the opinions and can just discuss the ones that are freshest in their minds.

Transcript   [1 minute 20 seconds]

Woman: Sometimes the participants aren't sure what the purpose of the meeting is.
Man: People always start to argue and then they get angry with each other.
★★★
Woman: What often happens is that the chairperson dominates the group.
Man: Yes, and the chairperson rushes through the agenda so that the meeting can finish on time.
★★★
Woman: Lots of meetings I go to have no written agenda.
Man: Well, for a start, there are too many items on the agenda. We can't possibly cover everything.
★★★
Woman: Well, often some members are late and then the meeting doesn't start until everyone has arrived. So we just have to sit there waiting until they come.

★★★
Man: Look, the meeting finishes late because too much time is allowed for discussion.
Woman: Yes, but not all the items on the agenda are dealt with.
★★★
Man: Well, you see, the chairperson encourages everyone to speak when they want to and proposals aren't made 'through the chair'.
Woman: The chairperson doesn't control the discussion and everyone talks at once.
Man: Because the chairperson asks the more senior people to speak first, the more junior ones are afraid to give their ideas.
★★★
Woman: No one is asked to take notes and keep the minutes of the meeting.

B The whole class should work together for this integrated activity. The purpose of the activity is to simulate the steps that are gone through to prepare a meeting from scratch and then hold it.

If possible, students should be encouraged to organize a REAL picnic, dinner or outing so that what is done in class has a direct, enjoyable outcome.

If your students feel that this is not a 'serious' enough topic for the meeting (i.e. not 'businessy' enough), you might like to choose a different topic.

For example, a class of students who are not themselves working could arrange a 'Careers afternoon' in which former students with jobs return to discuss their experiences, local employers are invited to send speakers, a careers expert is invited to talk about applying for jobs and interview skills, and so on.

Or students who are working in the same company might like to discuss a problem that is bedevilling members of staff at the moment (such as car parking arrangements, canteen facilities, etc.).

The procedure is explained in the Student's Book, but here is an overview of what happens:

1   Together, an agenda is drafted. The nature of the event needn't be decided until the meeting is held. Don't forget contingency plans in the event of rain, etc.

2 The point of having two groups is to give everyone a chance to exchange experiences later.

One student in each group is assigned the role of chairperson, who can be referred to the 'tips for chairing' in File **80**.

3 The meeting is held. Set a deadline, making sure this allows enough time for the remaining steps.

4 When the pairs compare notes, the chairperson can join in with one of the pairs.

5 In this step the two chairpeople work as a pair.

6 Probably as homework, everyone drafts a summary of their meeting in the style of a report that will be circulated among both the participants and the other people who weren't present.

7 Enjoy the picnic, or whatever!

C To round things off, here are some opinions from a magazine article about meetings – some of them are quite cynical. See which of them your students agree with. Perhaps ask them to pick out the three most valuable or interesting opinions.

Follow-up discussion

- What do you personally enjoy and dislike about meetings?
- What should you do to prepare for an important meeting?
- What is the ideal kind of room for a meeting? What equipment should it have? Should smoking be allowed? Should drinks be available?
- What advice would you give to someone who is going to take the minutes of a meeting for the first time?
- What advice would you give to someone who is going to chair a meeting for the first time?

Workbook contents for this unit

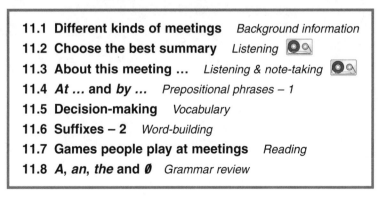

11.1 **Different kinds of meetings**   *Background information*

11.2 **Choose the best summary**   *Listening*

11.3 **About this meeting ...**   *Listening & note-taking*

11.4 ***At ...* and *by ...***   *Prepositional phrases – 1*

11.5 **Decision-making**   *Vocabulary*

11.6 **Suffixes – 2**   *Word-building*

11.7 **Games people play at meetings**   *Reading*

11.8 ***A, an, the* and *Ø***   *Grammar review*

12

Processes and operations

This unit aims to present and practise English as it is used both in the explanation of modern everyday machines and the processes they carry out. It also covers describing the operations needed to get machines to work and to show others how to undertake certain business operations.

The topics chosen inevitably appear to be specialized industrial and business processes. While it's not the specific task of this Business English course to prepare students to use 'technical English', there is an area of business activities where, for example, explaining how things work and instructing someone how to carry out certain operations will need to be mastered. This is dealt with in the first two sections.

Describing more abstract business-specific operations and talking about manufacturing processes are skills which are often required in business settings: for example, when receiving visitors or informing clients before a sale.

In addition, the ability to cope with and refer in English to problems that arise in the course of production processes is an activity which students need some practice in.

Background information

Draw everyone's attention to the Background information in the Workbook on processes and operations. This is important for students who have had little work experience.

Video

Programme 12 on the *New International Business English Video* introduces the theme of this unit. It deals with Swatch AG.

12.1 How does it work?

This section deals with everyday gadgets and machines: explaining how they work and the processes they carry out.

Vocabulary

electrical charges   *fax machine*
drum   *hard disk*
coated

Procedure – *about 90 minutes*

⚠ In each step, encourage students not to get held up with the details of the technical vocabulary, as far as is possible. Emphasize that knowing the technical terms doesn't necessarily help if you're explaining something to a client, or to someone who is new to the firm. They may need you to explain the process in *non-technical terms*.

Students will learn (or have learned) the technical terms they need on the job. Each process and industry has its own special jargon. Indeed each firm or even department may well have too. You have to know the jargon to talk to people within your 'business'. But remember that you also have to be able to use non-technical terms to people outside your firm, such as clients and visitors.

A This warm-up activity encourages students to think about and discuss some processes and objects similar to those they'll encounter later in the unit.

1 Photos:
a) an opened up VHS cassette
b) the gears on a mountain bike
c) an opened up photocopier
d) a TV remote control
e) an opened up fax machine

2 Encourage students to try out an explanation on each other. Perhaps ask a pair to perform in front of the class if you think their explanation is helpful.

3 Exact answers are not required. Indeed a couple of the gadgets will figure in the later steps. But if you want to help your interested students, the following may be of use.

VHS cassette: a digitally processed TV image is stored on special magnetic tape.
Gears on a mountain bike: they enable the wheel of the bike to be turned around by employing less energy and effort when pedalling.
Photocopier: the original is scanned electronically and a photographic image is then produced on paper by an electrostatic process using a special chemical powder (toner).
TV remote control: an infra-red ray connects the remote control to the TV set and allows you to adjust the controls without having to touch the TV set itself.
A fax machine: the original is scanned electronically and the image is converted into digital signals which are sent down a telephone line. At the other end a light source recreates the image in rows of tiny dots printed on heat-sensitive paper.

4 It is difficult to know exactly where to begin. Also you do not always know how much previous knowledge or experience your listener may already have of the machine. Such things make it hard to describe even simple operations in easy language for some people.

B **1 & 2** Students study together the explanations of how a photocopier works. Before starting this step check that most of the words for the processes and the words for the gadgets can be understood. There seems to be no perfect set of explanations that appeals to everyone. Some people hate pictures, others find it easier to follow only numbered steps, while still others have no apparent difficulty with discursively formulated writing. Of course in a foreign language a number of further factors come into play when reading technical explanations. Allow time for the pairs to ask questions about vocabulary and perhaps other things, before they go on to pool their views with another pair.

If time allows, perhaps select one or two groups to summarize the main things they liked about one of the explanations.

Most learners of English at this level can be expected to be familiar with, or may even have had experience of using a photocopier.

C 🔊 Play the recording in which someone explains the same process, namely how a photocopier works. There are two people: one explaining, the other listening and reacting. The recording shows how to explain something, preparing students to attempt a similar task in **D**, but there is one slight snag: the speaker makes three mistakes.

Answers

The three mistakes:

1 Instead of 'negative static electric charge' he should have said 'positive' charge.
2 He says 'the electrostatic charge destroys the light' instead of 'the light destroys the electrostatic charge'.
3 He forgets to explain that the coated paper has to be heated to make it permanent.

Transcript   [2 minutes]

Questioner: So how does a photocopier work?
Explainer: Well, basically they work on the principle of electrical charges. Modern photocopiers make use of static electricity – no ink is involved, as it used to be.
Questioner: Well, how do the marks get onto the paper?
Explainer: Well, if you open up the inside of the photocopier underneath where you lay the sheet of paper you want copying, you'll see...ooh, you'll see a lot of things going on.
Questioner: Well, what actually happens when you press the start button?
Explainer: Well, there's a drum, which is specially coated with a material which conducts electricity when light shines on it. This drum turns around. First it's given a negative static electric charge. That's very important.
Questioner: What does the light do?
Explainer: Well, you see, at the same time as the drum is being charged, your original which you've laid face down over the glass top is exposed a little at a time to a light which moves over the document. This image is projected onto the drum as it revolves and the electrostatic charge destroys the light.
Questioner: Right. But...um you said that the image, or printed material, that it no longer comes from ink, as it used to, so how do the marks get onto the paper?
Explainer: Mhm. Yeah, well before that can happen toner powder which is negatively charged is dusted or brushed onto the drum. And it is attracted to the charged parts on the drum. That is the toner sticks to those parts. And those are the marks on the document, that is, the parts that have kept their el...their static electric charge.
Questioner: Right. Yup.
Explainer: And w...after that comes the transfer stage. The sheet of copy paper is positively charged. And in this way it attracts the toner.
Questioner: And is that when it actually comes out of the photocopier?
Explainer: That's right.
Questioner: But why's the paper hot when it comes out of the machine?
Explainer: Ah, well, . . .

D For this role-play divide the students up into groups of four or five. One pair should look at File **26** and the others at File **56**. The role-play is divided into two phases:

1 First they have to work out in pairs or in a group an explanation of how a fax machine or a hard disk works using the diagrams. Later they'll have to explain how it works in their own words.
2 Give them sufficient time and then ask them to form new pairs with one of the other members of the group. Students should attempt to explain their product to their partner(s) in their own words.

12.2 What do I have to do?

This section gives students the opportunity to practise the skills of explaining operations, such as how to use a gadget and giving instructions.

Vocabulary

digital display	*beep*	*alarm*	*flashing*
feed it into the slot	*disconnect*	MODE	*up-date*

Procedure – *about 90 minutes*

A 1  Play the first conversation and ask students what the product was and how long it took them to work out that it was a photocopier. What clues helped them to work it out? Do the same thing with the other two conversations: a fax machine and the alarm on a Walkman.

2 Then play the first and second conversations again. Students should make notes on the four main points in each explanation. These are <u>underlined</u> in the Transcript.

The third conversation, where the woman is giving a hands-on demonstration of the alarm on a Walkman, doesn't lend itself to note-taking. But if you bring your own or a borrowed alarm or clock radio to class it can be used for a real hands-on demonstration.

Here's a picture of the one the speakers were talking about. The buttons the woman pressed were MODE, MINUTE (+), HOUR (−) and ALARM ON/OFF.

Transcript   [2 minutes 30 seconds]

First conversation

Woman: OK, Bob. So first of all, you <u>make sure that there's paper</u>.

Man: Yeah, uhuh.

Woman: Yes, fine...there. And then you <u>put the document down. Face down</u>.

Man: Mhm.

Woman: Right. And then you <u>indicate in the digital display here how many copies you want</u>.

Man: Mhm.

Woman: So that's...er...what? Two. We want two.

Man: Fine.

Woman: And <u>then you press the button</u>.

Man: Easy as that?

Woman: Yeah.

Second conversation

Man: OK, so you've got your document. OK. Two pages. So, <u>the first page</u>, OK, <u>you turn face up</u>.

Woman: Yeah.

Man: And you <u>feed it into the slot here</u>, and it takes it in automatically.

Woman: Oh, right.

Man: Yeah? And then you <u>dial the number</u> that you want.

Woman: What here?

Man: Just there, yeah. And you...you <u>press the green button</u>.

Woman: Right.

Man: OK. And it dials the number automatically.

Woman: Yes.

Man: And it connects with the fax at the other end. And...um ...and then it automatically sends the first page. It just feeds through.

Woman: Oh, right, yes.

Man: And then when the first page is finished, there's a 'beep'...and...er...and it's simple, you just feed in the second page.

Woman: Straight away after the other one?

Man: In the same way, that's right. That's right.

Woman: Right.

Man: Yeah. And then at the end there's another beep, which you ignore and wait for the...just wait for the line to disconnect and then you see the display there says: FAX DONE. And that's it.

Woman: Oh, right. Oh, I think I can manage that.

Third conversation

Woman: OK, so you want me to set the alarm for tomorrow morning?

Man: Show me how to do it, yeah.

Woman: OK, I'll show you. First of all, you press MODE.

Man: Yeah.

Woman: That's what it's set at now, 6.07.

Man: No, no, no.

Woman: Too early?

Man: Too early.

Woman: Right. I press this button. Now, 7.07?

Man: No. 7...7.30.

Woman: 7.30. OK. So I press the other button. 8, 9, 10 . . .

Man: It's a bit like the video.

Woman: It is a bit, isn't it? You just have to keep on pressing that button, until we get to 28, 29, 30. OK? Now press MODE again. But the numbers are still flashing. So . . .

Man: Right.

Woman: Press MODE again.

Man: Right.

Woman: That's 2.19 now. And then I press that and the alarm is set to come on.

Man: All right.

Woman: Tomorrow morning at 7.30.

Man: Excellent.

Woman: A pleasure.

Man: Thanks.

B Remind the students that they will be expected to use some of these expressions later in step **D**.

C For this step students work in pairs. One of them should look at File **62**, the other at File **68**. They follow the instructions there.

This activity may look like a game, but it's actually very challenging and simulates the kind of language used when explaining a technical operation to someone who doesn't know anything about it.

If your students find it difficult to get started, give them a clue, e.g. *Place your pencil on the paper just to the left-hand side above the small n, then go up under c, through d, over e, through the middle of f and below g . . .*

D **1** Students work in pairs and look at a diagram representing the process of booking a ticket for a flight. (The diagram is called an algorithm.) They have to try and work out where the three missing bits of information fit in.

Answers

a) Add to Provisional List
b) Up-Date Cash Record
c) Add to Firm List

2 Students work in pairs to see how the operation can best be described.

3 Students find a new partner to practise describing the operation. Allow sufficient time to answer questions arising from this activity.

Extra activity

Ask the students, in pairs, to draft a short set of notes explaining the process of booking a flight, which they could use to instruct a new employee in their company.

Then rearrange the pairs into groups of four. Students show their draft to another pair and compare drafts. Encourage them to say how helpful or otherwise they would find the explanation and to provide reasons for their opinions.

E The intention here is to give students practice in a 'hands-on' situation where they explain to their partner how to operate another machine or gadget, or how to carry out a process or an operation.

This step needs preparation and enough time to do justice to it – maybe postpone it to another lesson. Ideally, they need the thing itself in front of them to do this task.

Some suggestions:
- how to set the alarm on a wristwatch
- how to find out the price before VAT on some things you've bought, using a calculator
- how to record and play back voices on a cassette recorder
- how to make an aeroplane, a boat or a fortune-teller using a sheet of paper
- programming a video – ask several students to bring their video remote controls to class to use as realia

➡ Finally, allow time for the class to raise any questions concerning problems they may have had doing the activities.

Two more extra activities

1 Written instructions

❶ *Work in pairs* Read this fax from your distributors in France about the translation of the instructions for a new product. Find out why the writer was amused:

Dear Herr Gebhardt,

Today we had another ten minutes filled with laughter, thanks to your samples of instructions in French that we received today. They are full of linguistic errors which would make the product unsellable on the French market.

This is not the first time that we have drawn your attention to this. We refer you to our memo 'Notes on Instructions in French' dated July 3. We are relying on you to use your influence to prevent this happening again.

We certainly hope that you have not yet had these leaflets printed because such literature will put us on a level with importers of low-quality products from overseas — and our customers will not be amused.

Sincerely yours,

Jeanne Duvalier

P.S. I tried to phone you about this but you were not in the office.

❷ Here are seven genuine extracts from instructions in English. Find the errors and then correct them.

1 If the iron is standing on it's heel, pull the tank away from the iron.

2 Position stabilisation shelf on pins an tighten keyways. Prevent snapping out bey screwing locking bolt.

3 Even if the oven is provided with self-aeration, it is necessary that the furniture disposes of a chimney for the natural ventilation so as to exhaust the heat passing throught the oven thermal insulation.

4 So, no readjusted is usually required if you use the unit in the country where you brought it.

5 Finally lets summarize certain advices for a goog and safe procedure:
   – Clen away any grease or piant which covers the part
   – Never lay the vaiorus cables on parts which has just been welded

6 As soon as this glue has been dryed, which can be done with conventional equipment, it doesn't stick anymore.

7 If warning light and buzzer come on, drain water in fuel filter by loosing drain cook (1) and pumping knob (2).

The seven extracts haven't been modified: they're quite typical of what can be found in such leaflets. To show that this kind of thing isn't restricted to any particular places, we've shown the country of origin in the answers below.

Maybe the cause of all this is that instructions are written by a technical specialist, who then uses a dictionary to translate them into other languages. The moral presumably is to have all printed material checked by a native speaker before it goes to the printers. And later to have the printer's proofs checked too!

Suggested answers

These are corrected versions with more suggested amendments in brackets:

1 If the iron is standing on its heel (base?), pull the tank (water container?) away from the iron. (*Germany*)
2 Position the stabilisation shelf on the pins and tighten them clockwise (?). Prevent the shelf from snapping (slipping?) out by screwing the locking bolt. (*Germany*)
3 Even if (Even though??) the oven is self-ventilating, the room should be equipped with a chimney for natural ventilation so that the heat passing through the oven's thermal insulation disperses. (*Italy*)
4 Consequently no readjustment is usually required if the unit is used in the country of purchase. (*Japan*)
5 Finally, here is a summary of advice for successful (?) and safe operation:
   – Clean away any grease or paint which covers the part (unit?)
   – Never lay the various cables on parts which have just been welded
   (*not known*)
6 Once the glue has dried, which can be done with conventional equipment, it is no longer sticky. (*not known*)
7 If warning light and buzzer come on, drain water in fuel filter by loosening the drainage cock (tap?) and the pump knob. (*Cuba*)

New International Business English   This document may be photocopied.

2 Explaining

Work in pairs

1 Consider the following situations and explain to your partner what to do.
   • Explain to a friend who has bought a new camera how to put the film in.
   • Explain to a visitor how to use the automatic ticket machine on the underground/tram/bus/train system of your town or a town in your country.
   • Explain to a visitor to your country how to play a typical card game or chess.
   • Explain how to operate a compact disc player or video recorder.
   • Explain how to operate an old-fashioned record player.
   Take it in turns to explain.

2 Write down the main points that can't be left out of the instructions.

3 *Work in groups* Find another pair who have dealt with the same things. Compare the notes you've just made.

© Cambridge University Press 2000

➡ Perhaps ask some of the pairs to try out their explanations in front of the whole class.

12.3 A production process

This section presents the language used for describing modern manufacturing processes in one of the most common text types likely to be found in business English, namely the PR or advertising material aimed at the general public rather than the technical or specialist audience. The product chosen is an everyday consumer product – chocolate.

It's important to note that when highly specialized industrial and technological processes are being discussed there may be a heavy use of specialist language, terms and even jargon. This is unavoidable in technical descriptions, whatever the product. The description of chocolate production is no exception, but students should be encouraged not to let the technical terms distract them. It's important to remember that such specialized language will be encountered in whatever 'new' process one comes across. Chocolate has been chosen as a well-known product, but even here it's obvious that the tendency to special terms can't be avoided.

Vocabulary

ingredients	chocolate bars	precision
texture	chocolate assortments	bubbles
grinding / ground	product processing	crucial
roasting	processing and control technology	
	microprocessors	
	monitor	

Procedure – *about 90 minutes*

A Students work in pairs answering the questions about the production of chocolate by way of introduction to the product. This is a warm-up activity for the listening to come.

The first and last questions are open-ended. Only the second has predictable answers: cocoa, sugar and milk.

B Before playing the recording perhaps go through the technical terms for the stages of production and show how they are pronounced. On the recording an expert explains the various operations involved in the manufacture of chocolate. The recording may have to be played twice.

1 Students look at the flowchart of the process and number the operations listed in the box. They may find it helpful to write the names of the stages on the flowchart.

2 After the second hearing students should be able to distinguish clearly which of the stages belong to the actual chocolate production process and which to the preparing of the ingredients. In the Transcript the stages of the production process are numbered and printed in bold type, and the technical terms used are also underlined.

Answers

Stages 1 – 8 refer to the preparing of the ingredients.
Stages 9 – 12 refer to the actual chocolate production process.
The stages are all numbered in the Transcript on the next page.

Transcript [4 minutes 50 seconds]

Speaker: In the case of all Cadbury's chocolate products the basic ingredients are, of course, <u>cocoa beans</u>. We buy our cocoa beans from Ghana and some from Malaysia. 50,000 tonnes of cocoa beans are processed each year at the factory but that's before the actual chocolate-making process can be started.

When they arrive at the cocoa factory the cocoa beans are sorted and <u>cleaned</u> [1]. And then they're <u>roasted</u> [2] in revolving drums at a temperature of about 135 degrees. The actual time for roasting depends on whether the use at the end is for cocoa or chocolate.

Now after that, the next processes are called <u>kibbling</u> [3] and <u>winnowing</u> [4]. Well first, in the kibbling stage the beans are broken down into small pieces. And at the same time the shells are blown away by air currents. The technical term for that process is 'winnowing'. And so, then you've got the broken pieces of cocoa beans. And those are known as '<u>nibs</u>'. OK?

Well, now in the next stage the nibs are taken and **ground** [5] in mills until the friction and the heat of milling reduces them to a thick chocolate coloured liquid. The result of the grinding stage is known as '<u>mass</u>'. Now, this contains 55 to 58% cocoa butter and, of course, that solidifies as it cools. And it's the basis of all chocolate and cocoa products.

Cocoa *powder* is made by extracting about half the cocoa butter through <u>pressing</u> [6] in heavy presses. And that cocoa butter is later added back in the chocolate-making process.

Right then, now after the mass has been produced, we come to the actual chocolate-making process itself. I'm going to tell you about the production of *milk* chocolate.

Well, at the milk factory the mass, the cocoa mass, is <u>mixed</u> [7] with liquid full cream milk and sugar which has already been <u>evaporated</u> [8] to a very thick liquid. The resulting chocolatey creamy liquid is then dried. At that stage it's called 'chocolate <u>crumb</u>'. Then that's taken to our factories at Bournville and Somerdale in Bristol.

There, the 'crumb' is mixed with the additional cocoa butter and special chocolate flavourings. And this is then turned into a kind of <u>paste</u> [9]. And it's <u>ground</u> [10] again and pulverized further.

The chocolate, which has had sugar and cocoa butter added to the mass before grinding and pulverizing, now undergoes the final special production stages. Now, the most important component of chocolate as far as the texture is concerned, is the addition of fats. The final processes of '<u>conching</u>' [11] and then '<u>tempering</u>' [12] are essential in the process: they control the texture and <u>viscosity</u> of the chocolate before it can be used in the manufacturing process. Are you with me so far? Good!

Now 'conching' involves mixing and beating the semi-liquid mixture to develop flavour and reduce the viscosity and the size of the <u>particles</u>. Well basically, what this means is that it stops it becoming too sticky and enables it to be manipulated. And then comes the tempering. This is the last stage and it's crucial: what it means is mixing and cooling the liquid chocolate under very carefully controlled conditions to produce chocolate in which the fat has set in its most stable <u>crystalline</u> form.

It is the tempering of the chocolate that gives it the famous Cadbury smoothness, and gloss and the snap. Without this last process the chocolate would be very soft and gritty, and there'd be large crystals inside it and it would have a very dull grey appearance.

Well then, there we are, that's how milk chocolate is made . . .

C Students work in pairs and read the text about the recent production developments at Cadbury.

1 The first reading is to encourage reading for gist and 'tone'. The suggested answers include terms that underline the positive aspect of the processes described. Many of the words are typical of PR jargon, which tends to represent the sunny side of automation and labour-saving process manufacturing.

Suggested answers

- modernization programme
- the rationalization of production
- individual product processing
- the most modern processing and control technology
- specialist machinery
- the highest standards of quality control
- with such precision
- automation
- one person supervises the whole operation
- automation of the packing systems

2 If the highlighting of items in step **1** has not yet made it clear, students should be encouraged to focus on quality, precision ('speed') and increased productivity – a word which isn't used anywhere in the text, but which is clearly understood.

3 There follows a detailed reading phase. Students read the text once more and answer the true or false questions.

Suggested answers

True: 3 4 5 6 7
False: 1 2

D Students can be put into larger groups, say four or six, to compare their answers to the questions.

As not many students will perhaps have had experience of highly automated manufacturing processes, remind them that they could be concerned with the ways in which such manufacturing processes *may, might, can, could, should* or *ought to* be utilized, *if* they *should* be installed in new factories or be encouraged more generally in industry. You may wish to use these questions in a round-up session in which groups report back their conclusions to the rest of the class.

Suggested answers

If you wish to encourage discussion, in what is actually quite a controversial subject, you could interpolate some of these suggested answers.

1 It is clear that this is a controversial area. For one side of industry, automation cuts down on labour costs, for the other it destroys jobs. This can result in higher unemployment in some regions. But greater productivity may mean a better return on investment for the company shareholders. Swings and roundabouts, some might say.

2 Most people have their favourites. Minimizing risks to health and safety are arguments for some automation. Dangerous and toxic production processes, involving harmful chemicals and paints, are areas where they should be used more.

3 Workers freed from semi-skilled or unskilled jobs could retrain for socially useful jobs in hospitals and house-building, etc.

4 Potentially, there is no need for repetitive and monotonous work to be done by humans. In societies where such work is eliminated there may well, however, be a transitional problem concerning alternative occupations. For instance, criminality, violence and drug addiction have followed in cities in the USA where this road has been taken. Is this what our industrialists want? Do they care?

5 More highly skilled staff will perhaps be required for the management of automated and computerized processing.

6 This is a controversial question. In our contemporary economic system, despite the threat to the environment we are all aware of, little thought is being given to why we need more and more cars, machines and consumer goods.

7 This question is controversial. If you are out to maximize return on investment, minimizing your costs is important. If you do not wish poverty to spread throughout the world, you will perhaps wish to organize work processes so that everyone in society is engaged in socially useful occupations.

8 This is an open question. It all depends . . .

E Students can be asked to do this writing activity as homework if you don't have sufficient time in class.

At the end, ask the class what they learned from the activity.

12.4 When things go wrong ... What do we do?

This section allows students to engage in a report-writing activity in which they rehearse situations and practise the language connected with industrial operations.

Vocabulary

a wide range	*facilities*
streamline production	*standby crews*
handling equipment	*install*

Procedure – *about 90 minutes*

The newspaper article acts as a scene-setter for the subsequent documents. Be prepared to explain vocabulary and answer queries concerning the documents.

1 Students work in pairs for the first two steps. After reading the newspaper article they read the consultant's report. Ask them to try and decide what the difference is between a 'breakdown' and a 'bottleneck'. To get them to understand the gist, ask them to locate what has been going wrong and to attempt to find out what the cause could have been, as they read the remaining documents.

2 Students make notes and draft a report from the Chief Executive Officer explaining what happened.

3 Reassemble the students in groups of four (each pair with another pair) to compare notes. They read the report they have drafted and offer suggestions for improvements.

Allow time at the end for the class to raise any queries or difficulties which may have arisen in the course of the activity.

If you have students in the class who work in manufacturing companies or have knowledge of such processes, divide the class up into groups so that each group can interview them about whether they know of such breakdowns and difficulties or whether everything has always run smoothly.

Workbook contents for this unit

12.1 How things work   *Background information*
12.2 Doing things   *Vocabulary*
12.3 Explaining   *Functions & listening*
12.4 In ...   *Prepositional phrases – 2*
12.5 Anti-noise   *Listening*
12.6 About time   *Reading*
12.7 Modal verbs   *Grammar review*

Model report

12.4 When things go wrong ... What do we do?

**From the Chief Executive Officer
DELTA TOOLS
Southford SF4 HK3**

Vance Ballard
European Regional Director
Delta Tools Inc.
Monsstraat
Brussels
BELGIUM   20 May 20--

Dear Mr Ballard,

Problems at Southford Plant

You asked for a brief report concerning the recent events at the Southford plant.
   We have consulted the files and spoken to relevant members of the higher
management and thus feel able to provide an explanation for the breakdown reported
in the press on 17 May of this year.
   The cause of the breakdown was very simple. The handling equipment used to
deliver the components to the assembly line has been known to be in need of an
overhaul for the past six months.
   The plant has been working to full capacity to finish the American orders
according to schedule. As you know, we had commissioned a study by Industrial
Research Consultants. They submitted their report on April 5.
   In it they warned that there was not enough space available to store
sufficient components. They also recommended expanding the present two-shift
system to a three-shift one.
   We had decided to install a fully automated robot system. However, at the same
time it was clear to our production director that with the present maintenance
staff we would not have sufficient staff available if big problems were to arise.
The firm has been advertising for maintenance engineers for some weeks. We were
still only working a two-shift system so that the machines were not getting the
necessary cover.
   We all agree that the breakdown was extremely unfortunate and yet we must
admit that, under the circumstances, it was not entirely unexpected.
   We now believe that we have managed to sort out the major problems which we
had been having with the conveyor equipment. And also when the new robots are
installed in September, we feel certain that such problems will become a thing of
the past. Added to this the fact that the personnel department has been successful
in recruiting some highly qualified maintenance staff makes us confident that a
repetition of the events of 17 May now seems entirely unlikely.

Sincerely,

Hank Cruyff

Hank Cruyff

13 Jobs and careers

This unit covers all aspects of applying for a new or different job or for a promotion or new position within one's existing company. We consider the interview situation from the point of view of both interviewer and candidate. Most of the activities are also relevant to students who are unlikely to be interviewed for a job in English – though many international companies conduct part or all of their interviews in English these days, and may expect applications to be made in English too.

It should be borne in mind that different conventions apply to the processes of applying and interviewing in different countries. There are no international norms.

Background information

Students who haven't worked should study this information, which describes the process of applying for jobs and interviews and introduces some of the basic vocabulary.

Video

Programme 13 on the *Video* introduces the theme of this unit.

13.1 The ideal job?

Vocabulary

redundancies	*new initiative*	*on the dole*
volunteered	*recession*	*recruit*
transition	*flight slots*	*seasonal work*
academic	*cabin crew*	
jump at the chance	*from scratch*	

Procedure – *about 45 minutes*

To save time in the lesson, the article should be prepared for homework.

A This discussion is more than just a warm-up because it encourages students to consider some of the reasons why they, and other people, work.

Among the other aspects that might be added to the list are:

responsibility   being part of a team   being able to learn new things being able to tell other people what to do   a pleasant working environment good prospects for promotion   long holidays

B Although there may be a lot of unfamiliar vocabulary in this text, try to persuade everyone not to be distracted by this, but just to concentrate on finding the answers to the questions. A good way for students to show that they've found the answers is to underline the relevant parts of the text, rather than laboriously write them out.

Answers

1 a) the recession
 b) not getting flight slots at Heathrow
2 a) take up to six months unpaid leave
 b) share jobs
3 450
4 They seemed to enjoy work more on their return
5 Nine months' salary a year makes them better off than when they were in college or unemployed
6 Maybe – this partly depends on finding new recruits to participate

C Some of the reasons why this scheme worked so well for Virgin are: many of the staff are young and unmarried (so they can survive on less pay than breadwinners can); airline staff get cheap or free travel all over the world; it's easier to sell new ideas to young or new staff than to older, experienced staff.

At the end of this discussion, ask each group to report to the rest of the class:

- What were the most interesting points that were made?
- Which was the most controversial question they discussed?

➡ If you need more material now for the second half of a 90-minute lesson, you could start work on **13.2** right away – or you may prefer to use one of the following Extra activities.

Two extra activities

1 Application forms

We have not included an application form in this course, as forms are all so different from each other that showing an example would not be very helpful – it's much better if students can see a variety of authentic forms that they can relate to.

Ask each member of the class to bring in an application form that is used in their firm – if they can find one in English that would be wonderful. Also get some yourself (your Director of Studies may be able to let you have some) and show them to the class.

Look at these forms with the class and discuss how the various sections should be completed. Photocopy one or two of the forms you have discussed and get the class to practise filling them in.

2 Your own career history – *see overleaf*

It's important to realize that different countries have different conventions when it comes to CVs/résumés, application letters and supplementary information sheets. It's important to observe these conventions, as not just the information, but also the style of each may be important: which has to be handwritten or typed, which can be dot matrix printed, etc.?

1 This gives students a chance to discuss what the conventions are in their country. If possible, arrange the pairs so that those with less knowledge have a more experienced partner – it may be preferable to have groups of three to achieve this.

2 The drafts can be done in class, if there is time, or as homework. Once the drafts have been checked, students should produce a final version, preferably typed or word-processed.

➡ Once completed, these CVs will come in very handy in the simulation in **13.4**.

Your own career history

❶ *Work in pairs* Discuss what your own CVs/résumés will include. Make notes.

- What information will your CV/résumé include?
- What elements of the résumé in **13.2**B and the CV on this page will it include? What further details would you include in yours?
- How much space will you allow for your education and training, and how much for your work experience?
- How long will your CV be – can you fit everything onto a single side?

❷ Draft your CV and give it to your teacher to be checked.

❸ Rewrite your draft CV and, if possible, have it typed or word-processed.

CURRICULUM VITAE

Name: MARY BRENDA SCOTT

Address: 44 London Road, Winchester SO16 7HJ
Telephone: 01962 888990 (home)   01703 778777(work)
e-mail: 44maryscott@aol.com

Date of birth: 30 August 1979
Marital status: single

EDUCATION

Churchill Comprehensive School, Basingstoke   1990–1995
Winchester Technical College   1995–1997

QUALIFICATIONS

GCSE Maths, English, French, Geography, History, Spanish, Chemistry   1995
BTEC National Secretarial practice, Office Practice   1997

EXPERIENCE

Office assistant   Totton Engineering, Totton   1997–1998

Secretary to Sales Director   Totton Engineering, Totton   1998–1999

Personal Assistant to Export Manager Millbank Foods, Southampton   1999 to date

My work with Millbank Foods has involved responsibility for giving instructions to junior
staff and dealing with clients and suppliers in person and on the telephone. I have
accompanied the Export Manager to Food Trade fairs in Germany, France and the USA.

OTHER INFORMATION

I speak and write French and Spanish quite well (intermediate level). I am now taking an
evening course in German conversation.

OTHER ACTIVITIES AND INTERESTS

I play club basketball regularly and I sing and play guitar with a local country and western
band.

REFERENCES

Mr S.J. Grant, Personnel Manager, Millbank Foods, 34–42 South Dock Drive, Southampton SO8 9QT

Mr John Robinson, Sales Director, Totton Engineering, Cadnam Street, Totton SO23 4GT

Miss P.L. MacPherson, Head Teacher, Churchill Comprehensive School, Independence Way,
Basingstoke RG20 9UJ

13.2 Applying for a job

This section covers the writing of a job application letter and focuses on aspects of style that can be emulated or avoided in writing one's own letters and CVs. Step **C** looks at some of the problems people encounter when applying for jobs if they are discriminated against on the grounds of age, sex, disability, etc.

> ⚠ IMPORTANT: Ask everyone to read the various documents in this section through BEFORE the lesson: the job ad, the résumé and the application letter in **B** and the newspaper article in **C** – and if possible they should answer the comprehension questions in **C1** too.

This preparation is ESSENTIAL if you want to have enough time during the lesson for discussion.

Vocabulary

laser-printed	scratch a living	traineeships
CV	incident-packed	lagging behind
résumé	single-strand career structure	the oppressed
long-term prospects	criminology	discrimination
career history	sliding pay-scale	obsessed
administrative work	steady pensionable employment	high-flyers
product development	ageism	strenuous aptitude and fitness tests
presentations	culprit	a blanket upper limit
dynamic	irrespective of sex	arbitrarily
	creed	the rot sets in at 32
	ethnic origin	pressing concern
		alleviate

Procedure – *about 90 minutes*

A Again, this isn't just a warm-up. These questions encourage students to get to grips with some of the fundamental issues of self-presentation in writing. Different countries, different industries and different grades of job approach job applications in different ways.

B **1** After the pairs have discussed the ad, ask the whole class to say what the drawbacks might be – and then to say what the attractions seem to be.

2 The kinds of questions that one would like to ask Kevin might concern the kind of work he did with Valentine and Chicago, his period of unemployment, why he decided to become a travel guide, what subjects he enjoyed most at school, and maybe about his interests and hobbies.

3 Arthur Dent seems pretty suitable unless he's lying about his experience.

4 There are two possible approaches to this letter-writing task. It should be prepared in class but the actual writing should be written as homework.

There's a model application letter in File **81**.

EITHER
You may prefer your students to work on this from scratch. When they've finished they compare their work with the model letter in File **81**.

OR
If they need more guidance, you may want them to look first at File **81** and then adapt the model letter there.

C 1 If possible, students should have read the article before the lesson. The article contains a lot of tricky vocabulary, but the questions concentrate on the basic information and ideas in the text, in order to discourage students from getting bogged down in the vocabulary.

➡ This is an excellent text to use for 'guessing the meanings of words'. The meanings of most of the tricky words can be worked out from the context, without using a dictionary.
   Get the students to highlight any words they don't understand, and then work in pairs to try and guess the meanings.

Answers

The even-numbered statements are all true.
The odd-numbered statements are all false – note that Question 9 is *partly* true: you can get a job in the Civil Service up to 32, and in the Probation Service at any age.

2 The last question may raise some sensitive issues. But, if appropriate, you might like to discuss the wording of the British employment ads in the Student's Book and compare them with similar ads in your students' country.

13.3 Interviews

Vocabulary

assessment form	*use my initiative*	*eligible*	*long-range goals*
consultancy work	*commitment*	*bonus scheme*	*supplementary questions*
more scope	*get down to the nitty-gritty*		

Procedure – *about 90 minutes*

A We begin by exchanging experiences of interviews. If possible, arrange the groups so that each one contains at least one person who's undergone one or more interviews. If only a handful of people have ever been interviewed, do this as a whole-class activity. If no one, apart from yourself, has been interviewed, the class could ask you the questions.

B 🎧 The first interview is fairly humane and affable. We hear the beginning of the interview, which fades out before the end.
   In the second interview, the interviewer is giving the candidate a harder time. We join the interview just before the end.
   There are no suggested answers for the task, as it's a matter of opinion who performed better – but do spend time discussing which interviewer seemed more successful.

Extra activity

🎧 Play the two interviews again, but this time with pauses. Pause the recording at the places shown by ☆☆ in the Transcript. Ask students to suggest how they might answer each question. Then play the real response so that they can compare what they said with the answer on the recording.

Transcript [6 minutes]

First interview
Interviewer: Good morning, Miss...
Sue Jones: Miss Jones. Good morning.
Interviewer: Miss Jones, yes, right. Hi. Um...now, you'd like to join our team, I gather.
Sue Jones: Yes, I would.

Interviewer: That's...that's very good. Er...I'd like to know a little bit about you. Perhaps you could tell me...perhaps we could start...if you could tell me a bit about your education. ☆☆
Sue Jones: Oh yes, right. Well, I left school at 18 and for the first two years I went to Gibsons, you might know them,

they're an engineering firm.

Interviewer: Ah, yes, right.

Sue Jones: Um...and after that, I wanted to do a course, so I...I did a one-year full-time PA course and went back to Gibsons. I was PA to the Export Director. I stayed there for another two years and...and then moved on to my present company. Um...that's Europa Marketing...um...Mr Adair, the marketing director, offered me a job because Gibsons had...had worked quite a lot with Europa Marketing.

Interviewer: Oh, yes, Europa Marketing...yes.

Sue Jones: And I've been with them for three years now...um...first with the Marketing Director and...and now I'm with the Sales Director.

Interviewer: That's all very interesting, Miss Jones. Um...I...I'd like to know, what did you enjoy most at school? What was the course that you enjoyed most? ☆☆

Sue Jones: Ah...foreign languages I liked best.

Interviewer: Foreign languages?

Sue Jones: We did French and German. Yes.

Interviewer: Mhm. And are you quite fluent in those now or . . . ?

Sue Jones: Yes, a bit rusty now, but...um...obviously the more travel I can do the more I can use my languages and I'd like to learn another language. I'd like to add Italian as well.

Interviewer: Italian?

Sue Jones: Yes.

Interviewer: Very good, very good, that...that might be very useful. Now...er...tell me a little bit about...er...the work you're doing at present. ☆☆

Sue Jones: Um...well Europa Marketing is a marketing and publ...public relations company.

Interviewer: Yes, I've heard of it.

Sue Jones: And they do...they do consultancy work for companies operating in the UK and European markets. Er...our clients come from all over the world...um...we deal with some of them by...by post, but most of them come to our offices and at least once during a project. I assist the Sales Director by arranging these visits, setting up meetings and presentations and I...I deal with all her correspondence. I've not been able to go with her on any...on any of her trips abroad, but I...I've been to firms in this country, several times on my own...um...to make these arrangements.

Interviewer: It sounds as if you're very happy there, Miss Jones. I'm curious why you'd like to leave them and join our company? ☆☆

Sue Jones: Well...um...I know the reputation of Anglo-European and it has a very good reputation. And I feel that I would have more scope and opportunity in your company and the work would be more challenging for me. I might be able to possibly travel and use my languages because at the moment most of my work is...is rather routine secretarial-type work and I like the idea of more...um...challenges in my life really . . .

Interviewer: Yes, aha, aha.

Second interview

Interviewer: . . . yes, well, your CV seems pretty well up to scratch. Now, I wonder, can you tell me more about yourself? ☆☆

Tom Richards: Um...well, I...

Interviewer: Yes?

Tom Richards: I...I'm...well, I think I'm serious...serious-minded, I...calm . . .

Interviewer: You're calm?

Tom Richards: Yes, well, yes, I like a joke, though, good sense of humour. I don't panic in a crisis and I...I enjoy working with all kinds of people. I...I even like...um...p...people who are, you know, bad-tempered or something like that.

Interviewer: Yes, but wh...where do you see yourself in let's say five years' time? ☆☆

Tom Richards: Um...well, I...sort of the long-range thing. Well, I...I see myself in the public relations and...er...well, one day I must admit I would rather like to open up my own consultancy in my own home town.

Interviewer: Mhm, what is it specifically about Anglo-European PR that attracted you? ☆☆

Tom Richards: Er...well, first of all, I want to leave my present employers because they're a small company and...er...I know about Anglo-European PR, I mean, they're a...they're a good company, larger. I think I'll have more scope...er...the work will be more challenging. I mean, quite a lot of what I do at present is quite boring, it's...it's routine secretarial work.

Interviewer: And...and you'd like to move on?

Tom Richards: Yes, if I could, you know, hopefully to a job that gives me more opportunity. So I can use my initiative.

Interviewer: Mhm.

Tom Richards: Can I just ask you this question? Excuse me...I'd like to know if I get this job with Anglo-European, would I be able to...um...work abroad in one of your overseas branches?

Interviewer: Oh, yes, certainly.

Tom Richards: Oh, good.

Interviewer: Um...our staff regularly do six-month placements in other branches.

Tom Richards: Six. Oh well, that's good.

Interviewer: So I'm sure you might . . .

Tom Richards: Um...that's what I'm interested in.

Interviewer: Mhm. Can I...d...I know we're all human beings here and I'd like to know wh...what you consider your strengths and your weaknesses. ☆☆

Tom Richards: Um...strengths and weaknesses? Haha. Well, I...I mentioned before, I think my sense of humour...er...and my ability to work with all types of people is a particular strength.

Interviewer: Yes.

Tom Richards: My weakness? I don't know, I suppose I'm a bit of a perfectionist...I...I'm quite often dissatisfied with what I've done. I always think I can do it better, you know, or in a different way.

Interviewer: I wouldn't call that a weakness, I'd call that a strength.

Tom Richards: Well...ah...well, that's good, well...I mean, apart from that I...I suppose I get a little bit sort of full of the 'Wanderlust' and that's why I want to travel. I'm easily bored with repetition and...er...and procedure.

Interviewer: Do you have a lack of commitment? ☆☆

Tom Richards: No, not at all. No...er...once my goals are set and I've got the right sort of initiative then...er...I...I'm as committed as anybody.

Interviewer: Not one of these people who wanders off? ☆☆

Tom Richards: No, not at all.

Interviewer: Now...um...i...is there anything else you'd like to ask me? ☆☆

Tom Richards: Aha...yes, if I can just get down to the nitty-gritty: would the salary be reviewed at the end of the year?

Interviewer: Yes, the salary wi...the salary would be reviewed every six months. And after six months you'd also be eligible to share in the company's bonus scheme.

Tom Richards: Oh, I didn't know that. Oh, that's good, yes.

Interviewer: Right, well...um...time is pressing on, I'm afraid, so thank you very much for coming to see me and we'll be in touch with you before the end of the week.

Tom Richards: Good. Well, thank you for seeing me.

Interviewer: Goodbye.

Tom Richards: Bye.

C Now everyone thinks of advice they would give to a novice interviewee: get the groups to compare ideas afterwards.

Some more tips that might be added are:

- Make sure you know in advance exactly where the interview is to take place
- Take a pen
- Take your school and college certificates with you, and any testimonials you may have, and samples of your work
- Show your best side – don't stress your shortcomings, like how you hate getting up early in the morning
- Give a clear answer to each question – avoid answering Yes or No
- If you don't know the answer to a question, don't try to bluff your way out of it

Oh, and don't be tempted to have a drink beforehand to give yourself courage

D The difficult questions are recorded (the recording lasts 1 minute 50 seconds). Play them through before the pairs discuss the questions.

More nasty questions might be:

Does your present employer know you've applied for this job?
If you were me, what other questions would you ask?!
How would you describe the ideal person for this job?
What has been your most valuable experience?
When did you last lose your temper? Describe what happened.
What was the worst problem you have had in your present job and how did you solve it?
Describe your present job – what do you find rewarding about it?
What do you do in your spare time?
Describe your ideal boss.
What makes you think you'd enjoy working for us?
How would you describe your own personality?
What worries you about the job you're doing now?
What is the best idea you've had in the past month?

Pairs who can't answer some of the questions should ask another pair for advice. At the end, just check round the class which of the questions seemed the hardest.

> ⚠ Some of the questions are very challenging: you may feel you want to 'protect' some students from the experience of being put on the spot in this way.

E Rearrange the students. This role-play should be done with different partners, so that the probing seems more realistic.

Make sure there's time for everyone to have a turn at being interviewed. If necessary, postpone this to another lesson – but this must be done before **13.4**, which itself takes a good 90 minutes.

Finally, find out if any students have attended interviews where such difficult questions were asked. Do such questions serve a useful purpose, or is the difficulty self-defeating?

Two extra activities

1 Being interviewed

Work in small groups How would you feel in the following situations during an interview for a job you really want to get? What *exactly* would you say or do in each situation?

1 You are still waiting for the interview to begin half an hour after your appointment.
2 Unexpectedly, you find that you're going to be interviewed in a group with several other candidates.
3 You have to sit in an uncomfortable, low chair.
4 The interviewer hasn't prepared for the interview: he/she doesn't seem to have read your CV and application letter.
5 You take an instant dislike to the interviewer.
6 The interviewer never looks you straight in the eye.
7 You have a terrible headache. The room is very hot and stuffy and the windows are closed.
8 You are asked about your political and religious beliefs.
9 The interviewer receives a phone call which seems to be going on too long.
10 The interviewer talks too much and keeps interrupting you.
11 The interviewer keeps asking questions you can answer with Yes or No.
12 At the end of the interview you still don't have a clear picture of the nature of the job.
13 The interviewer doesn't tell you when you may expect to hear his/her decision.

2 Advice for interviewers

Work in small groups Here is some advice that might be given to an inexperienced interviewer. Tick the points that you agree with. If you only partly agree, give your reasons.

1 Make sure you are not interrupted or phoned during the interview.
2 Read the candidate's CV and application letter before the interview begins.
3 Ask the candidate to explain why he/she keeps changing jobs.
4 Make sure you have a clear picture of the nature of the job.
5 Ask each candidate the same questions.
6 Decide on a maximum of four key qualities required for the job.
7 Make sure the candidate has an uncomfortable, low chair.
8 Ask the candidate about his political and religious beliefs.
9 Only trust a candidate who looks you straight in the eye.
10 Trust your first impressions.
11 Never let the candidate feel relaxed.
12 Avoid talking too much yourself.
13 Avoid asking questions that can be answered with Yes or No.
14 Find out the candidate's opinions on a variety of topics.
15 Encourage the candidate to ask you about fringe benefits, the pension scheme and promotion prospects.
16 Tell the candidate about the scope of the job and its terms and conditions.
17 Interview groups of candidates, rather than one-by-one.
18 Tell the candidate when he/she may expect to hear your decision.

13.4 The Real Thing   *Simulation*

At first glance, this simulation may look a bit complicated. However, if you work out a realistic timetable on the basis of the suggestions below, it will go smoothly.

If you think all your students should have experience of both interviewing and being interviewed, you will need to do the simulation twice – but this may not be necessary as the 'interviewers' can learn a great deal about being interviewed by being an interviewer.

Vocabulary

panel of interviewers   corridor
give them a hard time   short-listed
look promising

Arranging the room

Depending on the size of the class, the room should be arranged so that the interviews can take place in relatively private conditions – in far corners of the room, for example. The candidates should congregate in a different part of the room, or better still, in another room or in the corridor outside the room. Ideally, each panel would receive candidates in a different room, but this may not be possible to organize.

Equipment required

Access to a photocopier *or* large sheets of paper, notice board / bulletin board and pins.

Timing

To give a rough idea of how long each step should take, here is a suggested timetable for the simulation in a 90-minute lesson with about 12 participants, divided into six candidates and two panels of interviewers.

This timing is given simply as a guide, and everything will depend on the time you have available and the number of participants.

A   15 minutes – Ideally, this should be done in a previous lesson, to allow more time for the interviews in **B3**.

B1   10 minutes

B2   15 minutes

B3   30 minutes (each panel conducts six five-minute interviews) – **This is the crucial part of the simulation: make sure you have a good 30 minutes for this, if necessary at the expense of previous and subsequent steps.**

B4   8 minutes

B5   2 minutes

B6   10 minutes

Documents

To save having to circulate documents between groups, and to add to the realism of the simulation, it is desirable to quickly photocopy the advertisements that the participants compose in step **A**, and their letters and CVs after step **B1**. This is not absolutely essential, however.

Roles

In **B**, the participants will be playing the roles of interviewers or candidates.
The INTERVIEWERS are 'Consultants' who will work as a panel of three (or two) to

choose the right person for the job on the employer's behalf. As the procedure is very thorough, each candidate may be interviewed by more than one panel. Each CANDIDATE has applied for one of the two jobs advertised.

Procedure – *about 90 minutes*

A For this preparatory step, the class is divided into two groups – each will produce a different job advertisement. If you can't photocopy the completed job ads, ask students to use large handwriting, so that the ads will be easily legible when posted on the class bulletin board.

If possible, do this step in a previous lesson so that there is more time for the six steps in **B** – particularly the interviews themselves.

B In the procedure given here, there is additional information for the teacher as the CONTROLLER of the simulations.

Before step 1 Rearrange the class into two groups and assign roles – this should be done at random and the two groups should not be the same as the ones in step **A**. There should be an even number of candidates; each interview panel will consist of three members, or possibly just two. If in doubt, have more interviewers than candidates.

➡ If your students wrote their own CVs in **13.1** (Extra activity) the CANDIDATES should use them here. If they don't have their own CVs available, just application letters will be OK.

If your CANDIDATES need more time to write *long* application letters, these should be drafted beforehand as homework – otherwise the ten minutes allowed for this in step **B1** won't be long enough.

1 Each panel of INTERVIEWERS discusses what they will be looking for and what questions they will ask. Meanwhile, each CANDIDATE writes a (short) application letter.

Before step 2 Collect the application letters (and CVs if your students have these). If possible, photocopy them so that each panel of interviewers has a complete set of these.

If this isn't feasible, then circulate the letters and CVs between the panels until they've seen them all – in this case the candidates will have to take their own letters and CVs to each interview in step **3**.

2 Each panel of INTERVIEWERS reads and assesses the application letters. Meanwhile, each CANDIDATE works with another candidate to prepare themselves for the interviews. They look again at the difficult questions in **13.3**.

Before step 3 Arrange the panels of interviewers and candidates in different parts of the room (or different rooms if possible, see above). The timetable should be announced and displayed, so that the interviewers know exactly how long they have for each interview. Ideally, each panel would see every candidate, but if this isn't feasible, make sure each panel sees at least three candidates – and preferably each candidate should be interviewed twice.

3 Each panel of INTERVIEWERS receives a different candidate in turn. There is further guidance for the INTERVIEWERS in File **82**, where they are advised to assess each candidate's experience, personality and potential.

Meanwhile, the CANDIDATES wait to be called to one or other panel and, between interviews, sit silently or chat (nervously?) with other waiting candidates.

4 All the panels of INTERVIEWERS meet together in the same part of the room to discuss the various candidates for the two jobs and make a short list of three for both.

Meanwhile, the CANDIDATES meet 'in a café' to discuss their own performance at the interviews and to decide which panel performed best.

5 The whole class reassembles for a feedback session: the INTERVIEWERS announce their short lists and the CANDIDATES announce their preferred interviewers.

6 In the follow-up discussion, find out how everyone felt at the different stages of the simulation: relaxed, confident, authoritative, nervous, etc.

Workbook contents for this unit

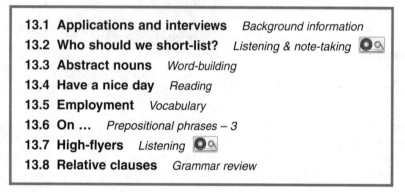

13.1 **Applications and interviews**   *Background information*
13.2 **Who should we short-list?**   *Listening & note-taking*
13.3 **Abstract nouns**   *Word-building*
13.4 **Have a nice day**   *Reading*
13.5 **Employment**   *Vocabulary*
13.6 **On ...**   *Prepositional phrases – 3*
13.7 **High-flyers**   *Listening*
13.8 **Relative clauses**   *Grammar review*

Extra activity: A progress interview

It's quite common for companies to hold progress interviews, to see how their employees are getting on. And trainees on long-term training courses are also interviewed.

Procedure *– about 60 minutes*

A This is an introduction to the topic.

B Everyone, working in pairs, makes a list of some suitable questions. Discuss these with the whole class before beginning step **C**.

C This step depends on having groups of three (or four) – the pair who are participating in the interview are 'observed' by their partner(s), who afterwards make comments and evaluate both participants. The observer(s) should sit slightly apart from the participants so as not to put them off. Perhaps point out that in business it's not uncommon for there to be an observer who disconcertingly doesn't participate in the interview.

File **A** contains role information for the interviewer. File **B** contains role information for the interviewee. File **C** contains guidelines for the observer.
   As there may need to be four interviews (in groups of four), allow plenty of time for this.

D The written reports would probably be done as homework, though prepared in pairs in class.

E Finally, there is a follow-up discussion.

Progress interviews / Staff assessment

Employees often take part in a 'progress interview' (also called a 'review' or an 'assessment interview') at least once a year, during which they can discuss their performance and the development of their career. Participants on training courses often take part in similar mid-course/mid-term interviews too.

A *Work in pairs* Read these comments on progress interviews and put them in order of importance:

For employees, it's necessary:	The company and the managers can:
☐ to know how they are getting on in their jobs	☐ benefit from closer contact with individual employees
☐ to have the opportunity to discuss their work in detail with the boss	☐ find out what their employees do well or could do better
☐ to discover their own weaknesses	☐ review the performance of their staff by interviewing them
☐ to find out what the boss thinks of them	☐ benefit from interviews, because they create closer working relationships
☐ to find out how to work more effectively	☐ find out which people should be promoted
☐ to discuss their future within the organization	☐ make employees believe in the company more
☐ to see how their careers are developing	☐ find out which employees can benefit most from further training

B *Work in pairs* Make a list of ten questions that might be asked at such an interview in your firm (or during the course you're doing now).
`Here are some examples:

What have been your most valuable experiences with us so far?
Which parts of the course have been least valuable to you?
What particular difficulties have you had?
How well do you get on with the other members of staff/participants?

C *Work in groups of three* You will be taking part in three separate interviews: as interviewer, as interviewee – and as 'observer'.
The observer's role is to make notes and give advice to the other two on their performance in the interview.
When it's your turn to be the interviewer, look at File **A**; when you're the interviewee look at File **B**; when you're the observer look at File **C**. This flowchart shows how the activity works:

❶ Student A plays the role of interviewer, B is the interviewee and C is the observer.
⬇
The observer gives feedback to A and B.
⬇
❷ Student A is the interviewee, B is the observer and C is the interviewer.
⬇
The observer gives feedback to A and C.
⬇
❸ Student A is the observer, B is the interviewer and C is the interviewee.
⬇
The observer gives feedback to B and C.

D *Work in pairs* Draft a report of the interview from the perspective of the manager. Decide whether you would recommend the employee for promotion. Give reasons for your decision.

E *Work in groups* Look at another pair's report and discuss these questions:
- What decisions did they come to?
- What experience do any of you have of such interviews?
- What is your opinion of them?
- How is progress monitored in your country/company?

A You are the BOSS.

Imagine that you are interviewing a member of your staff about his or her progress in the job so far. Give your opinion of his or her performance and find out what he or she thinks of the work so far.

Perhaps start like this:
'Come in and have a seat. I'd just like to talk to you about your work so far . . .'

B You are the EMPLOYEE.

Imagine that you are being interviewed by your present boss about your progress in your work so far. Find out how well you have been doing and let your boss know what you think of the work so far.

C You are the 'OBSERVER'.

As you listen to the interview, make notes on these points:
- What impression did each person give?
- If they were nervous, how did this affect their performance?
- Were there too many Yes/No questions?
- Which questions did they answer badly?
- Which questions did they answer well?
- What advice would you give them for their next real interview?

Unit 13   Jobs and careers

Sales and negotiation

This unit looks at various aspects of sales, including the preliminary demonstration and the stages of commercial negotiations. Both face-to-face and telephone negotiation are covered, in which agreement on prices, quality of product and delivery, etc. are sought co-operatively by both parties.

Background information

Before beginning this unit, students should read the Background information in the Workbook. This is particularly important for students without business experience.

Video

Programme 14 on the *New International Business English Video* introduces the theme of this unit.

14.1 Selling and buying

This section introduces the activity of selling and encourages students to think about both sides of the sales process.

Vocabulary

service engineer
cheated
'hard sell'
'soft sell'

Procedure – *about 45 minutes*

A This warm-up activity helps to focus students' attention on the widespread and diverse forms that selling and buying can take. The range from everyday to specialized products reflects numerous possibilities for using English in international and other business situations.

B Students can work individually or in pairs or groups. Point out that the text is from a training manual for sales staff.

Points you might want to stress in a discussion:
- The importance of building up a good relationship with your clients.
- Belief in one's own product is often stressed at training sessions. This will include being fully informed about its specifications, etc.
- It is important to be adaptable. With one particular customer you may need to emphasize the price of the product, while with another the delivery times may be central.

Draw attention also to the mention in the text of the importance of questions. This is a point which will be taken up in more detail in **14.3**.

14.2 The sales process

This section deals with the stages which a sales interview ideally goes through, when you meet a client or when a salesperson visits you to sell you something. We see that there are three stages: the Opening Stage, the Building Stage and the Closing Stage.

Either before or perhaps after step **C**, it may be helpful to make explicit the distinction between 'sales pitch' and 'negotiation'. The first is a case of demonstrating the product. This is presented in **14.1**, as we have seen. Section **14.3** gives students a further opportunity to practise the sales demonstration aspect of selling. In business, demonstration and order placing are often separated in time or even in terms of personnel. That is to say, the demonstration prepares the way for the negotiation. In international business interaction this division of labour is likely to be the norm.

This section focuses explicitly in a non-technical fashion on the stages or phases involved in taking and placing orders. This is itself perhaps the most common kind of commercial 'negotiation'. Indeed, even non-business people regularly engage in such transactions, so they are seldom dignified by the term 'negotiation'. (See the Background information in the Workbook.) The section anticipates **14.5**, with its more serious and 'technical' treatment of what is, after all, the same basic activity.

Vocabulary

rehearse

Procedure *– about 45 minutes*

A Students work in pairs. This is a pre-listening activity designed to focus students' attention on the general gist of what is involved in the sales process before they listen to the recording.

Answers

1 product   2 weaknesses   3 buying   4 before   5 wants
6 client   7 individual

B 🔊 Students work in pairs. This is a listening-for-gist activity.

Answers

1 A typical sales interview where you meet a client or a salesperson visits you
2 The Opening Stage, the Building Stage and the Closing Stage

C 🔊 Students work in pairs. Before you play the recording a second time give the students time to read through the summary.

Answers

The missing words are in italics.
1 The *Opening* Stage:
  usually a phone call. You have to talk to *your client* in person – not his/her *secretary*. Identify yourself and arrange an *appointment*.
2 The *Building* Stage:
  a) prepare and *rehearse* with a *friend* or *relation*.
  b) dress suitably for the *occasion*.
  c) behave in a *friendly*, confident but *business-like* manner.
  d) don't spend too long on *social conversation*.

e) show that you're a *responsible, trustworthy* person.

f) mention *well-known* firms who use your product.

g) tell the client about the *benefits* of your product.

h) encourage your client to talk by *asking (him/her) questions* and only talk *half* the time yourself.

3 The *Closing* Stage:

recognizing exactly when your client is ready to *place* the order.

This depends on *timing*.

Finally, *thank* your client for the order and leave.

Transcript   [4 minutes 20 seconds]

Workshop leader: . . . All right then everybody, if...um...we look at a typical sales interview where you meet a client or where a salesperson visits you to sell you something, we see that there are three stages: the Opening Stage, the Building Stage and the Closing Stage. And we should add to these stages other activities that will take place when you are not actually meeting or talking to a client: Preparation and Planning.

So let's look at these stages one by one. If you have any questions don't be afraid to interrupt. Now, the first stage, one, is the Opening Stage. Usually this is a phone call. But you might be preceding it with a letter, or a brochure or something like that. The first thing you have to do is get past the secretary, that's the most important. Find out when exactly you can talk to your prospect. Don't accept a promise to ring you back, ever. And you need to explain who you are and what you're selling. And arrange an appointment. Right?

And two is what we call the Building Stage. In other words the sales interview itself. It's important to prepare well and rehearse doing this sales interview. OK? And you can role-play it with a friend or a relation. Erm...and now this person should try to be unfriendly and unco-operative and difficult, to give you the right sort of practice. OK? Then dress suitably for the occasion. OK, think about that. Behave in a...in a friendly, confident but business-like manner. Right? And remember not to spend too long on social conversation, it makes people impatient, before getting down to business. And remember that your client is a busy person. So respect that. Try and show the client that you're a responsible, trustworthy person, which of course you are. Tell the client about all the other well-known firms who use your product. Let the client know the benefits of the product. But, make care...be careful that you don't do all the talking. Ask him questions. And make sure they're open questions, not ones he can just answer with a yes or no, to find out what his needs are. So that you can match your product to those needs and to find out how large and how frequent an order he may place. That's important. You should talk only about half the time. Make sure of that.

Man: Oh...erm...what about objections? I always find that the hardest thing to deal with, when a client starts giving you reasons why he doesn't need to buy your product. Um...how do you deal with...er...objections?

Workshop leader: Well, objections suggest an interest in the product. The client may be...may be looking for arguments to use to justify to his superiors or his colleagues, for buying your product. And if you can answer these objections, you're well on the way to making a sale. But the important thing is to prepare answers to all foreseeable objections.

Man: Right, yeah.

Workshop leader: And give your prepared answer or if you don't have an answer, tell the client about a...a further benefit. I think the important thing is not to spend too long trying to answer an objection. It gives it too much importance. And, remember, don't argue with the client. And finally, you get to stage three: the Closing Stage – recognizing that your client wants to buy and is on the point of confirming that order. Now, this is the hardest part, because it depends on timing. You have to judge when your client is ready to place that order. Then you can thank him for the order and go on to your next appointment. Now there's one more thing. Once you have a promise of the order, if it's a new client, do remember to check their financial status. And sometimes even if it's an old client, don't start work until you have a written confirmation of the order. That's very important . . .

14.3 Selling your product

This section starts off with a listening activity which provides a model for a sales demonstration.

The activity in step **B** requires students to do preparation at home. Announce this in good time – or postpone the demonstrations to another lesson, perhaps before doing **14.4**.

Vocabulary

sales rep	*exposure and focusing*	*up-market*	*random objection*
end-user	*processed*	*down-market range*	
viewfinder	*micro-lens*	*appeal to*	

Procedure – *about 45 minutes*

A

1 Students work in pairs. They are listening for overall gist. Play the recording for the first time and discuss the questions. The notes of the customer's questions will be of use when hearing the demonstrations in step **B3**.

Answers

The aspects NOT covered are: *after-sales service* and a *guarantee period*.

2 Play the recording a second time and give students time to number the summary notes.

Answers

1 When you look at a Nimslo 3-D print you get an amazing feeling of depth and realism.
2 The cost to the end-user will be under £100. Plus the usual trade discount.
3 It's not possible to let you have the goods on sale or return.
4 We're running a national advertising campaign.
5 It uses normal 35 mm film.
6 Special introductory offer: first three films are processed free.

Transcript   [2 minutes 20 seconds]

Salesman: . . . yes, well, the best thing to do is er...take a look at this print here. You see you get an amazing feeling of depth and realism. And, well, I mean it's as if you're really there, isn't it? You don't need any special glasses, you know, anything like that.

Customer: Hmm. That's very impressive. Mm...what's the price and...and what sort of discount are you offering?

Salesman: The cost to the end-user would be under £100. And we're obviously offering the usual trade discount.

Customer: Mhm, I see. Well, I might be prepared to take...er...let's see, well, ten on a sale or return basis for each branch...er...that's 50 altogether.

Salesman: Ah, er...problem: I'm afraid...er...can't let you have the goods on sale or return because, well, the demand's going to be very heavy.

Customer: Well, the problem is, you see, it does look a bit complicated for the beginner to use.

Salesman: Oh no, not at all, no. Look, if I could just show you, you see, you just look through the viewfinder here, press the button and...er...the automatic exposure and focusing system takes care of the rest.

Customer: Mm...er...do you have any point of sale advertising material?

Salesman: Yes, we have this showcard and a nice colourful poster.

Customer: Oh yes, that's very good, I like that, yeah.

Salesman: And we're running a national advertising campaign, so...er...end-users will be fully aware of the product. And...oh...there'll be this double-page spread in the Sunday colour magazines next month. You see, it answers all the questions people may want to ask about the product.

Customer: Mm, I see. Well now, presumably the camera needs a special film?

Salesman: No, no, it uses normal 35 mm colour print film. Er...the films are processed by us in our computer-controlled laboratory. The four images...er...from the four lenses here, they're printed onto a special micro-lens material to form one single image. And...oh...and we're running a special introductory offer – end-users' first three films are processed free.

Customer: Yeah, that's good. Well, I'd like to know...mm... what'll happen if the product doesn't take off and...er...you stop manufacturing it – will the laboratory still operate? Um...I mean, will my customers be left with a piece of equipment that they can't use?

Salesman: No, there's absolutely no danger of that whatsoever. This product is going to be a big success. Er...the reviews in the trade press have been fantastic. Take a look at this one, for instance . . .

B As suggested above, the first two stages should be done at home before the lesson. Students who wish to work together on this should be encouraged to do so. Maybe you could demonstrate a product you have recently acquired, to start the ball rolling (perhaps a toy belonging to a child, or a cassette or CD). As the demonstration stage may be intimidating and very time-consuming in a large class, it should be done in groups.

C In this role-play students will be acting out two sales meetings. Arrange the class into an even number of pairs (pairs of pairs). Any groups of three can share roles and become a 'double act' in each part of the role-play. Remind them to try to use questions like the ones they noted down in **A1**.

1 Student A, looking at File **28**, plays the role of salesperson, representing an importer. Student B, looking at File **83** plays the role of a customer: chief buyer for a mail order company. The sales rep has to describe the features and benefits of a new product, while the customer has a list of queries. The product described and illustrated in File **28** is a miniature telephone recorder.

2 Now the roles are reversed: student A becomes the customer and looks at File **83**, while student B becomes the salesperson and looks at File **58**. The product described and illustrated in File **58** is a Bulldog Alarm.

Give the students this task for homework:

Draft a short report on one of the meetings you had in **14.3C**, describing what happened and the outcome. Imagine that this report will be read by your superior, who is away this week.

Extra activity

The three case studies below can be shared out among the groups if time is limited. Call on your most experienced students to decide which of the suggested courses of action are wise or unwise.

As homework, students could be asked to select one of the cases and write up their explanation of what they would do. There are by definition no 'correct answers', but, notwithstanding this proviso, some rather subjective scenarios are provided overleaf.

New International Business English   This document may be photocopied.

Three customers – three case studies

Work in groups What would you do in these situations? How would you deal with these customers?

Mr A always keeps you waiting 20 minutes when you've made an appointment to see him. He never looks at the literature you leave him but seems equally unfamiliar with your competitors' products. He seems very cautious and says he has to consult his colleagues before making a firm decision, but regardless of this, when you make your next visit he always says he hasn't had time to do so.

Mrs B regularly places small orders with you, but could order substantially more. Instead she orders from your main competition. She seems to enjoy telling you that your products are too up-market for her customers. Your product range is very competitive, and anyway you do have a more down-market range that you know she knows about. She always says she's in a hurry, but can still find time to criticise your company.

Mr C keeps raising objections to your products: he says they are too expensive, that he's worried about your after-sales service, that your new technology may not be reliable, that your design may not appeal to his customers. Just when you think it's time to close the deal, he raises yet another random objection and declines to place an order.

© Cambridge University Press 2000

Suggested possible scenarios

Mr A

State that you are glad to wait for him, as it will mean that it will be worthwhile this time, you hope. But add that if it is likely to happen again that he is so busy, perhaps it may be preferable to ask to see his assistant next time. It may even be advisable to send the promotional literature in advance to his superior. If he would prefer this to happen, you can offer to leave and to return on an occasion more convenient to all concerned.

Mrs B

You might offer her an increased discount, if she is prepared to order more next time. Offer to show her the catalogue for products in the lower price range, in case she has lost the one you sent in advance. Tell her that she would be able to benefit from taking a longer look this time at the products which are clearly qualitatively far better than anything the competition currently has on offer. Emphasize that your competitors are still offering largely out-of-date models as the latest design. This is a method your own company would never engage in.

Mr C

Tell him that you understand his fears concerning the price, but since the beginning of the year you have acquired some new after-sales engineers and the problems he mentions with after-sales service are now a thing of the past. Moreover, the slight difficulties with the new technology were simply teething troubles which have now been satisfactorily resolved. It's perhaps worth giving the new-look product a chance, since in the trade journals it has been certified as being twice as fast as the old model, despite appearances. It is, after all, performance that counts. Despite his unwillingness to place an order this time, tell him that you are convinced that you will be able to do business in the future. Thank him for his time and promise to call again next month, when you will be able to offer him a number of new articles which you feel will be just the kind of item he will be able to use.

14.4 Negotiating on the phone

This section presents telephone negotiation and the use of follow-up faxes, followed by an integrated activity.

Preparation: Ask your students to read the Background information in the Workbook. (There are different types of commercial negotiations, negotiation styles and negotiation situations.)

Procedure – *about 45 minutes*

A   In this listening activity we hear a Central European buyer and a Dutch salesperson negotiating a large order for yogurt. Students should be encouraged to listen to the overall pattern of the conversation. Note that there are no 'correct answers' to the questions in the Student's Book.

Suggested answers

1 Price, quantities and delivery date
2 Many significant points are made by both sides: the supplier makes it clear that they need exact figures, the buyer wants an acceptable price, and so on.
3 Both people have important points to make. This demonstrates the mutual interest in a successful outcome.
4 In particular the salesperson needs to think, and probably to decide with a colleague what to do next. This will be followed up in a fax.
5 The fax contains the next step in the negotiation. 2,000 tonnes can be delivered and a price, quality (Splendide variety) and a delivery date are proposed.

Transcript [2 minutes 30 seconds]

Irena: Let us talk about the yogurt deliveries for the Central European market and the North European market.

Jan: Yes, sure.

Irena: Is that OK?

Jan: Yeah, you know for the North European market I can deliver the yogurt fairly quickly.

Irena: The North European area is not going to be a problem, I have approval. But I need to know about the Central European area.

Jan: Yes.

Irena: I am sure we can do a good job.

Jan: Yeah, but you will have to give me some idea about amounts or quantities, because that way it is easier to get it through our organization, you know. They need sometimes time, but if they know something about quantity, they will be more interested.

Irena: Well, I can't say exactly. They depend on price and quality.

Jan: Oh, yes, of course.

Irena: If you like, I'll send you a fax and I shall be very open.

Jan: Er...yes.

Irena: I can put in writing to you, that, say, in quantity terms, that we can take two thousand depending on the price and quality. And then if you come back to me by fax, I can tell you in my fax what I think. And I can tell you, if your quality is not good and your prices are not competitive, then that'll be the end of our business.

Jan: Sure, of course, I understand. But if the quantity is interesting, I am sure that our organization . . .

Irena: In that case.

Jan: Mrs Eichelberger...I'm sure we can be flexible, because we need, and want, figures or quantities.

Irena: I, that is, we are not talking less than one thousand tonnes . . .

Jan: Good.

Irena: I am ready to say even a minimum of one thousand tonnes.

Jan: Yes, good.

Irena: But what if the matter is pushed through quickly? Will everything be OK?

Jan: Yes, of course.

Irena: Perhaps things will move too fast for you and then maybe we'll find that the prices you are quoting us are much too high and the quality is not good and then . . .

Jan: And then you will have to tell us.

Irena: Yes, then maybe we will stop the order, I tell you, because of that.

Jan: Yes, I see.

Irena: And so can't you let us have one thousand tonnes now?

Jan: That might not be easy, because . . .

Irena: You don't want to do it, that's all.

Jan: It depends, you see.

Irena: OK, then, we'll give you time to decide. How long do you need?

B This is a telephone role-play in which student A, looking at File **29**, plays the role of customer or buyer, negotiating an order for yogurt. Student B, looking at File **59**, plays the role of a salesperson or supplier, and student C, looking at File **84**, as the non-participating 'Observer' eavesdrops, makes notes and comments afterwards on the transaction.

For students who still have little imagination, even at this late stage in the course, perhaps indicate how the role-play might get started:

Buyer: Good morning. I'm calling about a large order for yogurt.
Salesperson: Can you give me some idea about the quantities you require?
Buyer: Yes, I need 10,000 cartons for a customer in three weeks from now.
Salesperson: I'm sorry, but we can only let you have 5,000 at such short notice.
Buyer: What price can you quote me?
Salesperson: . . .

C The 'Observer' can double up with students A and B, and together they draft a follow-up fax to the buyer or customer confirming the call and what was agreed on. They send their fax to another group to respond to.

14.5 Getting it right in negotiations

This section deals with the activity of negotiating. If you have not yet encouraged students to read the Background information on negotiation, now is the time to get them to do so.

In the first part of this section we encounter a situation where only one side can win. The fact that this is a conflict situation is partly reflected in the tone of voice Bob Kellerman employs towards the supplier. It is to be hoped that students will recognize the scene as a parody! Where a dispute about delivery of faulty components exists, as is the case here, there is normally only one possible outcome: Mr Wiley, the supplier, should accept full responsibility and replace them. So the conversation is somewhat one-sided. By contrast the desirable 'win-win' scenario of negotiation, which comes in step **C**, demonstrates 'how to get it right'. This is built up to in the next step, which gives an explicit presentation of the phases which sales negotiation can contain. Then finally, a 'co-operative' negotiation is presented. Hopefully, this is more likely to serve as an example for what your students will be engaging in.

Procedure – *about 90 minutes*

A 🔊

1 Play the first part of the recording to the whole class. Note that the woman's voice is indistinct, as if it's heard down the line. Ask the students to imagine that they're 'eavesdropping' on Mr Kellerman's phone call.

Suggested answers

- Substandard components seem to have been delivered.
- The supplier doesn't appear to be very efficient or honest!
- Check the facts once more as reported by Michelle with the individuals she mentions.
- He'll probably ask to speak to the supplier's rep.

Transcript [2 minutes]

Bob: Good morning. Buying department.
Michelle: Hello, can I speak to Bob Kellerman?
Bob: Speaking. Hi Michelle. How are you?
Michelle: Fine. It's about those new components.
Bob: You mean the X77s – the ones from Coyote Enterprises?
Michelle: Yes.
Bob: Uhuh, why, are there any problems with them?
Michelle: There's a big problem with the quality of the wiring.
Bob: Yeah, but we tested all the samples and my assistant told me there were no problems at all with the wiring. And the price is very good, Michelle. No, it...it may be Coyote's...er...quality control that's at fault. Er...is it just the wiring that's faulty?
Michelle: No, there have been problems with the switches too.
Bob: No, not the switches! What, is there a safety problem or something?
Michelle: The assembly people are having to reject 20% of them.
Bob: Wait a minute, did you say 20%?
Michelle: Yes.

Bob: Well, if you're rejecting that many, then there's no...there's no cost saving i...in getting the components from Coyote. A...and if any of the switches don't work properly, then, well, we'll be getting some customer complaints.
Michelle: We already have. There's obviously a design fault.
Bob: A design fault in the switches? But if there is a design fault, I'm...Geoff – you know Geoff in assembly – well, he would have told me. So, are you sure?
Michelle: Yes.
Bob: Oh, no! All right, I'll look into it. I...is there any...anything else?
Michelle: Well, the paint matching isn't quite right.
Bob: Well, if the paint doesn't match, that's not so serious, we can deal with that. But with everything else – well, OK, I'll get onto this right away. Um...I'll get my assistant to look into it and...er...I'll get back to you...um...well, I'm not sure, but as soon as I can, is that all right?
Michelle: As soon as you can, Bob.
Bob: OK, Michelle. Listen, I'm really sorry about all this. I'll clear it up.
Michelle: Bye.
Bob: Bye bye. I'll talk to you later. Bye bye.

---

2 ◉◎ Play the second part of the recording to the whole class.

Suggested answers

- Mr Wiley thinks his components are extremely popular and good value.
- Bob Kellerman informs him about the complaints about the wiring.
- Mr Wiley says the first batch were not manufactured by Coyote Products.
- Bob Kellerman wants to know who was responsible for quality.

If you were Mr Wiley you would either know what had happened or be extremely stupid. So you would probably feel that you had no choice but to offer a solution.

Concerning the conflict, the simple answer is that it probably can't be solved by negotiation. If Mr Wiley's company has delivered inadequate components, he'll have to give in.

These are some of the questions the students might ask Mr Wiley:

- Could you be more specific about how reliable the components really were?
- Would you please clarify exactly who was responsible for quality control?
- What suggestions would you make to solve the problem?

Transcript   [1 minute 20 seconds]

Secretary: Bob, it's Mr Wiley of Coyote Enterprises. Are you free?

Bob: Mr Wiley?

Secretary: Yes, you know, the sales rep from Coyote Enterprises.

Bob: Haha. Right! Yeah! Wheel him in, he's...he's picked just the right day to call . . . Ah, well, Mr Wiley, ha...er...it's nice to...er...to see you again. Come on in, sit down.

Mr Wiley: Mr Kellerman, how are you?

Bob: I'm fine, I'm fine.

Mr Wiley: Great.

Bob: Well now, about these components...er...we've been getting from you.

Mr Wiley: What the...er...the X77s? Yeah, well, they've been extremely popular – good value too, I think you'll agree.

Bob: Have you had any problems with...er...reliability?

Mr Wiley: Er...no, none at all, why?

Bob: Well...er...you see, our salespeople have been getting all sorts of complaints. First, about the wiring.

Mr Wiley: Well, I mean, that's very strange because as far as I know the X77s are completely reliable.

Bob: Well, that's not the information we've got. Now, where is the wiring manufactured?

Mr Wiley: Well, I'm...now we do all the wiring in our own factory. Er...but...er...well, let's see because you got some of the first batch, didn't you?

Bob: First batch, yeah.

Mr Wiley: Which I believe were manufactured by our...one of our sub-contractors.

Bob: Ah, well, that's very interesting. So, who was responsible for quality control? Was it their people or was it yours?

Mr Wiley: Er...well, I'm not sure about that, normally of course we'd be responsible, but in this case . . .

B **1** The object of this reading exercise is to focus attention on the four phases of negotiation. These are the ways that negotiators ideally work together towards a result which will be satisfactory for both sides.

The question about *debating* and *bargaining* is a preliminary orienting question. Hopefully, students will be able to see that the term *debating* refers to an early stage of the process in which you and your customer are both still trying to find out what the conditions for the sale are likely to be (this is why open questions are used at this stage). The term *bargaining* refers to the final stage of agreement (this is where actual conditions are stated and perhaps finalized in writing).

2 Suggested answers

1 in the proposal and bargaining phases
2 in the proposal phase
3 to hear what they might be prepared to trade
4 in the preparation phase
5 to write down the agreement
6 open questions

7 to try to find out in what areas the other side may be prepared to move
8 in the bargaining phase

Between the two stages of *debating* and *bargaining* comes the proposal phase. This is where you test out how far you can go. Key phrases to mark phases 1, 2, 3 and 4 are:

- The preparation phase: *want* – i.e. what is desirable
- The debating phase: *may be prepared to* – i.e. what is possible
- The proposal phase: *could/might be prepared to* – i.e. what is probable
- The bargaining phase: *will actually* – i.e. what is the case

Impress upon students that this is an idealized view of what goes on. They shouldn't be disappointed if reality fails to live up to textbook models. After all, factors such as how well you know the other person, how much you like them, how much they like you, how much time you have, what you have eaten for lunch, etc., affect all individual transactions!

C Now the students hear a negotiation taking place about the sale of lavender. Perhaps, if you think it necessary for your students, ask them to listen to the recording and answer these preliminary questions:

- How well do the people appear to know each other? (Answer: very well)
- What is the product? (Answer: lavender)

1 It may be best to play the recording twice. The first time is for gist listening. The students have to decide the order in which the points are raised. The second time the students are concentrating on which speaker says what.

Suggested answers

ORDER THE POINTS ARE MENTIONED		WHO FIRST RAISES THE POINTS
4	discount	M
5	good price	M
1	competitive prices	F
8	guarantees	M
7	importance of quality	F
3	the need for firm figures	M
6	perfect condition	F
2	the point about the organization being flexible	M

2 Play the recording once more.

Suggested answers

1 b   2 d   3 c   4 a

Transcript [2 minutes 40 seconds]

Fritz: Well, I can say, Marianne, I can let you have orders for at least...um...a hundred fifty tonnes depending on the price and quality, like I said last time. I told you, as we mentioned at the last meeting, if your quality is no good and your prices are not competitive, that's the end of our deal.

Marianne: But, of course, Fritz, I understand, naturally. Now, if we know how much you are putting in an order for, I mean what are you saying, what sort of quantity are we talking about?

Fritz: I can safely say my clients...er...that is one large client, needs by next month, at first, eighty to a hundred tonnes of lavender.

Marianne: That's all right. We are flexible and we can do that.

Fritz: In that case, Marianne . . .

Marianne: And if the quantity is interesting, I am sure that we can do business. But, Fritz, I must stress, we do require firm figures or quantities, I mean, especially if you want a discount, Fritz.

Fritz: Well, I am not talking less than one hundred tonnes.

Marianne: That's good. We'll give you a good price on that.

Fritz: If we order immediately two hundred in total, then can I expect a discount?

Marianne: If the order is made, yes, that is not going to be a problem.

Fritz: One more thing, the condition of the produce must be perfect, A1 quality. Otherwise we can't do business.

Marianne: Of course, naturally, but you know, we only deliver perfect A1 condition. We do have a good reputation, you know.

Fritz: But, if we find that the prices you are quoting us are much too high and the quality is not good, Marianne, then we . . .

Marianne: Then, then you must tell us, Fritz.

Fritz: But we are trusting you, Marianne, we have done business with your organization before.

Marianne: I think you will see our lavender is guaranteed A1.

Fritz: If there's a guarantee, then we are prepared to take two hundred tonnes.

Marianne: OK. That's good, Fritz, we can give you a 5% discount, then, on the total.

Fritz: But last time we received 7%. Why so little now, Marianne?

Marianne: Ah, well, I'm sorry. But that was on a larger quantity, you see, and this is just two hundred tonnes.

Fritz: Look, I'll sign for two hundred and fifty tonnes and you give me 6% discount, what do you say, Marianne?

Marianne: OK. Agreed, we'll do that, Fritz.

D **1** For this role-play students should be in pairs – if possible there should be an even number of pairs (pairs of pairs). One pair (A) are the sellers, the other pair (B) are the buyers. Allow everyone time to decide which pair is which. To aid the decision-making process they can toss a coin. Both pairs are involved in preparing a sales negotiation. The product involved is an electrical component.

Before the sales negotiation proper starts with the people from the other firm, both the sellers and the buyers have to decide together what the margins for the sale are going to be. File **30** contains information about the limits or margins within which the sellers can negotiate (pair A). File **60** contains information about the limits or margins within which the buyers can negotiate (pair B). Both pairs must agree on these.

2 In this step the real negotiation starts. One of the sellers (pair A) now joins one of the buyers (pair B). File **32** contains information for the seller (student A). File **61** contains information for the buyer (student B). If you have odd numbers, two people can negotiate with an individual buyer or one salesperson and two buyers. This might be the situation when experienced salespeople or buyers accompany inexperienced ones.

Alternatively, with groups of three, one student can be an 'observer' and look at file **84** and eavesdrop on the negotiation and report back afterwards on the success or otherwise of the transaction.

3 For this step students can either rejoin their original partners or form larger seller or buyer groups and report on how 'successful' they were.

E Finally, there is a follow-up discussion which can be 'keyed in' by the quotation, which actually comes from a bona fide advertisement for negotiations skills courses.

14.6 Negotiating an international deal   *Simulation*

The simulation to come allows practice in co-operative negotiation. First there is a short preparatory step. The idea is to consider how people's behaviour in international and cross-cultural negotiation may be different from what you expect. In the situation where people use English as an international lingua franca, in particular, you may encounter individuals or groups who have a style which is different from your own.

Procedure – *about 90 minutes*

A 🔲 Students work in pairs for this activity. This step deals with behavioural differences in negotiation styles. It presents a set of mini-case studies.

A facilitating activity may be necessary with some groups of students. Tell them they are going to hear people engaged in negotiations. Before they hear the conversations ask them to imagine they are in the following situations. (The suggested possible thoughts given in brackets are subjective. Many alternatives are possible.) What would they think if:

1 they encounter someone who finishes their sentences for them (*they are impatient*)
2 someone interrupts them (*they are not interested in hearing your proposals*)
3 someone always goes 'um and er' and hesitates (*they are unprepared and wasting your time*)
4 someone speaks incredibly fast without pausing for breath (*they are trying to make up your mind for you!*)
5 someone speaks very loudly (*they think you are deaf, or they were in the army!*)
6 someone speaks so softly or quietly they can hardly hear them (*they are shy, or afraid of making mistakes in English*)
7 someone says nothing and expects them to do most of the talking (*they are uncertain or first want to find out what you think*)

After they have heard the recorded conversations and made notes, students discuss their reactions to the speakers before moving on to discuss different behavioural styles in negotiation.

Transcript   [3 minutes 40 seconds]

1 *A:* . . . Because I believe that...er . . .
B: . . . we can do a better job.
A: Well, yes, and you...ah . . .
B: . . . we have the skilled workforce to assemble the components.
A: Yes, if the...er . . .
B: . . . specifications are cleared up at your end.
A: Yes, we feel sure . . .
B: . . . that we can do a good job for you. That's most gratifying!

2 *A:* I can let you have half the merchandise . . .
B: No way, I tell you.
A: Look, we can come to some sort of agreement surely . . .
B: Not if you can't get the quantities.
A: Look, we have bought . . .
B: I'm telling you, I don't see it.
A: Look, I'm sure that there's a . . .
B: My boss won't buy it.

3 *A:* Shall we say 500 cartons?
B: Well, you know, I think...er...you know.
A: Well, we can let you have 1,000 cartons.
B: Well, if...if they are...erm...I mean if they...if you know if they're...obviously if they're . . .
A: Well, can you name the required date of delivery?
B: Well, of course, er...no if...if I knew, well . . .
A: So that's 1,000 cartons on the 15 February?
B: Er...well, maybe, I mean...er...you know, if...could I, perhaps...um...you know, you know if I could just . . .

4 *A:* But I don't get it.
B: If you can't buy quantities, they're not interested. These people aren't interested. I mean, if you're only gonna order three or four hundred pieces, or five hundred, they're not interested. Especially the factories we deal with. They are the biggest factories in the country. They need quantities. That's why we're important to them, you know. We gave them almost two million dollars worth of business right on the spot. That's what they're interested in.

5 *A:* Well, we are certainly thinking about it.
B: The only thing I know is that whatever quantities you place and whatever delivery dates we give you, you can be sure you'll get it on that date. So think about it. You've got to be more definite.

6 *A:* So how will you do it?
B: Eh? Oh...er...yeah, OK. Er...er...w...as a first stage I'd like to...I'd like to...um...introduce the idea to our head office and...er...er...well, you know, so that...I sound... I sound...I sou...don't I? Well, is it possible to market...market it or...or...er...or produce it locally so...so that...um...er, well, at the first stage I'd...I'd like to have some samples and I'll deliver them to our head office and then...er...well...er . . .

7 *A:* We'd like to sell in your country.
B: Uhuh.
A: Or to manufacture it in your country.
B: Mmm.
A: Either way, whichever is best.
B: Mmm.
A: Maybe manufacture it here for six months.
B: Mmm.
A: Maybe we could send you some samples?
B: Uhuh.

Steps B and C

Timing

To give a rough idea of how long each step should take, here is a suggested timetable for the simulation in a lesson lasting between 70 and 80 minutes, after step **A** has been done.

This timing is given simply as a guide, and everything will depend on the time available, whether you can have students prepare step **B** in advance, and the number of participants.

B	10–15 minutes – Ideally this should be done in a previous lesson or should have been prepared at home to allow more time for the simulation in class.
C1–C2	10–15 minutes
C3	25 minutes – **This is the crucial part of the simulation. Make sure you have enough time for this, if necessary at the expense of subsequent steps.**
C4	5–10 minutes
C5	5–10 minutes

Roles

In step **C** participants will be playing the role of sellers or buyers. Both the SELLERS and the BUYERS work for firms negotiating with a foreign firm to finalize a deal on the sale or purchase of a product.

Procedure

B Arrange the class into two large groups for this step, which is preparation for the simulation. With a class of 12, two groups of six each will work. With a class of 24 divide up the two company teams of twelve into four groups of three each in the subsequent **C** steps; then you will only have one product to be negotiated about.

If you have time in a lesson beforehand it would help to prepare step **B**. It might be a good idea to ask the class to collect some sample pictures or ideas in the form of advertisements as homework. They have to decide on and write a very brief specification of the product. The specification is written or typed and photocopied to be used in step **C**. If you have an overhead projector the two companies can write their specifications on a transparency to be projected later.

If you have two rooms available, send one group into the other room for this stage. Tell the students that their main task is to agree on:

1 a product
2 a realistic price
3 quality you can supply
4 size of orders you can fulfil
5 delivery times you can offer
6 length of guarantee to be offered
7 amount of discount

The CONTROLLER blows a whistle (after 10 minutes) and tosses a coin to decide which of the two groups is selling and which is buying.

C The simulation proper now begins. With a class of 24 divide up the two company teams of 12 into four groups of three.

1 The SELLERS send a copy of the product and its price and other specifications to the BUYERS. For this stage if you have two rooms available, send one (or more) group into the other room. If not, separate them in different parts of the room.

2 The SELLERS work together with the product specification, deciding on their specifications and margins, as a team, for the negotiating process. They also decide on a delegation leader or leaders to initiate the discussions and speak first in the negotiation sessions.

Meanwhile . . . the BUYERS work together with the product specification they have received, deciding how far they can move in their demands for price, quantity and delivery dates in the negotiating process. They also decide how much discount they will ask for, etc. They then decide on a delegation leader or leaders to initiate the discussions and speak first in the negotiation sessions.

3 At this stage the two groups come together to negotiate. (As already stated, with a class of 12, two company teams of six each can be sub-divided into two groups of three each. With a class of 24, divide the SELLERS and BUYERS into two halves and then sub-divide into smaller groups of three.) One half meets their opposite numbers now. Allow what you think is a reasonable amount of time, probably up to 25 minutes. If the time is limited the CONTROLLER blows a whistle about 10 minutes before the time is up so the teams know how long they have to reach an agreement.

4 When the negotiation is over, all the SELLERS and the BUYERS should meet in separate areas and report back to each other on their results. If no satisfactory result has been achieved, discuss what to do next, or go on to step **5**.

5 In the follow-up discussion, find out how everyone felt at the different stages of the simulation.

NOTE: If time allows, or if you choose to, you can repeat the simulation from step **C1** onwards with the SELLERS and the BUYERS changing roles. In this way everyone gets the opportunity to experience both the salesperson and the purchaser roles in sales negotiation.

Extra activity

After the simulation you can give the students the following task for individual homework.

SELLERS: Draft a report of the negotiation for head office. Summarize the progress and the results that were reached. What recommendation will you make?

BUYERS: Draft a report of the negotiation for head office. Summarize the progress and the results that were reached. What recommendation will you make?

Workbook contents for this unit

14.1 **Selling and negotiating**	*Background information*
14.2 ***Of, out of ...***	*Prepositional phrases – 4*
14.3 **Asking for and giving advice**	*Functions & listening*
14.4 **Talking shop**	*Vocabulary*
14.5 **Co-operation and competition**	*Reading*
14.6 **International styles of negotiating**	*Listening*
14.7 **Order of adverbs**	*Grammar review*

A special project

Video

Programme 15 on the *New International Business English Video* deals with **Giving Presentations**. See the *Video Teacher's Guide* for full information.

This unit revises many of the main areas of business that have been covered in the previous units. Besides using the basic business skills introduced in Units 1 to 4, this unit revises and consolidates work done in Units 5, 6, 8, 9, 10, 11, 13 and 14.

It takes the form of a simulation which is spread over several lessons – each part of the simulation taking place in a different 'month'. Students will be working in teams, one based in the USA and the other in the UK.

As simulations go, this is quite a straightforward one.

Procedure

The procedure for each step is described in the Student's Book and below, in more detail.

Time

You'll need three 90-minute lessons for the five 'Months' of the simulation.

Photocopies and documents

You'll need to make photocopies of the documents for this simulation.

Class numbers

A class of eight to 20 students should be divided into two teams of four to ten participants.

A larger class could be split into two groups, each sub-divided into two teams, and at the very end the two groups discuss what they did and why they made their decisions.

A smaller class should be split into two teams, but in this case the APRIL tasks can be done by everyone in each team, because you can't sub-divide three students into two pairs.

➡ If there is another class in your institute or college using *New International Business English*, here's a great opportunity to combine the two classes for this simulation, thus putting two separate rooms at your disposal – the two Controllers can share their duties and responsibilities.

JANUARY & FEBRUARY

Students who are working in the same company may prefer to choose their own product for the simulation, rather than a food product. However, the relative simplicity of discussing a food product may be preferable to the necessity of adapting the scenario to suit a different product.

Vocabulary

location	*criterion / criteria*	*local authority*	*on line*
microwave	*expertise*	*refurbishment*	

Procedure – *about 90 minutes*

JANUARY: The product

1 Divide the class into small groups.

2 Have each group do a short 'Presentation' of their product. The others should make notes and ask questions afterwards.

3 Take a vote or agree by consensus on one product range to deal with during the rest of the 'year'.

FEBRUARY: Finding a location

1 For steps **1** and **2**, it is not yet necessary to assign the participants to teams – the rubric in the Student's Book explains what will be happening later.

   Working as whole class or in groups, students consider their criteria in choosing a location.

2 Then they look at the maps to see which sites seem to fulfil their criteria – if you have large-scale maps of the areas that the class can consult, that would make the task more realistic.

3 Divide the class into two teams: the GB TEAM and the US TEAM.

Give copies of MARCH Documents (GB) and MARCH Documents (US) to the appropriate team – these should be photocopied from pages 208 to 221. If the teams are small, one copy of each document should be enough and these can be circulated within the team – as if being circulated in the company.

Then, for homework, they study the Documents so they are ready to discuss them in March (the next lesson).

MARCH

Vocabulary

shell-building	*corporate government incentives*	*well-sited*
cost-wise	*government grants*	

Don't be tempted to 'pre-teach' (explain in advance) the vocabulary in the photocopied documents or in the recordings for this unit.

   The documents for photocopying in the Teacher's Book include unsimplified authentic extracts from publicity material and brochures, containing a lot of vocabulary which may be unfamiliar to your students. Discourage your students from looking up all the new words (or asking you to explain them). Perhaps explain to everyone that the reading should be treated as a real-life task: the purpose is to extract the main points from the documents without worrying about words you don't fully understand.

   The recordings also contain words that may be unfamiliar. Again, students should concentrate on the main points that are made and not worry about details they don't understand. Remind everyone that in real life you can't keep asking speakers what they mean, or asking them to stop talking whilst you use a dictionary!

Unit 15   A special project

1 The memo explains the parameters of the tasks that have to be accomplished.

MARCH: Choosing the location

2 **NOTE:** Participants can only use the information supplied in the documents and in the recordings. In a real-life situation, there would be hundreds of pages of documents and financial information to wade through and deal with, experts and advisers to consult, dozens or even hundreds of locations to evaluate and choose between, etc. – what we're attempting to do here is to give a *flavour* of the real thing only.

Participants who complain *'But there's some important information missing, we need to know so and so'* may be placated with this advice:

'Actually almost all the information you'd really need is missing – you'll have to make do with what you've got. Remember that this is a language exercise, not a business exercise. I think you should assume that whatever's missing IS THE SAME FOR EACH SITE.'

3 🖭 The teams get more information about the locations in recorded reports from a colleague 'on the spot'.

The recorded reports should ideally be played to the separate groups in different parts of the room (on separate cassette or CD players). If this isn't feasible, there's no harm in everyone hearing everything as it may help them to form a better impression of what the others are up to.

Transcript

Reports on Telford and Wigan for the GB team [4 minutes]

Leslie Maxwell: Hello, I'm here inside the Shopping Centre at Telford. I was expecting this town to be a bit of a concrete jungle, like some of the other new towns I've visited. But the mixture of housing, good roads, parks and clean modern industry make this really a very pleasant place. Right here next to the indoor shopping centre is the town park and just up the road is some of the best scenery in England – and unspoilt countryside just outside the town boundary.

Also, nearby is the world's first iron bridge, built in 1779, and a symbol of the industrial revolution that started in the area in 1709.

Telford has the biggest concentration of Japanese companies in the United Kingdom: Epson Telford (they invested £15m in a new plant manufacturing computer printers), NEC (they've invested over £50m in a plant manufacturing computer monitors and printers, mobile telephones and fax machines) they employ around 750 people here, Hitachi Maxell have their European headquarters here and make video cassettes and floppy disks, and Ricoh manufactures photocopiers for sale throughout Europe. Also here are Tatung, from Taiwan, with 400 workers making TVs.

Although Telford's quite a good place for sports and leisure (Telford even has its own dry ski slope), it's not too good for entertainments and cultural activities. You have to go to Birmingham 30 miles away for that kind of thing, but the shops here are good and this shopping mall I'm in now is quite impressive.

As you know, Telford has its own motorway, the M54 connecting it to the M6, but although it has a brand new Central Station, connections to London are not very regular or quick. Birmingham Airport and the National Exhibition Centre are 40 minutes away – if there aren't any hold-ups on the motorway!

Leslie Maxwell: I'm sitting outside the Orwell Pub at Wigan Pier on the Leeds and Liverpool canal having a drink. This is the place George Orwell wrote about during the Great Depression in the 30s and to me Wigan still had a bad image of being a run-down coal mining town. This is the first time I've been here and I must say that I'm quite impressed. It's very clean and it has a great atmosphere. You get the feeling that the people are proud of their history and are keen to make a visitor feel welcome. Lancashire people are famous for their warmth and hospitality.

Wigan itself is a down-to-earth, no-nonsense sort of town, many of the houses are Victorian and beginning to show their age, but there's been a lot of urban renewal with modern houses outside the town and good sports facilities. It's not very far to the Lancashire coast and the Pennine Hills, so it's quite easy to get away from the town by car and enjoy some fresh air and scenery. The shops are a nice mixture of the old and the new too.

You're also mid-way between Liverpool and Manchester, which both have fine theatres and symphony orchestras. The main line from London to Glasgow passes through Wigan, and you can be in London in just under 3 hours. Manchester Airport is just 40 minutes away – with connections to all parts of Europe and even to Singapore and North America.

Reports on Binghamton and Trenton for the US team [4 minutes 40 seconds]

Lee Carter: I'm here now in Binghamton, in Upstate New York. I'm sitting in Ely Park overlooking the city. This is a charming little city, it's safe and pretty – though maybe it's a little dull.

The people are kind of slow and hospitable and it's hard to believe that you're just a couple of hours from downtown Manhattan and that practically every city from Chicago in the west to Boston in the east and from Washington in the south to Toronto and Montreal in the north can be reached by overnight truck.

In spite of the first impression you get of being in the heart of the country, there's plenty of high tech industry here in town: there's a new IBM plant and Singer-Link make their famous flight simulators right here.

Here too there are plenty of people without special technical skills – one of the largest employers in the area is Fisher Price Toys whose workforce is largely semi-skilled. One thing that strikes me about the people hereabouts is that they are dependable and loyal and they're not afraid of hard work – indeed many of them come from farming communities where even the children have to work.

One of the big attractions of the area is the beautiful scenery. The forests in the fall are glorious and in winter the main skiing resorts of the Eastern United States are just an hour's drive away. There are some lovely lakes too.

People are moving out of New York City to get away from commuting and urban crime and to get closer to nature.

Lee Carter: I'm sitting beside the Delaware River in Trenton, New Jersey. I've just been finding out about the huge range of industry here in this state, which is the size of Wales but has about the same population as Sweden. New Jersey is one of the most popular states for foreign companies to establish their headquarters: BASF, Mercedes-Benz, Volvo, Volkswagen, Toyota, Nissan, Fiat all have their US headquarters here. Big foreign companies with factories here are Oki Data & Sharp from Japan and Samsung & Daewoo from Korea.

New Jersey is the number one state in the Union for pharmaceuticals with Hoffman-La Roche, Ciba-Geigy, Johnson & Johnson and Merck. Throughout the state each year $4 billion being spent on research in academic and industrial R&D labs, including Bell Laboratories, ITT, AT&T, RCA – the people are very proud that 11 Nobel Prize winners live in New Jersey.

Here in Trenton I've been looking at the amazing DHC (district heating and cooling system) operating in our premises. Heating and cooling costs will be low because surplus heat generated by electric power stations is turned into steam, hot water and even cooled water for distribution by pipes to homes and industrial premises.

New Jersey calls itself the Garden State and it's true that once you get beyond the urban areas of Newark and Jersey City, the countryside begins. One great plus is the ocean – New Jersey has 127 miles of coast. And with the huge air network of Newark International Airport close, it's easy to get anywhere in North America and to anywhere in the world on a direct flight. From here it's just a short drive to Philadelphia or New York City.

Trenton itself is a pleasant city, though parts of it are a bit run-down. The people here are good workers and there's a long industrial tradition in the state. It's a nice place and not too large – it's quite a lively sort of place and there's a highly varied mixture of different races and nationalities.

---

4 The two teams discuss the relative merits of the sites.

At least twice during the month, a member of each group has to telephone his or her counterpart in the other country. Designate one corner of the classroom for the phone conversations to be made in.

Remind the participants that the time has come for this by giving a suitable signal or making a suitable announcement.

MARCH: The personnel

5 Now the two teams make further decisions about the organization and staffing of their projected establishments. They draft an outline of how they'll organize the business to foster staff motivation and efficiency.

They inform the other team by 'faxing' or 'e-mailing' the outline to them.

6 At the end of the month there is a meeting where the two teams exchange experiences.

7 In April, the GB team will be divided into two groups: GB 1 and GB 2 and the US team into two groups: US 1 and US 2. Each group will be dealing with a different aspect of the plans for relocating in their respective countries.

Sub-divide the teams and then give out the copies of the appropriate Documents (on pages 222 and 223).

Document 1 should be given to the members of groups GB 1 and US 1: one copy for each participant.

In April (the next lesson), these smaller groups will discuss their policy on materials, supplies and distribution in the next 'month'.

Document 2 should be given to the members of groups GB 2 and US 2: one copy for each participant.

In April (the next lesson), these smaller groups will discuss their policy on marketing and sales.

APRIL & MAY

⚠ It may be necessary to speed up or skip some steps, so that there is enough time for the Meeting and De-briefing. The Meeting itself needs 20 to 30 minutes and the De-briefing about 10 minutes.

Procedure – *about 90 minutes*

APRIL: Suppliers & distribution / Marketing & sales

1 Both groups will be discussing and making decisions, and making phone calls.

At least twice during the month, a member of each group has to telephone his or her counterparts in the other country. Designate one corner of the classroom for the phone conversations to be made in.

Remind the participants that the time has come for this by giving a suitable signal or making a suitable announcement.

➡ If time is getting short, omit step **2** and go straight on to MAY step **1**. Interrupt the groups by handing them a copy of the fax from Frank Miller (MAY Document 1) and take it from there.

2 The original teams meet together to find out what each group has been doing (US 1 meets US 2, while GB 1 meets GB 2).

MAY: The meeting

In this part of the simulation, there is a spanner in the works: the teams discover that their months of planning may have been in vain – something that is not unprecedented in the real business world! Now each team is going to have to argue its case and fight for the location it has chosen at a Big Meeting.

1 So that the surprise works realistically, get the teams to sit together in their by-now-customary places. Then deliver the fax for everyone to read (MAY Document 1). Only two copies are needed per team. Be prepared for an angry reaction from some participants, as the fax from head office rules that only one of the branches may be established – a meeting must be held to decide which one.

2 The memo has called for a meeting. The two teams prepare their contributions.

Before the meeting starts, the chairperson should be appointed from the two nominated by the teams. To make this seem fair, a coin could be tossed.

The chosen chairperson is given a copy of MAY Document 2 – this document contains special instructions for the chairperson. Tell the chairperson what time the meeting should end, so that you have enough time after it for a de-briefing/follow-up discussion.

3 **THE MEETING** is held. This is the climax of the whole simulation: allow 20 to 30 minutes for this step so that all the arguments can be presented and thrashed out.

The two teams put forward their arguments and a final decision is reached, perhaps by voting or by consensus.

DE-BRIEFING: Follow-up discussion

At the end of the simulation, make sure there is time for participants to step out of role and analyse what they did.

Follow-up written work – Highly recommended

Each participant should write a report of his or her work in the simulation. This may be done 'in role' from the point of view of a member of the project team. Or it could be a report on the simulation written in retrospect.

Workbook

Workbook contents for this unit

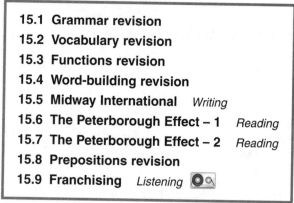

15.1 **Grammar revision**
15.2 **Vocabulary revision**
15.3 **Functions revision**
15.4 **Word-building revision**
15.5 **Midway International** *Writing*
15.6 **The Peterborough Effect – 1** *Reading*
15.7 **The Peterborough Effect – 2** *Reading*
15.8 **Prepositions revision**
15.9 **Franchising** *Listening*

The Workbook exercises for Unit 15 consist of revision material, which can be used as a 'progress test' of the work that has been done while using *New International Business English*.

If you wish to conduct a progress test of your students' ORAL work, you can supplement the written and recorded exercises in the Workbook with the two role-play exercises on the next page, to be done in pairs. While your students are doing these, their proficiency can be assessed by yourself or by another teacher. Alternatively, you could get a student to play the longer role while you (or another teacher) play the shorter one in each role-play.

Unit 15

1st Role-play

A You are on a visit to a foreign country and you have been unavoidably delayed because of a train strike. You have been invited to dinner at 8 pm but now you won't be able to make it. Phone your host/hostess to explain the delay and apologize. The time now is 7.00 and the earliest you could get there would be 10 pm, which would be too late for dinner.

Tell your host/hostess that ...

- You'll arrive at the factory tomorrow morning at 8 am – or will that be too early for your host/hostess?
- You're catching the 17.30 plane tomorrow, so the meeting will have to be in the morning.
- You're staying at the Sheraton Hotel – phone number 447618.
- You've booked a table at the Excelsior Hotel for lunch for your host/hostess and colleagues at 12.30 tomorrow.
- You'll phone your host/hostess from the station when you finally do arrive.

B You are expecting a visitor from abroad as your guest of honour for dinner. The visitor is due to meet you and your colleagues formally tomorrow afternoon at the factory. You have invited several colleagues who will be arriving at 7.45. The time now is 7.00. Answer the phone. Make a note of any information you are given.

© Cambridge University Press 2000

Unit 15

2nd Role-play

A You are expecting a visitor from abroad who is coming to your office. Your assistant has already left for the airport to meet the visitor when his/her plane arrives at 12.00. The time now is 10.00.
    Answer the phone. Make a note of any information you are given.

B Your flight to a foreign country is delayed and you're waiting at the airport for it to leave. Your host/hostess is going to meet your flight, which is due to arrive at noon. Phone your host/hostess and explain that you'll be late and he/she shouldn't come to the airport to meet you. You will make your own way to the office when you eventually arrive. The time now is 10 am and the plane isn't going to leave till about 11.00.

Tell your host/hostess that ...

- You'll need photocopies of the technical report for the meeting tomorrow morning.
- Your boss (Jean du Maurier) is calling you at 1 pm – can your host/hostess take a message?
- You'll be staying at the Metropole Hotel, near the station – phone number 801829.
- Your return flight tomorrow is at 15.30, so you'll have to leave straight after lunch – will there be enough time to settle everything by then?

© Cambridge University Press 2000

Unit 15 A special project
MARCH Documents for the GB team

I am pleased to report that we have found suitable buildings in two locations. The two sites are Bradley Hall Trading Estate, Standish, in Wigan (Greater Manchester) and Stafford Park Industrial Estate in Telford (West Midlands). There is a shell building available at both sites that is ideal for our purposes.

Our own research and advice from local consultants suggest that cost-wise there is nothing to choose between the two sites: both offer the same corporate taxation incentives, and government grants are available at each location for setting up a new plant and training staff. Labour costs and power costs are similar in both sites.

Wigan is mid-way between Liverpool and Manchester. It has a population of over 300,000. Telford is a New Town to the west of Birmingham with a population of about 110,000. Both are well-sited for the motorway network: Wigan is close to the M6 and Telford is connected by the M54 to the M5 and M6.

I will be visiting both sites soon and I will send you a tape giving you my personal impressions of both locations.

In the meantime, I enclose some background information about each place.

With best wishes,

Leslie Maxwell

TELFORD

TELFORD
WELCOME

Telford – a town with technology for tomorrow – and the historic Ironbridge Gorge where the Industrial Revolution began.

An international town full of new investment – surrounded by beautiful Shropshire.

A town with its own motorway – and no traffic jams.

A town which can always find you a factory or an office – or a place to build one.

A town with a young, growing workforce – getting on with the job.

A town in green – where tree-planting started before the environment was an issue.

A town for people with a future.

TELFORD

Amongst the UK's most successful towns, Telford's dynamism and environment have attracted worldwide investment. Telford sits in beautiful Shropshire countryside, with long established communities, like the market town of Wellington and historic Ironbridge, carefully blended with modern shopping and leisure, schools and a new hospital and university campus.

Here, in 1709, in the Ironbridge Gorge, Abraham Darby perfected a new iron-making technique which began the Industrial Revolution. This remarkable area is now a World Heritage Site and an international tourist attraction. Massive public and private sector investment is forging a second, high technology revolution, with a service sector to match – creating a town which values lifestyle and environment. A unique sculpture of the famous engineer Thomas Telford, whose name was taken for the Town, stands in Telford Square and serves as a reminder of the past and a symbol for the future.

"Our detailed research led us to establish Maxell's European manufacturing HQ in Telford because the environment and transport links make a superb location for us. We confidently expect to grow here."

H Yamaguchi, Managing Director, Maxell (UK) Ltd

TELFORD
LOCATION

Telford is in Central England, with its own motorway link to customers, suppliers, seaports, airports – and an internal road system far ahead of its time.

Within an easy drive of most major cities, Telford is an altogether different, greener world – with tulips and trees but no traffic jams. International airports are close by and Telford Central gets you a train connection to London most hours.

So you can get away to do the business – in the UK or Europe – and your people get to work relaxed, in minutes, from anywhere in town.

TELFORD – all the right connections.

TELFORD
INDUSTRIAL

Telford's superb sites in green, landscaped settings have attracted some of the most interesting UK and overseas investments in recent years – and you can rent or buy from a wide choice of modern, first-class property if you don't want to build.

Telford's Japanese companies alone are World-famous, part of a success story which has been running for 20 years. And with plenty of room for everyone, Telford will continue to be a market leader for new manufacturing investment well into the 21st century.

So, why not join us? It's easy!

TELFORD – Where new investment comes naturally.

"Gibson Greetings International is a new company serving British, Irish and continental markets. We chose Telford for its road links and proximity to the international airports at Birmingham and Manchester."

Peter Osman,
Managing Director,
Gibson Greetings
International

Companies recognise that Telford's excellent location and communications give unrivalled access to the UK and beyond. The M54 links Telford into the UK motorway system, bringing 66% of the population

"When NDMF was formed we needed a very big site. Telford offered that quickly – in a town which made us welcome, with just the sort of clean, green environment in which we wanted to work."

Henry Ohiwa,
Chairman and
Managing Director,
NDM Manufacturing
Ltd

Telford has 40% of the highest quality development land in the West Midlands, over 1,000 acres, already serviced and mostly with simplified planning

within four hours drive by HGV and giving easy access to seaports and the Channel Tunnel. London is two hours away, Birmingham, with its enormous industrial base, 30 minutes. All Telford's business parks are within five minutes of the motorway. Birmingham International Airport is 45 minutes away, Manchester's 75 minutes – with direct flights to North America, major European destinations and the Far East. Heathrow is 2 hours 30 minutes away. Cross-town travel is easy: most journeys taking under ten minutes – with ample free parking throughout the district.

procedures. There are sites for the small company or the multinational giant needing a campus of its own, properties of all sizes, many with flexible leases or room for expansion. Land prices, rents and business rates are amongst the most competitive in the UK offering real, long-term benefits. Over 1,000 companies have located here – 130 of them from 18 foreign countries, including World-class manufacturers like NEC, Dunlop, Tatung, Nestlé, Maxell, Epson and Ricoh.

TELFORD
WORKFORCE

People make Telford. This is a town of young families and a multi-skilled, ambitious, loyal and fast-growing workforce. The people here were undaunted by the challenge of making the World's first iron bridge – and the same goes for the challenges of today.

Excellent productivity and competitive wages keep overall labour costs down and a steady inflow of modern manufacturing industry means an adaptable workforce.

New working practices, shift patterns and high standards are the norm here – not the exception. Educational standards are high – with quality and choice from pre-school to university, and, in this growing, high-tech town, education works closely with industry.

TELFORD – getting on with the job.

TELFORD
SUCCESS

Telford is a great international success story, a high-tech town of the 21st century, growing and attracting investment from around the World, designed from the beginning to offer all the advantages of a big-city location with none of the problems.

The people of Telford and the leaders of the new industries are intensely proud of their achievements – and determined that Telford's environment, quality of life and business advantages will be preserved. In a gentle, green sort of way, Telford symbolises the Britain of the future.

We think you will like it here.

TELFORD – the way it's going to be.

> *"Our customers demand high standards which we achieve in Telford with a top quality, enthusiastic and flexible workforce. That was one of the key things which brought us here."*
>
> *Stephen Dyne, General Manager, Reliance Electric (UK) Ltd*

Telford has an increasing number of school leavers and a workforce growing at eight times the national average. The population is 120,000, rising to 140,000 by 2001. The workforce is 60,000 with 14,000 people commuting in – and a catchment labour market of 500,000 living within 30 minutes.

Industrial relations are outstanding with disputes almost at zero.

Telford has several colleges and one of the UK's largest Information Technology Centres, specialising in electronics, business computing and office skills. The new university offers business and management courses and will cater for 2,500 students. The British Polymer Training Association has its national headquarters here, providing the latest facilities and training for the plastics industry.

> *"Telford has a great environment for business. The costs of setting up here make real sense and this will keep us at the front of European investment locations well into the 21st century."*
>
> *Michael J Tandy, President, Shropshire Chamber of Industry and Commerce*

Telford's business advantages have brought spectacular investments and thousands of new jobs. The environment, the communications, the quality of the workforce and the lifestyle here are constantly being improved – keeping Telford as THE location for international companies serving Europe and for UK companies simply wanting something better.

Newcomers and new investments are made welcome here, without red-tape and bureaucracy. At the Telford Development Agency, we have a wealth of experience in helping new and expanding companies, from the UK and overseas. The TDA and its private-sector partners offer you the backing of a great team. Welcome to Telford!

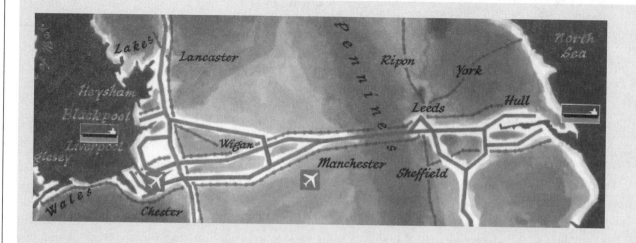

<u>Quality of Life</u>

People in Wigan have a first class ticket to a lifestyle of the highest quality, with its excellent transport network making everything easily accessible. There is a splendid choice of housing in Wigan, but it is also within easy commuting distance of some of the most prestigious and reasonably priced property in the country. Every kind of development can be found in North West England from waterside apartments to spacious detached houses.

Wigan and the Region's many towns and cities offer all possible amenities, but there is a wealth of pretty villages in the Lake District and the Pennines where residents can enjoy rural life. All within commuting distance of Wigan.

Wigan is among the UK's top ten local authorities in terms of academic achievement. There are 180 schools in Wigan alone and there are 8 universities in the Region. North West England was also the birthplace of the National Health Service, and this is reflected in Wigan's acknowledged excellence in healthcare and public services, ensuring the needs of the family or the individual are catered for at the highest level.

Complementing this is an impressive range of cultural and sporting facilities in Wigan and across the Region. North West England's reputation as an international centre of sporting excellence is underlined by the choice of Manchester as the latest British Olympic Bid, with Wigan as the venue for a number of the events.

The choice of sporting activities is impressive including the World's most famous

horse race – the Grand National, championship golf, test cricket, and international tennis. For those with a more active interest in sport there is sailing, mountaineering, and even opportunities to fly as well as the more widely known sports.

The arts, in all forms, are well represented in Wigan and North West England. There are orchestras and theatres throughout the Region and regular performances from international ballet and opera companies as well as Wigan's annual international jazz festival.

Wigan is rightly proud of its shopping facilities with attractive, recent developments which include The Galleries and Spinning Gate. They combine architectural elegance with the best known high street stores.

The Economy

Wigan is the centre of Britain's second largest region, with a population of nearly seven million people. Within a short radius, there is an excellent pool of skilled and versatile labour. Wigan itself has a population of 300,000 and a potential workforce of over 140,000.

Many of the world's largest companies, including H.J. Heinz, PPG Industries, and ICI, have recognised the benefits of being based in Wigan. This has led to the continued growth of Wigan's economic base, and to a reputation for excellence at the leading edge of both manufacturing and service industries.

There are excellent links between industry and North West England's academic institutions, many of which offer the very best in research and development. With such organisations as The National Computing Centre and NIMTECH, the Region has long been able to attract companies at the forefront of technology.

Metrotec (Wigan) Ltd., Wigan's Training and Enterprise Council, helps to ensure a relevantly skilled workforce. The Region's workforce has a proven adaptability to meet the requirements of new industries. At the same time, Wigan has an exceptionally good labour relations record that is demonstrated in the willingness of employers and employees to maintain good communications.

The strength of Wigan's partnership between public and private sectors is reflected in 1992's successful City Challenge Bid. This provides £37.5m of central government funding for Wigan to embark on major urban regeneration projects, which will lever some £200m in private and additional public sector investment.

The partnership is exemplified by the close working relationships between the Council, Metrotec (Wigan) Ltd., the Education Business Partnership and the Employers Association (which incorporates the Chamber of Commerce, Tourism Association and the Wigan and Leigh Small Firms Club).

Building on these firm foundations, Wigan's City Challenge will be delivered by the Douglas Valley Partnership, acting in concert with its many partners.

The City Challenge area is at the heart of the Wigan Borough and forms a belt running across central Wigan stretching from the Heinz factory at Marsh Green including the communities of Marsh Green and Worsley Hall, through to Wigan Pier, Westwood Park, the fringe of Wigan town centre and the communities of Scholes and Ince.

By 1998, through City Challenge, the Douglas Valley Partnership will have made Wigan into a prime location for investment in the North West and will have created at least 6,000 jobs, of which 2,500 are intended for local people.

City Challenge will have created a climate in which people want to invest, work and live.

Communications

Wigan is surrounded by a triangle of motorways, at the heart of the most comprehensive motorway network in Europe. Some of the UK's principal North–South and East–West road and rail links pass through it. The M62 running East–West, linking Liverpool with Hull, provides access to the East Coast ports, and passes through such key centres as Manchester and Leeds. The North–South M6 is the principal route to London, Scotland and the Midlands, with a drive time to the capital of only three and a half hours.

Running through the heart of Wigan is the main West Coast rail line, with a journey time to London of two and a half hours, and less than three and a half hours to Glasgow. It also provides direct access to the Channel Tunnel, with dedicated freight services available every day.

Few locations can claim to be within forty minutes drive of both the fastest growing airport in Europe and a Freeport which, each week, handles goods worth millions of pounds for hundreds of companies serving over 80 countries. From Manchester and Liverpool airports 94 airlines serve 170 destinations around the world. Manchester Airport, which handled over 12 million passengers last year, has more domestic flight routes than any other airport in the UK, including Heathrow, and is the third busiest airport in the UK.

Unit 15 A special project
MARCH Documents for the US team

I am pleased to report that we have found suitable buildings in two locations. The two sites are Interstate Industrial Park in Binghamton, NY and Delaware Corporate Park in Trenton, NJ. There is a shell building available at both sites that is ideal for our purposes.

Our own research and advice from local consultants suggest that cost-wise there is nothing to choose between the two sites: the tax advantages of New Jersey are balanced by the lower power and labor costs in Upstate New York. Grants are available at each location for setting up a new plant and training staff.

Binghamton is in Upstate New York. It has a population of 55,000 and good communications by interstate highway to all parts of the East Coast and Mid-West. Trenton is the State Capital of New Jersey, with a population of 110,000. It is mid-way between Philadelphia and New York City on the banks of the Delaware River and also well-sited for communications by truck or automobile.

I will be visiting both sites soon and I will send you a tape giving you my personal impressions of both locations.

In the meantime, I enclose some background information about each place.

Best,

Lee Carter

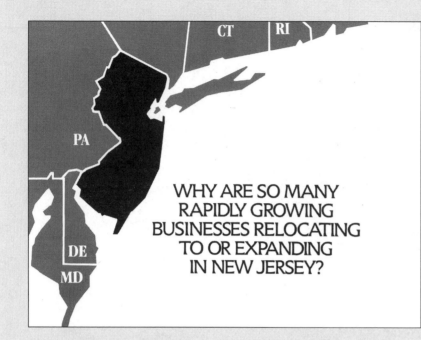

WHY ARE SO MANY RAPIDLY GROWING BUSINESSES RELOCATING TO OR EXPANDING IN NEW JERSEY?

NEW JERSEY HAS IT ALL . . .

- a location in the heart of the world's largest concentration of market wealth

- an international business environment of diverse industries

- a large pool of highly qualified professionals and technical specialists

- a close link between academia and new technology/research industries

- a state government committed to business growth

- a large roster of innovative financial institutions with resources earmarked for new and growing business

- a transportation network ideally suited and equipped for international trade and for rapidly reaching a part of the United States

- a high quality of life featuring an unmatched diversity of cultural, recreational and entertainment facilities – all within close proximity of each other

A NEW JERSEY PROFILE

New Jersey is the geographical center of a 250-mile circle constituting the world's greatest concentration of market wealth. This strategic location – the midway point of the megalopolis extending from Boston to Washington – has attracted major national and international companies to New Jersey and continues to do so.

How does one describe this small in size but economically powerful state?

- Many miles of railway and super-highway make New Jersey a transportation center.

- Natural waterways that form almost all of the state's boundaries make New Jersey a maritime state. Its ports are an overnight truck or rail ride to 40% of the nation's population and accessible to the country's largest cargo airport.

- As home to the headquarters of 23 of the FORTUNE 500 companies as well as numerous other national and multinational corporations, and with billions of dollars in foreign investments, New Jersey is a world class center of commerce.

- A long history of research and innovation has made the state a leader in technology with unsurpassed expertise in pharmaceuticals, telecommunications, chemicals and other industries.

New Jersey boasts a climate for scientific research that is unmatched anywhere in the United States. Today, an astonishing number of scientists and engineers – more than 100,000 – work in New Jersey. Many of these are employed in the more than 500 research laboratories across the state. One-tenth of all U.S. patents are issued to New Jersey inventors; we count eleven Nobel Prize winners among our residents.

The state has attracted the top talent in business and industry because it is a good place to work and live, and it is a great place to play!

It's one of the most beautiful states in the nation; there are breathtaking beaches, farms, mountains and pinelands. Of the state's total of 5 million acres, 2 million acres are in woods and forests and more than 1 million acres are under cultivation. State forests and parks account for over 25,000 acres with more land being conserved under the Green Acres Program. You can ski, sail, horseback ride or beachcomb all on the same day. New Jersey has 218 golf courses and has hosted the U.S. Open and many other major golf tournaments. The national headquarters of the United States Golf Association is located here, too. And, with 127 miles of ocean front, the shore area has attracted many who want it "all" including rapid accessibility to New York and Philadelphia.

Some of the most beautiful suburban areas in the country are found in New Jersey. An excellent highway system and ample public transportation have helped create a "commuter class" who work on Wall Street or Madison Avenue in New York City or work in nearby Philadelphia but want to enjoy the suburban New Jersey lifestyle.

An International Business Environment of Diverse Industries

There are more than 170,000 companies located in New Jersey, including more than 1,000 firms with foreign investments ranging up to 100% ownership. This makes New Jersey the 4th most popular state for foreign investment.

Of the 49 nations with investments in the state, Germany and Great Britain are the leading investors with 125 and 116 "foreign-owned" firms respectively, followed by Japan with 88 firms in New Jersey. These 1,000 firms employ more than 130,000 people.

Ports, Roads, Rail and Airports

New Jersey ports include the largest container port and the largest foreign trade port in the United States. As part of the collective New York/New Jersey seaport known throughout the world as Port of New York and New Jersey, the state handles 85% of the tonnage that passes through America's largest port complex. New Jersey's southern ports are part of the Ports of Philadelphia which extends from the Delaware Cape 135 miles north and west to the head of navigation at Trenton.

The state boasts 35,000 miles of the safest and best maintained highways anywhere in the United States, including four major interstate highways. New Jersey, which has more railroad track per square mile than any other state, is connected to all other states by rail by the passenger and freight lines of Amtrak. High-speed Metroliner service takes

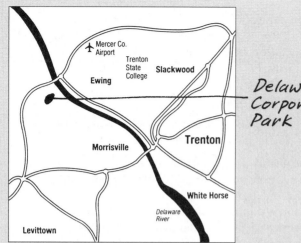

Delaware Corporate Park

passengers to Washington D.C. or Boston within an average of 3½ hours. Commuter rail lines operated by NJ Transit carry more than 65,000 passengers every work day.

Newark International Airport, the fastest growing international airport in the U.S., is expected to become America's busiest airport. Teterboro Airport, just a few miles from New York City, is one of several general aviation airports in the state and is already the busiest facility of its kind in the Northeast Corridor.

Climate

Moderate winters and warm summers are the norm for New Jersey which falls in the temperate zone. Within the state, the northern mountain lakes region is notably cooler in both summer and winter while the somewhat warmer 127-mile coastal area enjoys the moderating effect of the ocean year-round. Average monthly temperatures range from 22°F to 36°F in January and from 71°F to 77°F in July. Total precipitation, which includes rain and melted snow, varies from 51 inches over the northern highlands to 40 inches along the southeast coast. Snowfall ranges from an average

of 50 inches over the north-western hills (and ski country) to 13 inches in the southern coastal area.

Research and Development

New Jersey has been a leader in almost every facet that concerns the interests of mankind: medicine, pharmaceuticals, chemicals, electronics, communications, aerospace, physics, materials, education, urban planning, ecology and human behavior. The team concept of R & D began in New Jersey with the "invention factories" of Thomas Edison and continues with facilities such as Bell Laboratories. The list of those who were involved in high tech in New Jersey reads like a "Who's Who in Scientific America": Einstein in physics, Hyatt and Baekeland in plastics, Dumont in television, Weston in electrical instruments.

In addition to pure theoretical research taking place at the state's universities, most of the R & D going on within New Jersey is conducted by such corporate giants as AT&T, Exxon, Hoffman-LaRoche, Johnson & Johnson, Merck and RCA. Approximately 10% of the nation's research takes place here at a yearly expenditure

of more than $4 billion.

Innovations developed in New Jersey include the electronic switching system, the transistor, direct distance dialing and the automated switchboard. New Jersey has enjoyed a long-standing leadership position in telecommunications industry research; today that position is supplemented by an increasing emphasis on high technology skills such as laser, fiber optics, robotics and CAD/CAM.

Bell Laboratories in Murray Hill has grown and flourished and today is considered the most important research facility in the free world. Some of the exciting research projects currently underway in the state are in microfabrication technology, fiber optics, genetic engineering, communication systems, engineered plastics, space age materials and life-saving pharmaceuticals.

From the electric light to the construction of satellites, New Jersey continues to make a name for itself. That's why research-minded individuals with vision are locating in New Jersey.

NJ & You
Perfect Together

New York State . . . the Hub of U.S. Business

Welcome to New York State – truly the hub of business and industry in the U.S. This booklet provides a brief introduction to the exciting opportunities available in New York State for both new business ventures and the expansion of existing facilities.

All the conditions needed for successful business are available: a stable and highly productive workforce; a vast and efficient transport network; plentiful energy resources; and a State Government committed to supporting the development and growth of business.

New York State's proximity to the huge commercial and consumer markets in the U.S. and Canada has made it a favoured location for overseas companies seeking a foothold in North America. The wisdom of approaching such markets from a base in New York is clear. That is why more foreign companies have invested in New York State than in any other state.

Growth and prosperity await you in New York State. You'll find an attractive proposition on the following pages.

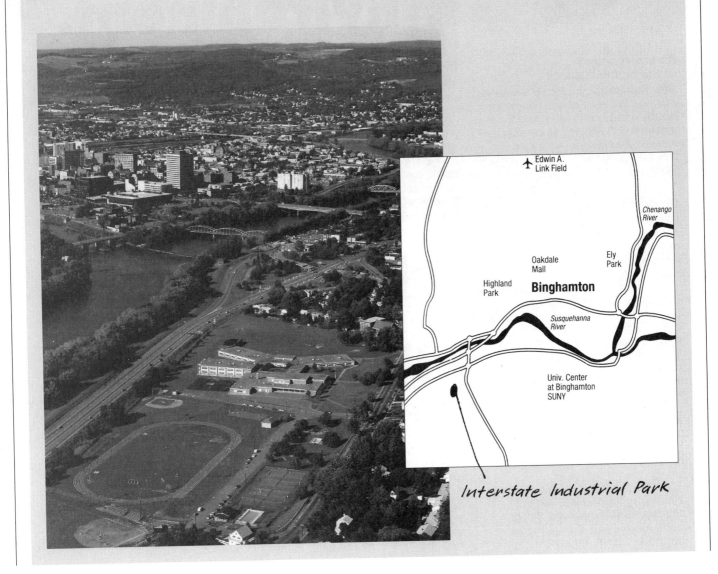

Interstate Industrial Park

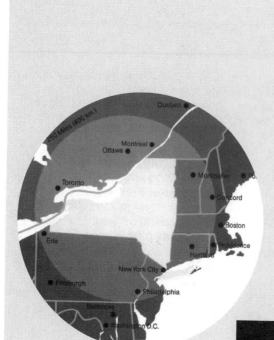

Living Environment.

Something for everyone in a state almost the size of England.

An environment of the highest quality

New York State is a place of amazing diversity. But whether you choose the big city or the countryside, suburb, or small town, the State has carefully preserved a high quality of life for those living and working within the State.

Outdoor recreation

85% of New York State is rural, wild, or forested. 150 State parks afford magnificent walking trails and facilities for camping, swimming, and, in winter, skiing.

The State has about 4,000 lakes, including Lake George, Oneida Lake, and the famous wine-growing region of the Finger Lakes. Fast-flowing streams yield trout and other game fish. Grouse, partridge, pheasant, wild duck and wild geese are plentiful, as well as whitetail deer in many parts of the State.

On Long Island, you can roam along more than 100 uninterrupted miles (161 km) of sandy beach. Long Island Sound has many beautiful harbours and great conditions for sailing.

The State has 4 thoroughbred and 7 harness race courses, 736 golf courses, 65 skiing centers, 9 hunt clubs, innumerable riding schools, squash and tennis courts.

A full range of cultural activities

A host of private cultural organisations, as well as the New York State Arts Council, sponsor opera, theatre, ballet and orchestral performances in communities throughout the State. They also organise exhibitions of art, architecture, film and photography as well as lecture series.

The Metropolitan Museum of Art, the American Museum of Natural History, and some of the world's most famous galleries, museums and performing arts centres are to be found in the State. The Rochester and Buffalo Philharmonic Orchestras, the Saratoga Performing Arts Center, Lincoln Center (home of the Metropolitan Opera, the New York Philharmonic Orchestra and the New York City Ballet) are among the outstanding cultural attractions.

Bright lights and excitement

New York State is the home of Broadway, Off-Broadway, Off-Off-Broadway, glittering nightclubs and glamorous revues.

It's also a great place to be a supporter of major-league sports. Take the children to a baseball game

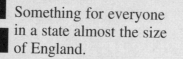

– it's an afternoon event, and your neighbours in the stands will be happy to explain.

American football combines skillful strategy with physical prowess, but be warned: it's addictive. And during the winter, take in a fast moving indoor soccer or hockey match.

Nostalgic touches

It's easy for an international business executive to feel at home in New York State. The seasons revolve in a familiar cycle, with an accent on sunny skies.

Once you get outside New York City, you'll be surprised how quickly the hubbub dies down. Food, prices, and style of life tend to be comfortably traditional. You'll soon feel at home with friendly neighbours and familiar pursuits.

Case Studies.

Success stories:
They're showing up all over New York State.

PHILLIPS CABLES LIMITED

When Phillips Cables, Canada's leading manufacturer of wire and cable, chose Watertown, New York, as the base for its entry into U.S. markets, it found ready assistance and cooperation from the local and State authorities.

The costs of setting up a new manufacturing plant for Phillips, a subsidiary of BICC of the U.K., were held well within the limits specified by the board, with the help of a financing package put together by the New York State Department of Commerce and the Industrial Development Agency of Jefferson County.

An issue of tax exempt bonds arranged by the IDA on Phillips' behalf, together with a loan from the Urban Development Authority, reduced interest charges significantly.

The State Department of Commerce provided funds for an on-the-job-training scheme which helped assure Phillips of an adequate supply of skilled labour during the start-up period of the new plant.

Mr. J. Leroy Olsen, President and Chief Executive Officer of Phillips Cables, pays tribute to "the excellent help and cooperation given by officials in the Watertown area, which have considerably eased our entry into this new venture."

INTERKNITTING, LTD.

The first links in the chain which drew Interknitting, the West German textile firm, from its home base to a new operating venture in Cobleskill, New York, were forged in the European office of New York State's Commerce Department.

Now, after eight years, Interknitting, a subsidiary of Paul Hofmann K/G of West Germany is soundly established in Cobleskill on a site originally found for it by the Commerce Department. The location included an existing textile plant, and offered an experienced labour force and close proximity to both suppliers and market outlets.

A substantial start-up cost was lifted from Interknitting's shoulders when the Commerce Department helped eliminate a required deposit from the local power utility.

Other valuable help came from the Schoharie County Industrial Development Agency which purchased the factory building and then leased it to Interknitting, which will eventually acquire ownership.

Since opening the business in Cobleskill, the German firm has increased its workforce nearly tenfold, helped by on-the-job training funds from the State authorities.

LAZZARONI SARONNO, LTD.

After nearly fifty years of selling its high quality pastries in the U.S., D. Lazzaroni of Saronno, near Milan, decided it could best serve its American markets from a manufacturing facility close to the New York City Metropolitan area.

Lazzaroni wanted to be near its major customers, but also wanted to take advantage of New York's business network and of New York State's business tax incentives.

Lazzaroni Saronno, the new U.S. subsidiary, achieved these goals when it opened for business in Rockland County, just one hour from Manhattan. From the new plant, the company expects to establish new markets in Canada as well as attract new business in the U.S.

Lazzaroni was helped by the New York State Commerce Department which arranged the issue of industrial revenue bonds to meet the initial $2.25 million investment cost.

Moreover, Lazzaroni qualified for a reduction of 95% of its New York State corporate income tax.

New York State was not the only venue considered for the new development by the Italian group. But Paolo Lazzaroni, chairman of the parent company, said, "the personal contacts and warm relationships" tipped the balance in the decision in favour of New York State.

QUO VADIS INC.

The opening of its new printing and production facility near Buffalo in Hamburg, New York, by Quo Vadis was the culmination of more than two years of planning by the company and the State Commerce Department.

Quo Vadis, whose parent company is based in Marseilles, obtained a financing package covering the total cost of the new facility which will handle production of its business diaries and desk calendars for markets throughout the U.S., as well as in Canada, Australia and the U.K. The financing was put together with the help of Erie County Industrial Development Agency and the New York Job Development Authority.

The New York State site location office helped the French firm find a suitable site to replace the small sales office originally opened eight years earlier, and put the company in touch with the local agencies which arranged the financing.

As a final touch, Quo Vadis expects to qualify for relief of at least 90% of its New York State corporate income tax under the Job Incentive Program.

Unit 15 A special project
APRIL Document 1
Materials, supplies and distribution

Discuss these questions:

1 Supplies

Local companies will supply you with office equipment, furniture, stationery, catering, cleaning, etc.

- What kinds of firms will you need to contact?
- What specialized services will you need to obtain locally: tax advice, translation services, etc.

2 Materials

Local companies will supply you with the basic ingredients for your manufacturing process and packaging.

- What are the basic ingredients for your product? What kinds of companies supply them?
- What materials will be required for packaging?

3 Distribution

45% of your output will be sold to the trade (hotels, restaurants and canteens), 35% to store groups and 25% to independent retailers. As freshness is vital, the product must be delivered quickly:

- Will you buy your own fleet of trucks, lease trucks for your staff to drive, or use trucking contractors to ship goods to customers?
- Can you supply direct to independent retailers, or should you deal through a wholesaler?
- How much warehouse space will you set aside for goods ready for dispatch?
- Will this be a completely separate building or area?

Keep in touch with your counterparts in the other country by phoning them at least twice to find out what decisions they have made.

Unit 15 A special project
APRIL Document 2
Marketing and sales

What are the main differences between the local market and the market in your own country? Discuss these questions:

1 Product

- Is your brand name suitable for the local market?
- Will the product need to be changed at all to suit local customers' tastes?
- What age groups and income groups will your customers be in?
- Will the product be bought by families or single people?
- Does your country have a good image, which can help create an interest in your product?

2 Price

- In the local market, what is your customers' attitude to high prices?
- What is their attitude to low prices?

3 Place

- In what kinds of retail or catering outlets should the product be available?
- Is there any chance of exporting the product from this base to neighbouring countries?

4 Promotion

- How important are packaging and design, compared with the home market?
- What methods of promotion can be used for this kind of product?
- What are the best ways of informing (a) trade customers, (b) retailers, and (c) end-users about the product?

Keep in touch with your counterparts in the other country by phoning them at least twice to find out what decisions they have made.

Unit 15 A special project
MAY Document 1

```
To: Special Project Team
From: Frank Miller, Head Office

The Board has looked at your plans for the new plant. They are very
impressed with the thoroughness of your arrangements.

Unfortunately, in view of the firm's poor results for the first
quarter of the year, it is now clear that the firm's original
expansion plans were too ambitious. The start-up costs for the two
projects are much higher than the Board foresaw. Consequently, I
regret to inform you that we cannot go ahead with both of these
projects.

It has been decided that only one of the plants can be set up at this
time. A meeting will be held in May to decide whether the new
location will be in the USA or in the UK.

All members of both teams will attend this meeting.
```

Frank Miller

Unit 15 A special project
MAY Document 2
for the Chairperson

You will be chairing the meeting between the two teams:

- Welcome everyone at the start of the meeting.
- Tell everyone at what time the meeting will finish.
- Announce that there will be a vote at the end to decide which location is to be chosen.
- To prevent any one person from dominating the meeting, anyone who wishes to speak must raise their hand and wait to be named by you. Inform everyone of this procedure.
- Make sure both teams have the same amount of time to put their case.